Phoenix

TECHNICAL REFERENCE SERIES

▶ System BIOS for IBM® PCs, Compatibles, and EISA Computers, *Second Edition*

The Complete Guide to ROM–Based System Software

PHOENIX TECHNOLOGIES LTD.

▲▼ Addison-Wesley Publishing Company, Inc.
Reading, Massachusetts   Menlo Park, California   New York
Don Mills, Ontario   Wokingham, England   Amsterdam   Bonn
Sydney   Singapore   Tokyo   Madrid   San Juan
Paris   Seoul   Milan   Mexico City   Taipei

Many of the designations used by manufacturers and sellers to distinguish their products are claimed as trademarks. Where those designations appear in this book and Addison–Wesley was aware of a trademark claim, the designations have been printed in initial capital letters.

Limitation of Liability
While every reasonable precaution has been taken in the preparation of this book, the author and the publishers assume no responsibility for errors or omissions, or for the uses made of the material contained herein or the decisions based on such use. **No warranties are made, express or implied, with regard to the contents of this work, its merchantability, or fitness for a particular purpose.** Neither the author nor the publishers shall be liable for direct, special, incidental, or consequential damages arising out of the use or inability to use the contents of this book.

Library of Congress Cataloging–in–Publication Data

System BIOS for IBM PCs, compatibles, and EISA computers : the
  complete guide to ROM–based system software / Phoenix Technologies
  Ltd. –– 2nd ed.
      p.   cm. –– (Phoenix technical reference series)
    2nd ed. of: System BIOS for IBM PC/XT/AT computers and
  compatibles.
    Includes bibliographical references and index.
    ISBN 0–201–57760–7
    1. IBM Personal Computer. 2. EISA (Computer bus) 3. Operating
  systems (Computers) I. Phoenix Technologies. II. Title: System
  BIOS for IBM PC/XT/AT computers and compatibles. III. Series.
  QA76.8.I2594S98   1991
  005.4′469––dc20   91–15679
                                                                    CIP

Cover design by Hannus Design Associates
Text design by Phoenix Technologies Ltd.
Set in 10–point Palatino by Phoenix Technologies Ltd.

ISBN 0–201–57760–7
1 2 3 4 5 6 7 8 9–MW–9594939291
First printing, May 1991

Trademarks

This manual acknowledges the following trademarks:

Ashton–Tate and Framework are registered trademarks of Ashton–Tate Corporation.

AST is a registered trademark of AST Research, Inc.

AT, IBM, Personal Systems/2, PS/2, and PC/AT are registered trademarks of the International Business Machines Corporation. PC–DOS, PC/XT, VGA, CGA, MCA, MDA, EGA, OS/2, and Micro Channel are trademarks of the International Business Machines Corporation.

Hercules, Hercules Graphic Card, and Hercules Graphic Adapter are trademarks of Hercules Computer Technology.

Intel is a registered trademark of Intel Corporation.

1–2–3, Lotus, and Symphony are registered trademarks of Lotus Development Corp.

Motorola is a registered trademark of Motorola Semiconductor Products, Inc.

MS, MS–DOS, XENIX, and Microsoft are registered trademarks of Microsoft Corporation.

NEC and Multisync are registered trademarks of Nippon Electric Corporation.

Quadram is a registered trademark of Quadram Corporation.

Table of Contents

Table of Contents, Continued

Table of Contents, Continued

Table of Contents, Continued

Table of Contents, Continued

14   System Services

15   Parallel Printer Service

Table of Contents, Continued

Preface

A word about the second edition

System BIOS for IBM PCs, Compatibles, and EISA Computers is a successor to *System BIOS for IBM PC/XT/AT Computers and Compatibles*, published in 1989. In addition to updating and correcting the original volume, this book has been revised to include information on the EISA bus specification.

Other volumes in this series

System BIOS for IBM PCs, Compatibles, and EISA Computers is one of three volumes in the Phoenix Technical Reference Series. The other volumes are:

ABIOS for IBM PS/2 Computers and Compatibles — a complete technical reference describing the portion of a PS/2 BIOS that supports multitasking operating systems such as OS/2.

CBIOS for IBM PS/2 Computers and Compatibles — a complete technical reference describing the portion of a PS/2 BIOS that supports single–tasking operating systems such as DOS.

continued

How to find information

System BIOS for IBM PCs, Compatibles, and EISA Computers is organized into several major parts. Chapter 1 provides a general summary of BIOS concepts. Chapter 2 discusses the hardware devices the BIOS supports. Chapters 3–7 describe BIOS and system data definitions, I/O port usage, and the power–on self test (POST). Chapters 8–17 serve as a technical reference to the individual BIOS services. Appendixes A and B provide comprehensive lists of potential error messages.

The service–specific chapters (8–17) include, where appropriate, a description of the service and the theory of operations for the service, a discussion of error handling for the service, and descriptions of each service function. The function descriptions include an explanation of what the function does, the function's required inputs and outputs, and any special programming considerations.

The purpose of this book

This book is intended to fill the gap between the many books on microcomputer hardware and PC operating systems, especially DOS. Programming and interfacing books sometimes include a description of BIOS function calls in an appendix, but advanced PC programmers still need detailed information on BIOS interrupt services. *System BIOS for IBM PCs, Compatibles, and EISA Computers* is an attempt to assemble a comprehensive source of information on PC system firmware.

Acknowledgments

This book was written and produced by the technical writing staff of Phoenix Technologies Ltd.: Marianne Adams, Ed Backus, Linda Foster, Dennis McCarthy, Marcia Mobilia, Sandie Zierak, and Kathy Schiff, manager.

Many Phoenix engineers contributed to the technical review of the second edition: Tom Block, Neal Buchalter, Dave Cardin, Bruce Cairns, Duffy Craven, Richard Cyr, Mark Easterday, Raul Garcia, Teresa Hopkins, Stan Lyness, Tim Otholt, Alex Rose, Debbie Schultz, Hank Sousa, Trevor Western, and Graciela Zaffarana.

Special thanks to Paula Bishop, Systems Architect, for her patient, knowledgeable guidance throughout this book project. Her expertise and persistent good humor were essential to its success.

KMS
Norwood, MA
April, 1991

Chapter 1

The ROM BIOS

Overview

PC architecture

The architecture of a single–board microcomputer like the IBM PC can be thought of as a series of functional layers. The lowest layer is the hardware — the actual machine. The highest layer is the application program that interfaces to the user. In between the hardware and application program is the system software. The system software itself is composed of several elements: the operating system kernel and shell, device drivers, and, perhaps, a multitasking supervisor.

The original IBM PC architecture also included a low–level software layer, between the hardware and system software, called the BIOS — the Basic Input/ Output System. The BIOS insulated the system and application software from the hardware by providing primitive I/O services and by programming the hardware's interrupt handling.

continued

Compatibility

By defining the hardware–software interface, the BIOS insured that PC software would be compatible with future generations of PC hardware. This enforced compatibility created a new industry. In 1984, Phoenix introduced its PC ROM BIOS, a BIOS program that was functionally equivalent to IBM's. Independent hardware manufacturers could now design and market PC–compatible, DOS–based computers.

Because of the BIOS, each generation of PC has been able to maintain a measure of backward compatibility. Its hardware–software interface has allowed each of the PC's components to incorporate the major features of its predecessors. The newest members of the Intel 80x86 microprocessor series can execute the original 8088/8086 instruction set, for example. And the current version of DOS still contains the commands and data structures of version 2.0.

Growth of the PC standard

Since 1984, the original 8–bit PC/XT standard has grown to include the 16–bit AT (or, more properly, the Industry Standard Architecture or ISA) specification, and the new 32–bit Extended Industry Standard Architecture, or EISA. These computer architectures and their mutual compatibility are defined by their processor, bus, and BIOS specifications.

The interrupt structure of the Intel 80x86 microprocessor family and the bus' routing of interrupt signals from the system's I/O devices provide the physical basis for PC compatibility. The BIOS's interrupt handling provides the logical basis.

Introduction

Computer systems based on the Intel 80x86 microprocessors are mainly controlled through the use of interrupts. Interrupts can be generated by the microprocessor, by the system hardware, or by software.

When an interrupt occurs, control of the computer is transferred to an interrupt handling routine. Once the routine has been executed, the processor's program counter and flag register are returned to their previous state.

Interrupt vectors

Every interrupt is assigned its own unique interrupt number, ranging from 00h to FFh. By convention, certain ranges of interrupt numbers are reserved for special use. The interrupt numbers ranging from 20h–3Fh, for example, are reserved for DOS.

An interrupt vector is the double word, segment:offset address of the routine assigned to a given interrupt number. Interrupt vectors are stored in a table in memory beginning at address 00:00h. The vector address for INT 00h is stored at location 00:00h to 00:03h; the address for INT 01h is stored at address 00:04h to 00:07h, and so forth.

While the BIOS executes its power–on self–test (POST) program, it creates the Interrupt Vector table in system RAM from its ROM–based table, and initializes the vector addresses of its interrupt–handling routines. Once booted, DOS initializes all the vector addresses of interrupts reserved for its use. Application programs that issue their own interrupts must initialize the associated vector addresses in the table.

continued

Invoking interrupts

Processor, hardware, and software interrupts are invoked differently.

Type	Description
Processor	Microprocessor or logical interrupts are invoked by the processor as a result of some unusual program result, such as an attempt to divide by zero.
	INTs 00h–04h are reserved for the processor.
Hardware	Hardware interrupts are invoked by peripheral devices that set their respective interrupt request lines (IRQ). Each time a key is pressed, for example, the keyboard hardware generates an interrupt. Hardware interrupts are vectored to Interrupt Service Routines (ISRs) that generally reside in the BIOS.
	INTs 08h–0Fh and 70h–77h are reserved by the BIOS for hardware interrupts.
Software	Software interrupts are invoked via the 80x86 INT instruction. Most software interrupts are vectored to Device Service Routines (DSRs) located in the BIOS, in DOS, or in application programs.
	However, software INTs 1Dh, 1Eh, 1Fh, 40h, 41h, 43h, and 46h do not service a particular device. Instead, each points to various ROM–resident hardware parameter tables.

For a list of the interrupts served by each interrupt vector, consult the Interrupt Vector table in Chapter 3.

BIOS Interrupt Service Routines

The BIOS Interrupt Service Routines (ISRs) handle interrupts issued by hardware devices. They use the microprocessor's registers and BIOS data areas, and save the program counter and flag registers.

ISRs are not invoked by operating system or application software.

BIOS Device Service Routines

Introduction

The BIOS Device Service Routines (DSRs) handle software interrupts issued by the INT instruction. The functions within a DSR are identified by a number that is passed as an argument to the DSR in register AH. Some functions contain sub-functions, also identified by numbers. The subfunction numbers are also passed as arguments, in register AL or BL.

The calling programs pass other arguments to the functions, and the functions return information to the calling program via the microprocessor's registers. The BIOS Device Service Routines store parameters and status information in the BIOS data areas.

Registers not used by the DSR are usually preserved.

Function descriptions

Throughout this book, the functions and subfunctions performed by the BIOS DSRs are described in terms of their input and output parameters. The sample description that follows is from Chapter 10, which describes BIOS Video Service.

continued

Example of a function description

INT 10h Function 02h — Set Cursor Position

Description

This function sets the cursor position for the display page indicated in BL. It saves the position as a two–byte row–by–column table entry in the cursor coordinates byte at 40:50h. Row and column coordinates are indicated in registers DH and DL respectively.

Function AH = 20h applies to both text and graphics video modes. In text modes, if the display page selected in BH is the active display page, the screen cursor will move to the coordinates indicated in registers DH and DL. In graphics modes, the cursor is invisible but is used to define a position on the screen.

Input/Output

Input:	AH	=	02h
	BH	=	Display page number (see Function AH = 05h)
	DH	=	Row (0 is top row of screen)
	DL	=	Column (0 is leftmost column)
Output:	None		

Cursor positioning

Positioning the cursor to screen coordinates 0,0 places it in the upper left corner of the screen in the 80x25 text mode. Selecting coordinates 79,24 in the 80x25 text mode will allow placement of the cursor in the lower right corner of the screen. The cursor can also be placed in the lower right corner of the screen using coordinates 39,24 in the 40x25 text mode.

The cursor can be turned off by moving it to an off–screen location or by changing its coordinates to a position such as 0,25. However, if it is moved too far off–screen, the actual position of the cursor may become unpredictable.

Additional information

The display page number must be set to 0 in CGA graphics mode.

continued

Example program

This assembly language program uses the INT 10h Function AH = 02h Set Cursor Position to move the cursor on video page 0 to row 3, column 14.

```
MOV AH, 2         ;Select "Set Cursor Position" function
MOV BH, 0         ;Input page number into BH register
MOV DH, 3         ;Input row parameter into DH register
MOV DL, 14        ;Input column parameter into DL
INT 10H           ;Invoke INT 10h,  Video Service
```

Unexpected–Interrupt Handlers

Description

The BIOS initializes all of the interrupt vectors that it will use to their appropriate addresses or parameters. Those vectors that the BIOS doesn't use are usually initialized to point to the BIOS's unexpected–interrupt handler. The unexpected–interrupt handler ensures complete error recovery.

Invoking an unexpected–interrupt handler

When an unexpected interrupt occurs, the BIOS's unexpected–interrupt handler is invoked. The BIOS will then either return control to the interrupted program with all registers preserved, or it will display a message indicating that an unexpected interrupt has occurred and requesting action from the user.

Interrupts 20h–3Fh, 45, 47h–6Fh, 72h–74h, and 77–FF are examples of reserved interrupt ranges that get revectored to unexpected–interrupt handlers.

Note: Some system manufacturers use a modified BIOS that initializes some unused vectors to zero rather than to an unexpected–interrupt handler address.

Summary: BIOS Services

The tables below briefly define BIOS services and list each function and
subfunction.

Print Screen Service		The BIOS Print Screen Service prints the contents of the current video screen to the printer. Invoked by the keyboard ISR (INT 9) when Shift–PRINT SCREEN is pressed.
INT	**PARAMETER**	**FUNCTION**
05h	None	Print Screen

Video Service		The BIOS Video Service provides I/O support for the MDA and CGA adapters. The BIOS support for EGA and VGA adapters is contained in adapter ROM.
INT	**PARAMETER**	**FUNCTION**
10h	AH = 00h	Set Video Mode
	AH = 01h	Set Cursor Type
	AH = 02h	Set Cursor Position
	AH = 03h	Read Current Cursor Position
	AH = 04h	Read Light Pen Position
	AH = 05h	Select New Video Page
	AH = 06h	Scroll Current Page Up
	AH = 07h	Scroll Current Page Down
	AH = 08h	Read Character/Attribute from Screen
	AH = 09h	Write Character/Attribute to Screen
	AH = 0Ah	Write Character Only to Screen
	AH = 0Bh	Set Color Palette
	AH = 0Ch	Write Pixel
	AH = 0Dh	Read Pixel
	AH = 0Eh	Write Teletype to Active Page
	AH = 0Fh	Return Video Status
	AH = 13h	Write String

continued

Equipment Check Service		The BIOS Equipment Check Service returns the system equipment list, as determined by the BIOS POST routine.
INT	**PARAMETER**	**FUNCTION**
11h	None	Equipment List Service

Memory Size Service		The BIOS Memory Size Service returns the amount of available base memory (in kilobytes), as determined by the POST routine.
INT	**PARAMETER**	**FUNCTION**
12h	None	Memory Size Service

Diskette Service		The BIOS Diskette Service performs BIOS–level read, write, format, initialization, and diagnostic support for up to two internal diskette drives.
		Note: If a fixed disk is installed, the BIOS automatically revectors all INT 13h Diskette Service requests to INT 40h. Revectoring is transparent to application programs. Application programs should continue to use INT 13h for both fixed disk and external diskette service requests.
INT	**PARAMETER**	**FUNCTION**
13h	AH = 00h	Reset Diskette System
	AH = 01h	Read Diskette Status
	AH = 02h	Read Diskette Sectors
	AH = 03h	Write Diskette Sectors
	AH = 04h	Verify Diskette Sectors
	AH = 05h	Format Diskette Track
	AH = 08h	Read Drive Parameters

continued

	The BIOS Diskette Service performs BIOS–level read, write, format, initialization, and diagnostic support for up to two internal diskette drives.
Diskette Service cont'd	**Note:** If a fixed disk is installed, the BIOS automatically revectors all INT 13h Diskette Service requests to INT 40h. Revectoring is transparent to application programs. Application programs should continue to use INT 13h for both fixed disk and external diskette service requests.

INT	PARAMETER	FUNCTION
13h	AH = 09h–14h	Reserved
	AH = 15h	Read Drive Type
	AH = 16h	Detect Media Change
	AH = 17h	Set Diskette Type
	AH = 18h	Set Media Type for Format

	The BIOS Fixed Disk Service performs BIOS–level read, write, format, initialization, and diagnostic functions for up to two fixed disk drives.
Fixed Disk Service	

INT	PARAMETER	FUNCTION
13h	AH = 00h	Reset System Fixed Disk
	AH = 01h	Read Disk Status
	AH = 02h	Read Disk Sectors
	AH = 03h	Write Disk Sectors
	AH = 04h	Verify Disk Sectors
	AH = 05h	Format Disk Cylinder
	AH = 06h	Format Bad Track
	AH = 07h	Format Drive
	AH = 08h	Read Drive Parameters
	AH = 09h	Initialize Drive Parameters

continued

Fixed Disk Service cont'd		The BIOS Fixed Disk Service performs BIOS–level read, write, format, initialization, and diagnostic functions for up to two fixed disk drives.
INT	**PARAMETER**	**FUNCTION**
13h	AH = 0Ah	Read Long Sector
	AH = 0Bh	Write Long Sector
	AH = 0Ch	Seek to Cylinder
	AH = 0Dh	Alternate Reset Fixed Disk
	AH = 0Eh	Diagnostics 1: Read Test Buffer
	AH = 0Fh	Diagnostics 2: Write Test Buffer
	AH = 10h	Test for Drive Ready
	AH = 11h	Recalibrate Drive
	AH = 12h	Controller RAM Diagnostic
	AH = 13h	Controller Drive Diagnostic
	AH = 14h	Controller Internal Diagnostic
	AH = 15h	Read Disk Type

Serial Communications Service		The BIOS Serial Communications Service performs RS–232C character I/O for IBM–compatible serial port adapters.
INT	**PARAMETER**	**FUNCTION**
14h	AH = 00h	Initialize Serial Adapter
	AH = 01h	Send Character
	AH = 02h	Receive Character
	AH = 03h	Return Serial Port Status

continued

System Services		The BIOS System Services is composed of several miscellaneous system–level subservices, all of which are invoked via the INT 15h instruction.
INT	**PARAMETER**	**FUNCTION**
15h	AH = 00h	Turn Cassette Motor On
	AH = 01h	Turn Cassette Motor Off
	AH = 02h	Read Cassette
	AH = 03h	Write to Cassette
	AH = 4Fh	Keyboard Intercept
	AH = 80h	Device Open
	AH = 81h	Device Close
	AH = 82h	Program Termination
	AH = 83h	Set Event Wait Interval
	AH = 84h	Joystick Support
	AH = 85h	System Request Key
	AH = 86h	Wait
	AH = 87h	Move Block
	AH = 88h	Read Extended Memory Size
	AH = 89h	Switch Processor to Protected Mode
	AH = 90h	Device Busy
	AH = 91h	Interrupt Complete
	AH = C0h	Return System Configuration Parameters Address
	AH = C1h	Return Extended BIOS Data Area Segment Address
	AH = C2h	Pointing Device Interface (if supported)
	AH = C3h	Fail–Safe Timer Control [EISA]
	AH = D8h	Access EISA System Information [EISA]

continued

Keyboard Service	The BIOS Keyboard Service interfaces the operating system and application programs with the keyboard.	
INT	**PARAMETER**	**FUNCTION**
16h	AH = 00h	Read Keyboard Input
	AH = 01h	Return Keyboard Status
	AH = 02h	Return Shift Flag Status
	AH = 03h	Set Typematic Rate and Delay
	AH = 05h	Store Key Data
	AH = 06h–0Fh	Reserved
	AH = 10h	Read Extended Keyboard Input
	AH = 11h	Return Extended Keyboard Status
	AH = 12h	Return Extended Shift Flag Status
	AH = 13h–FFh	Reserved

Parallel Printer Service	The BIOS Printer Service provides I/O support for parallel printer ports.	
INT	**PARAMETER**	**FUNCTION**
17h	AH = 00h	Print Character
	AH = 01h	Initialize Printer
	AH = 02h	Read Printer Status

Bootstrap Loader Service	The BIOS Bootstrap Loader Service loads the bootstrap code to memory from diskette or fixed disk.	
INT	**PARAMETER**	**FUNCTION**
19h	None	Bootstrap Loader Service

continued

<table>
<tr><td colspan="3">Time–of–Day Service</td><td>The BIOS Time–of–Day Service contains functions that support and maintain the time–of–day portion of the Motorola MC 146818A (or equivalent) CMOS clock chip.</td></tr>
</table>

INT	PARAMETER	FUNCTION
1Ah	AH = 00h	Read System Time Counter
	AH = 01h	Set System Time Counter
	AH = 02h	Read Real–Time Clock Time
	AH = 03h	Set Real–Time Clock Time
	AH = 04h	Read Real–Time Clock Date
	AH = 05h	Set Real–Time Clock Date
	AH = 06h	Set Real–Time Clock Alarm
	AH = 07h	Reset Real–Time Clock Alarm

2

Chapter 2
XT, ISA, and EISA Hardware

Overview

Description

The BIOS is the lowest software level in a PC, defining the boundary between device drivers and other system software, and the PC's hardware. The BIOS is customized to the system's circuitry — it must be aware of the physical devices present in the system, and their physical characteristics.

In this chapter

This chapter describes the hardware devices that are specified or allowed in an XT, ISA, or EISA system:

- Microprocessor
- Math Coprocessor
- XT, ISA, and EISA Buses
- I/O Devices
- Timers and Counters
- Programmable Interrupt Controllers
- Direct Memory Access
- EISA Bus Master Support
- Miscellaneous Additional Logic

Microprocessor

Introduction

The PC architecture is based on the Intel 80x86 family of microprocessors. This family grew from Intel's extremely successful 8080, an 8–bit microprocessor developed in the 1970s. The 8080 was followed by the 8086. Internally, the 8086 is a 16–bit processor; it has a 16–bit data bus and a 20–bit address bus.

Intel developed a simpler version of the 8086, the 8088, for the large number of applications that only required an 8–bit data path. The original PC, and its immediate successor the PC/XT, were based on the 8088.

The 8088

Like the 8086, the 8088 has a segment:offset scheme that makes it capable of addressing a 1–megabyte memory address space. The allocation of the original megabyte is still reflected in the real–mode feature of later generations of PCs.

The 8088 in the PC and XT had a system clock rate of 4.77 MHz. Later, some manufacturers enhanced the XT architecture by incorporating a 9.54, 10, or 12 MHz clock.

The 8088's most significant features are

- Maskable and nonmaskable interrupts
- Direct–memory access (DMA)
- Support for local bus coprocessors
- Support for both memory–mapped and direct I/O

The 80286

The next generation of PC architecture, PC/AT, was based on the Intel 80286. Like the 8086/8088, internally the 80286 is a 16–bit microprocessor. However, the 80286 incorporates several major improvements over the 8086/8088, including

- A 24–bit address bus, addressing 16mb of memory space
- A faster clock, 6 to 25 MHz
- Several new instructions supporting multitasking
- Fewer clock cycles per instruction
- Two clock cycles (versus four 8086/8088 clock cycles) per data–bus access
- A protected–mode virtual addressing scheme

continued

The 80386

At the time of its introduction, the 80286 was considered a major advance over the 8086/8088. However, its limitations became apparent as applications software attempted to address protected–mode memory. The 80286 is now considered an intermediate design between the definitive 8086 and 80386 architectures.

The 80386 is a 32–bit microprocessor: its internal registers, and external address and data paths are 32 bits wide. Its major features include

- Direct addressable memory space of 4 gigabytes
- Virtual memory space of 64 terabytes
- Virtual 8086 mode
- Fewer clock cycles per instruction
- Faster memory management
- Higher clock speeds — 20, 25, or 33 MHz
- Full compatibility with 8086/8088 and 80286 software

Intel Corporation has also created a lower–cost version of the 80386 called the 80386SX. The 80386SX is typically the basis for battery–powered and entry–level systems, and has clock–speeds of 16 MHz or 20 MHz.

Internally, the 80386SX is identical to the 80386 (sometimes called the 80386DX to distinguish it from the 80386SX). The SX version has a 16–bit data path, making it compatible with 80286–type peripherals. This 80286–80386SX–80386DX relationship is similar to the older 8080–8088–8086.

The 80486

Like the 80286, the 80486 is an enhancement of a benchmark architecture rather than a new generation of microprocessor. It only adds some minor modifications to the system control registers and eight new instructions to the 80386.

The 80486 contains an enhanced 80386 CPU core, an on–chip 80387 MPU, and an on–chip 8K instruction and data cache. The 80486 CPU allows many frequently-used instructions to execute in one clock cycle.

The most important features and performance improvements of the 80486 over the 80386 are related to Intel's use of newer silicon design and fabrication techniques.

Math Coprocessor

Introduction

The Intel 80x86 microprocessor family includes a parallel 80x87 family of math coprocessors (also called Math Processor Units, MPUs, or Floating–Point Units, FPUs). Each 80x86 processor, except the 80486, has an appropriate 80x87 coprocessor that operates at the same clock speed. The 80486 contains an on–chip 80387 MPU, as noted above.

8087 coprocessor hardware interface

The 8087 operates asynchronously and uses the same clock as the 8086 or 8088 CPU. It is internally divided into two independent functional areas: the Control Unit (CU) and the Numeric Execution Unit (NEU). The CU maintains synchronization with the CPU while the NEU processes numeric instructions.

The 8087 is wired in parallel with the CPU — the CPU's status (S0–S2) and queue status lines (QS0–QS1) enable the 8087 to obtain and decode instructions in synchronization with the CPU.

80287 and 80387 coprocessor hardware interface

The 80287 and 80387 coprocessors function as I/O devices. They are internally divided into two independent functional areas: the Bus Interface Unit (BIU) and Numeric Execution Unit (NEU). The BIU communicates with the CPU through I/O ports F8h, FAh, and FCh.

An 80287 or 80387 coprocessor can operate in either the real or protected address mode. It's in real address mode after a power–on, a reset, or when returning from protected address mode.

The 80287 and 80387 coprocessors generate an error signal that sets IRQ 13; the BUSY signal from the coprocessor is then held in the BUSY state. The BUSY signal can be cleared by a write of zero to I/O port F0h, which clears IRQ 13.

IRQ 13 is vectored to the INT 75h Exception ISR as part of system initialization. When IRQ 13 goes high, the INT 75h ISR clears the BUSY signal and issues a BIOS INT 02h Nonmaskable Interrupt ISR.

Note: Application programs that enable numeric exceptions must provide a method for intercepting and processing INT 75h (or INT 02h for 8087–based software).

XT, ISA, and EISA Buses

Introduction

The XT, ISA, and EISA buses aren't true backplane buses — they're expansion buses for single–board microcomputers. The only signal, timing, or electrical parameters specified are those for the physical bus connectors on the system board.

Typically, mounted on the system board are the processor, peripheral integrated circuits, and some memory. The expansion bus — the physical bus connectors — are used to add expansion boards that contain additional memory or peripheral circuits. An XT, ISA, or EISA system can even be built with a passive backplane, with the processor itself mounted on an expansion board.

The XT bus

The XT bus was carried over from the original PC. It's a straightforward design that is similar to native 8088 microprocessor buses. There are 20 address lines and eight data lines. The bus uses typical Intel–style control signals, and allows for DMA data transfers.

The physical expansion connector defined by the XT bus specification has 62 pins. These are divided between 31 component pins on one side of the connector and 31 circuit pins on the other. The component pins correspond to address and data pins on the 8088; the circuit pins correspond to control signals to and from peripheral circuits.

The ISA bus

IBM developed an extension of the XT bus for its 80286–based PC/AT system. When a committee was formed to design a 32–bit extension to the AT bus, it named the new bus "EISA" (see below) and renamed the AT bus "ISA," for Industry Standard Architecture.

The ISA bus adds four address and eight data lines to the XT bus to accommodate the capabilities of the 80286. There are also some unlatched address lines, three additional 16–bit DMA channels, and support for alternate bus masters.

The physical ISA expansion connector adds a second set of 36 pins to the 62–pin XT connector. These extra pins are separated from the XT pins by a gap of about a quarter of an inch, so that an 8–bit XT expansion board will fit into an ISA slot and still function properly.

continued

The need for a 32–bit bus

In 1987, IBM announced their PS/2 series of microcomputers, along with a new 16/32–bit bus specification called Micro Channel Architecture, or MCA. Unlike past announcements of new IBM products, most manufacturers of PC–compatible equipment didn't adopt MCA. This reluctance had three main causes:

- MCA isn't backward–compatible with the XT and ISA buses.
- IBM's licensing arrangement for MCA is expensive and restrictive.
- MCA–compatible expansion boards are not widely available.

Instead of adopting IBM's new standard, PC–compatible manufacturers continued to build systems with the ISA bus. However, many of the capabilities of the 80386 and 80486 can't be applied on the older, 16–bit bus. 80386– and 80486–based ISA systems have to be divided into "on–board" and "expansion–slot" portions. High–speed memory, for example, has to be implemented on the system board via a native 80386 bus because the ISA expansion bus is slow (8 MHz) and only has a 16–bit wide data path.

Several strategies have been applied to get around the expansion–slot bottleneck. The most successful of these has been the development of ISA "chip sets." New methods in CMOS design and fabrication have made it possible to integrate the functions of most of the AT peripheral circuits into a few, compact chips. Some integrated circuit manufacturers have even incorporated the entire set of AT peripheral circuits into a single chip.

Chip sets, by integrating the functions of many older chips into just a few newer ones, free up space on the system board. This system–board space can then be used for high–speed memory or other functions that would otherwise have to go onto slower expansion boards.

However, even these strategies are now insufficient. Applications, like network file servers, that require the full 32–bit capabilities of the 80386 and 80486 are severely restricted by the limitations of the ISA bus. So, AT–compatible system manufacturers have recognized the need for a new high–speed bus.

continued

The EISA bus

In September 1988, a consortium was formed (the so–called "Gang of Nine" — AST Research, Compaq, Epson, Hewlett–Packard, NEC, Olivetti, Tandy, Wyse, and Zenith Data Systems) to define a backward–compatible, 32–bit successor to the XT and ISA buses.

The result was Extended Industry Standard Architecture, or EISA. (The bus' name, and the divergence from IBM's leadership, required that the AT bus be renamed ISA.)

EISA adds several important new features to the ISA specification:

- 16 additional data lines that allow data transfers in 32–bit blocks
- 8 additional address lines that allow a 4 gigabyte address space
- Backward compatibility with the XT and ISA specifications
- Three new types of DMA transfers, including a 32–bit burst mode
- Level-sensitive, rather than edge-triggered, interrupts
- Sophisticated bus control arbitration

The physical EISA expansion connector adds 55 signals, on 90 new pins, to the ISA connector by incorporating a two–tier design. EISA slots will accept ISA or EISA expansion boards. EISA boards will fit into the lower tier of new connections, ISA boards will not.

continued

Summary table

IBM's original XT and AT used several discrete devices for peripheral functions such as interrupt handling, timing and direct memory access. These devices have largely been replaced in modern systems with more complex chip sets. However, the chip sets must maintain compatibility with the original specifications by providing the functionality of the original devices. This table is a list of these devices — all are Intel products except the Motorola 146818A and 6845, the NEC 765, and the National Semiconductor 8250.

I/O Addresses	Function	Original Implementation
0000h–000Fh	DMA controller	8237A
0020h–0021h	Peripheral Interrupt Controller	8259A
0040h–0043h	Programmable Interval Timer	8253
0060h–0063h	Programmable Peripheral Interface [XT]	8255
0060h and 0064h	Universal Programmable Interface [ISA, EISA]	8042
0070h–0071h	Real–Time Clock/Non–Volatile RAM [ISA, EISA]	146818A
00A0h–00A1h	Second Peripheral Interrupt Controller [ISA, EISA]	8259A
00C0h–00DEh	Second DMA Controller [ISA, EISA]	8237A
002F8h–02FFh	Asynchronous Serial Line Controller	8250
03B4h–03B5h	CRT Controller	6845
03D4h–03D5h	CRT Controller	6845
03F4h–03F5h	Diskette Controller	765
03F8h–03FFh	Asynchronous Serial Line Controller	8250

The following sections provide an overview of these devices. For a more detailed description of how the BIOS implements their functions, see Chapter 6.

I/O Devices

Description

The XT, ISA, and EISA specifications include the following I/O devices:

- Serial ports
- Parallel ports
- Diskette controller
- Fixed disk controller
- Video controller
- A keyboard controller

Serial ports

The XT, ISA, and EISA specifications include a National Semiconductor 8250 serial port controller or equivalent logic. The BIOS supports up to four serial ports, which are accessed through address ports 02F8h–02FFh and 03F8h–03FFh.

The NS 8250 handles data with the following characteristics:

- 5, 6, 7, or 8 bits
- 1, 1.5, or 2 stop bits
- Even, odd, or no parity

The serial port controller can operate at speeds of from 110 to 9,600 bps (XT) or 19,200 bps (ISA and EISA).

Note: The NS 8250 is compatible with the NS 16450 and the NS 16550.

continued

Parallel ports

The XT, ISA, and EISA specifications include parallel ports that can transfer 8 bits of data at standard TTL levels. The parallel ports can be called port 1, 2, or 3. Some adapters may provide a bidirectional data port. The BIOS will support up to four parallel ports with some customization.

The parallel ports are accessed through address ports 0278h–027Ah, 0378h–037Ah, and 03BCh–03BEh.

Diskette controller

The XT, ISA, and EISA specifications include an NEC 765 or equivalent diskette controller. Five types of diskette drives are supported:

- 720K 3.5 inch
- 1.44MB 3.5 inch
- 360K 5.25 inch
- 720K 5.25 inch
- 1.2MB 5.25 inch

Some enhanced BIOS programs for ISA and EISA systems also support the Intel 82077 diskette controller. This controller supports a 16–byte FIFO buffer that permits faster diskette performance in a multi–user environment. The FIFO buffer allows the system a larger DMA latency without causing diskette errors.

The diskette controller is accessed through address ports 03F4h–03F5h.

Fixed disk controller

The XT, ISA, and EISA specifications include up to two fixed disks in a system. The BIOS will support a Western Digital ST506 fixed disk adapter, RLL Controller, ESDI fixed disk and controller, or equivalent device.

continued

Keyboard controller

The XT architecture includes a keyboard subsystem based on the 8–bit Intel 8048 microcontroller, which

- Handles bidirectional keyboard communication
- Translates PC–compatible scan codes
- Performs interrupt processing with the appropriate scan code

The ISA and EISA architectures include a keyboard subsystem based on the Intel 8042, or equivalent, keyboard controller, which performs all of the XT keyboard functions and

- Controls the System Reset command
- May control address line A20

Many BIOS programs for ISA and EISA systems also support an optional PS/2–style pointing device, such as a mouse. The pointing device is controlled by the 8042 keyboard controller. The optional PS/2–style mouse support service consists of the INT 15h System Services Function C2h and the INT 74h ISR.

The keyboard controller is accessed through address ports 0060h and 0064h.

Timers and Counters

Description

The XT, ISA, and EISA specifications call for an oscillator, based on the Intel 8284A clock/reset circuit. This oscillator generates a clock signal from a quartz crystal that pulses at 14.31818 MHz. IBM chose this frequency for the original PC and it's still used in the PC's successors.

The original PC was intended to be a home/hobbyist machine — one that would likely use a color television as a monitor. The 14.31818 MHz clock signal is exactly four times 3.58 MHz, the subcarrier frequency used in color television signals.

The 14.31818 MHz signal is divided down to provide the clock signals used by the other circuits in the system. It's divided by three to create the 4.77 MHz clock signal used by the 8088 processor in the original PC. And, it's divided by 12 to create the 1.19 MHz signal for the system timer.

The XT system timer

The XT architecture is based on a single timer circuit, an Intel 8253 Programmable Interval Timer (PIT). The 8253 is addressed through I/O ports 0040h–0043h. Using the 8284A clock/reset circuit's 1.19 MHz oscillator signal as its input, the 8253 generates all of the XT's system timing signals.

The 8253 operates in any of six modes:

- Mode 0 — Interrupt on Terminal Count
- Mode 1 — Hardware Retriggerable One–Shot
- Mode 2 — Rate Generator
- Mode 3 — Square Wave
- Mode 4 — Software Retriggerable Strobe
- Mode 5 — Hardware Retriggerable Strobe

continued

ISA and EISA system timers

Instead of a single oscillator signal, ISA and EISA systems use three:

- The system clock signal — used to synchronize the microprocessor and the bus
- An XT–compatible 14.31818 MHz signal — divided down for the system timer
- Another XT–compatible 14.31818 MHz signal — used as a bus timer

The system clock signal is generated by an Intel 82284 Clock Generator circuit. The 82284 generates this signal by dividing the crystal frequency in half.

The XT–compatible signals are generated by an Intel 8254–2 PIT, a backward–compatible upgrade of the 8253 circuit used in the XT. Like the XT's 8253, the 8254–2 is addressed through I/O ports 0040h–0043h. The 8254–2 PIT also has the same six operating modes as the 8253.

Using the XT–compatible 1.19 MHz oscillator signal as its input, the 8254–2 generates three outputs:

- A signal that drives the time–of–day signal and interrupt
- A trigger for memory refresh cycles
- A signal that drives the speaker

These outputs are generated by dividing the input signal. A 16–bit register in the PIT is loaded with a number, and the PIT counts its input pulses until that number is reached. It then sends out a single output pulse. If the number is eight, the output signal will have a frequency of 148.75 KHz, one–eighth the 1.19MHz input signal. The time–of–day signal, for example, uses the maximum divider, 65,535, which produces an 18.2 Hz output signal.

The real–time clock

The ISA and EISA architectures include a Motorola MC146818A Real Time Clock circuit or its equivalent. The MC146818A is addressed through I/O ports 0070h–0071h.

The MC146818A contains 64 bytes of battery–backed CMOS RAM to store the time and date. The BIOS uses some of this CMOS RAM space to store configuration data — see Chapter 4. Some chip sets include extra CMOS RAM to store additional, chip set–specific configuration data.

Note: Many manufacturers have enhanced the XT specification to include an MC146818A or equivalent.

Programmable Interrupt Controllers

Description

The XT architecture includes a single 8259A Programmable Interrupt Controller (PIC), or its equivalent. The 8259A supports eight levels of interrupts, and is addressed through I/O ports 20h and 21h.

The ISA and EISA architectures include two cascaded Intel 8259As, or their equivalent. The two 8259As support 16 levels of interrupts, and are addressed through I/O ports 20h–21h and A0h–A1h.

Note: IRQ 12 is reserved in the ISA specification. The EISA specification, and some manufacturers' enhancements of the ISA specification, associate IRQ 12 with the 8042 Keyboard Auxiliary Device (mouse) controller.

Edge-triggered and level-triggered interrupts

The EISA standard supports both ISA-type edge-triggered interrupts and EISA-type level-sensitive interrupts.

Edge-triggered interrupts are signalled by the rising edge of the interrupt signal wave form. The system hardware's decoding circuitry determines the device from the assignment of the interrupt but is otherwise unaware of the interrupt's originator. A system of edge-triggered interrupts is simple to implement, but has some problems:

- Since the decoding logic isn't able to distinguish between devices, two peripherals cannot share an edge-triggered interrupt.
- False interrupts can be registered by transient electrical pulses and noise.
- Genuine interrupts can be lost when two interrupts occur simultaneously.

Level-sensitive interrupts are signalled by a continuous logic-level voltage. This method has the advantage of uniquely identifying the signal's originator. As a result, more than one peripheral can share the same interrupt. This method also has the advantage of being less susceptible to disruption by random electrical pulses and noise.

Direct Memory Access

Introduction

The XT–ISA–EISA specifications support direct memory access (DMA). A DMA controller takes control of the bus when the processor isn't using it, and transfers blocks of data between peripheral devices and memory.

The peripheral device requiring DMA service asserts a DMA request on the appropriate channel. The DMA controller then requests ownership of the bus from the processor and, when bus ownership is granted, transfers the data between the peripheral device and memory. At the end of the transfer, the DMA controller relinquishes bus ownership to the processor.

The XT specification called for a single Intel 8237 Direct Memory Access Controller, which provides four DMA channels. The ISA and EISA specifications add a second, slaved 8237 for a total of seven usable channels.

XT DMA

The XT's 8237 DMA controller provides four channels, only three of which are externally available on the bus:

- Channel 0 — used internally for memory refresh
- Channel 1 — available
- Channel 2 — supports data transfers between memory and diskette drive
- Channel 3 — available

ISA and EISA DMA controllers

The BIOS for ISA and EISA systems supports the equivalent of two Intel 8237 DMA controllers. This functionality provides seven usable channels:

- Channels 0–3 (Controller 1) — supports 8–bit data transfers
- Channel 4 (Controller 2) — used internally to cascade channels 0–3
- Channels 5–7 (Controller 2) — supports 16–bit data transfers

continued

ISA and EISA DMA controllers, cont'd

DMA controller 1 (master) contains channels 0–3 and uses I/O addresses 00h–0Fh, 81h, 82h, 83h and 87h. It supports 8–bit data transfers between 8–bit I/O adapters and 8–bit or 16–bit system memory.

DMA controller 2 (slave) contains channels 4–7 and uses I/O addresses C0h–DEh, 89h, 8Ah, and 8Bh. It supports data transfers between 16–bit I/O adapters and system memory on the 16–bit I/O channel.

EISA DMA modes

An EISA DMA controller can operate in the following modes:

DMA Modes	Description
Single Transfer	ISA–compatible. A DMA request cycle and a DMA acknowledge cycle are preformed for each DMA transfer cycle.
Block Transfer	The peripheral device requiring service issues a DMA request, and the DMA controller responds by performing a DMA acknowledge cycle. The DMA controller executes DMA transfer cycles continuously until the DMA request is removed or a terminal count is reached. A DMA device that uses ISA–compatible timing should not use this mode.
Demand Transfer	The peripheral device requiring service issues a DMA request, and the DMA controller responds by performing a DMA acknowledge cycle. The DMA acknowledge cycle is held, and bus transfers are executed, until the current word–count register reaches its terminal count. A DMA device that uses ISA–compatible timing should not use this mode unless the device periodically releases the bus.
Cascade	A bus master requiring bus ownership asserts a DMA request on the channel, the DMA controller performs a DMA acknowledge cycle, and bus ownership is transferred to the ISA bus–mastering requester.
	DMA channel 4 uses this mode to cascade DMA channels 0–3. A DMA channel can be programmed in cascade mode for use with external 16–bit ISA bus–master adapter cards.

continued

EISA DMA cycles

Each DMA cycle control sequence executes at a different timing pattern. The following describes the timing algorithm for each cycle type.

DMA Cycle	Timing Algorithm
Standard	One transfer cycle every 8 BCLK periods. Each wait state adds two BCLK periods. ISA DMA devices can use this cycle to transfer data to or from 8, 16, or 32–bit memory.
Type A	One transfer cycle for every 6 BCLK periods, except if the transferred data requires data size translation. ISA–compatible device can execute 1.3 times faster using this cycle, but this cycle requires that accessed memory is fast EISA memory.
Type B	One transfer cycle for every 4 BCLK periods, except if the transferred data requires data size translation. Some ISA–compatible devices can transfer data twice as fast as the Standard cycle using this cycle.
Type C	One transfer cycle for every 1 BCLK periods, except add one BCLK for each simultaneous transfer or wait state.

EISA 32–bit DMA transfers

When 32–bit DMA transfers are used, the following I/O address scheme applies:

- The DMA channel page register includes a 16–bit ISA–compatible current register, which contains the two low–order bytes of the DMA address.
- The low page register contains the next byte; the high page register contains the high–order byte of the DMA address.
- The extra page registers are used for the low and high page registers.

EISA Bus Master Support

Introduction

EISA architecture allows coprocessors residing on expansion cards in adapter slots to take over the system bus while the system microprocessor continues its operations.

Bus master use

EISA bus master capabilities support high–performance I/O devices that require optimum system performance and advanced memory access functions. EISA provides four types of DMA transfer cycles, including a 33–megabit–per–second burst cycle:

DMA Cycle	Maximum Data Transfer Rate
Standard	4 megabits per second
Type A	5.3 megabits per second
Type B	8 megabits per second
Type C	33 megabits per second

EISA supports up to six bus masters. Each priority level of the six arbitration levels has its own line to the central arbitration point.

Bus arbitration

EISA bus arbitration allows the latency for each device on the bus to be precisely determined. The EISA bus master then knows the system response time to allow for all devices on the bus. Several I/O processors can operate concurrently on the bus with other slave, DMA–connected, and CPU–connected devices.

continued

Arbitration priority

EISA DMA priorities are fixed. Memory refresh and DMA have the highest priority, followed by the six arbitration levels from master 0–5.

The following figure depicts the interconnections between the various devices on a typical EISA system board.

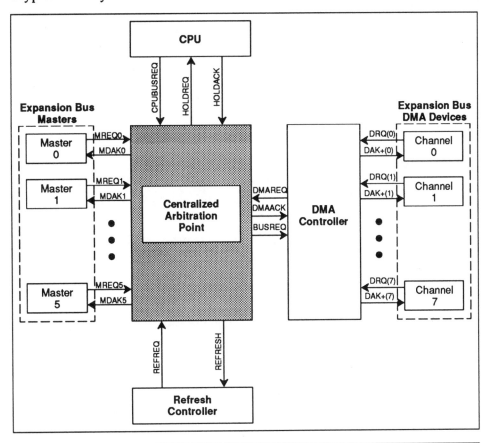

Miscellaneous Additional Logic

Introduction

The ISA and EISA architectures call for certain additional logic to be present in the system:

- An NMI mask
- A diagnostic port
- RTC CMOS RAM (also included in some enhanced XT systems)

NMI mask

The NMI input to the processor is masked off at power–on reset. Bit 7 of I/O port A0h (XT) or 70h (ISA and EISA) is set to zero to enable the NMI. A power–on reset sets this bit to one.

Diagnostic port

An I/O write of certain action codes to I/O port 80h is used to note progress within the boot and diagnostics (POST) process. This port can be read by an external device during a manufacturing test.

Note: Diagnostic messages and beep codes are described in Appendix A for ISA and EISA systems, and Appendix B for XT systems.

Accessing RTC CMOS RAM

To write to RTC CMOS RAM, application programs must

- Inhibit interrupts
- Write the target CMOS address to I/O port 70h, where the bit 7 setting indicates the NMI control
- Send the data to I/O port 71h

To read from RTC CMOS RAM, application programs must

- Inhibit interrupts
- Write the source CMOS address to I/O port 70h, where the bit 7 setting indicates the NMI control
- Read from I/O port 71h

Chapter 3
System RAM Data

Overview

Description

ROM BIOS uses three data areas in system RAM. These data areas are summarized below and described in the tables that follow.

Data Area	Location	Description
Interrupt Vector Table	0000h	Interrupt vectors stored in offset/segment format.
BIOS Data Area	0400h to 04FFh	BIOS work area. Contains data definitions related to fixed disk, diskette, keyboard, video and other BIOS features and functions.
Extended BIOS Data Area	Varies; 40Eh–40Fh contains segment address of extended BIOS data area. INT 15h, AH=C1h returns this value.	Extended BIOS work area. Contains pointing device (mouse), data definitions, and fail–safe timer data definitions. (Exists only if EISA and/or PS/2–style mouse or other special conditions require it.)

Interrupt Vector Table.

The following table provides a description of the Interrupt Vector table for ROM BIOS. It lists each interrupt number, describes its function, and tells what type of interrupt it is. ROM BIOS initializes the interrupt vector addresses during POST.

INT	Function	Type
00h	Divide by Zero	Processor
01h	Single Step	Processor
02h	Nonmaskable Interrupt (NMI)	Processor
03h	Breakpoint	Processor
04h	Overflow	Processor
05h	Print Screen	Software
05h	Bounds Exception (80386, 80486)	Processor
06h	Invalid Op Code (80386, 80486)	Processor
06h	Reserved (PC only)	Hardware
07h	Reserved (PC only)	Hardware
07h	Math Coprocessor Not Present	Processor
08h	System Timer (IRQ 0)	Hardware
08h	Double Exception Error (80386, 80486)	Processor
09h	Keyboard	Hardware
09h	Math Coprocessor Segment Overrun (80386, 80486)	Processor
0Ah	IRQ 2 Cascade from Second Programmable Interrupt Controller	Hardware
0Ah	Invalid Task Segment State (80386, 80486)	Processor
0Ah	IRQ 2 (Reserved) (PC Only)	Hardware
0Bh	Serial Communications (COM2)	Hardware
0Bh	Segment Not Present (80386, 80486)	Processor
0Ch	Serial Communications (COM1)	Hardware
0Ch	Stack Segment Overflow (80386, 80486)	Processor
0Dh	Parallel Printer (LPT2) (ISA, EISA)	Hardware
0Dh	IRQ 5 Fixed Disk (XT only)	Software
0Dh	General Protection Fault (80386, 80486)	Processor

continued

INT	Function	Type
0Eh	IRQ 6 Diskette	Hardware
0Eh	Page Fault (80386 only)	Processor
0Fh	Parallel Printer (LPT1) IRQ 7	Hardware
10h	Video	Software
10h	Numeric Coprocessor Fault (80386, 80486)	Processor
11h	Equipment Check	Software
12h	Memory Size	Software
13h	Diskette/Fixed Disk	Software
14h	Serial Communications	Software
15h	System Services	Software
16h	Keyboard	Software
17h	Parallel Printer	Software
18h	Process Boot Failure (XT, ISA, EISA)	Software
19h	Bootstrap Loader	Software
1Ah	Time-of-Day	Software
1Bh	Keyboard Break	Software
1Ch	User Timer Tick	Software
1Dh	Video Parameters Table	Software
1Eh	Diskette Parameters Table	Software
1Fh	Video Graphics Characters	Software
20h–3Fh	Reserved for DOS	Software
40h	Diskette BIOS Revector	Software
41h	Fixed Disk Parameters Table for fixed disk number 0	Software
42h	EGA Default Video Driver	Software
43h	Video Graphics Characters	Software
44h–45h	Reserved	Software
46h	Fixed Disk Parameters Table for fixed disk number 1	Software
47h–49h	Reserved	

continued

INT	Function	Type
4Ah	User Alarm	Software
4Bh–59h	Reserved	
5Ah	Cluster Adapter	Hardware
5Bh–5Fh	Reserved	
60h–66h	Reserved for User Program Interrupts	User
67h	LIM EMS Driver	Software
68h–6Fh	Reserved	
70h	Real–Time Clock	Hardware
71h	Redirect Cascade	Hardware
72h–73h	Reserved	
74h	Mouse DSR	Hardware
75h	Math Coprocessor Exception (external)	Hardware
76h	Fixed Disk	Hardware
77h–7Fh	Reserved	
80h–F0h	Reserved (BASIC)	
F1h–FFh	Reserved for User Program Interrupts	User

BIOS Data Area

The table below lists the data stored in the BIOS data area in offset order, starting from segment address 40:00h.

Location	Length	Description	BIOS Service
40:00h	4 Words	I/O address of up to 4 asynchronous communications adapters	INT 14h
40:08h	3 or 4 Words	I/O address of up to 4 printer adapters. (When extended data area is used, there can be only 3 printer addresses for a total length of 3 words. Otherwise, there are 4 printer addresses for a total length of 4 words.)	INT 17h
40:0Eh	1 Word	Segment address of extended data area (optional)	INT 74h
40:10h	1 Word	Number of devices installed, where: Bits 15–14 = Number of parallel printer adapters Bits 13–12 = Reserved Bits 11–9 = Number of serial adapters (RS–232) Bits 8 = Reserved Bits 7–6 = Number of disk drives, where: 00 1 disk drive 01 2 disk drives Bits 5–4 = Initial video mode, where: 00 EGA or PGA 01 40x25 color 10 80x25 color 11 80x25 black/white Bit 3 = Reserved Bit 2 = 1 Pointing device installed Bit 1 = 1 Math coprocessor installed Bit 0 = 1 Diskette available for boot	INT 0Eh INT10h INT 11h INT 13h INT 17h
40:12h	1 Byte	Reserved for manufacturer test, where: Bits 7–1 = Reserved Bit 0 = 1 Manufacturing test mode = 0 Non–test mode	POST
40:13h	1 Word	Installed memory in kilobytes (minus size of the extended BIOS data area, if implemented)	INT 12h
40:17h	1 Byte	Keyboard shift flags, where: Bit 7 = 1 Insert active Bit 6 = 1 Caps Lock active Bit 5 = 1 Num Lock active Bit 4 = 1 Scroll Lock active Bit 3 = 1 Alt pressed Bit 2 = 1 Ctrl pressed Bit 1 = 1 Left Shift pressed Bit 0 = 1 Right Shift pressed	INT 09h INT 16h

continued

Location	Length	Description	BIOS Service
40:18h	1 Byte	More keyboard shift flags, where: Bit 7 = 1 Insert pressed Bit 6 = 1 Caps Lock pressed Bit 5 = 1 Num Lock pressed Bit 4 = 1 Scroll Lock pressed Bit 3 = 1 Ctrl–Num Lock state active Bit 2 = 1 Sys Req pressed (enhanced keyboard) Bit 1 = 1 Left Alt pressed (enhanced keyboard) Bit 0 = 1 Left Ctrl pressed (enhanced keyboard)	INT 09h INT 16h
40:19h	1 Byte	Work area for Alt key and numeric keypad input	INT 09h
40:1Ah	1 Word	Pointer to next character in keyboard buffer	INT 09h INT 16h
40:1Ch	1 Word	Pointer to first available spot in keyboard buffer	INT 09h INT 16h
40:1Eh	16 Words	Keyboard buffer of 16 word entries (a maximum of 15 are used at a time)	INT 09h INT 16h
40:3Eh	1 Byte	Diskette drive recalibrate status, where: Bit 7 = 1 Diskette hardware interrupt has occurred Bits 6–4 = Not used Bits 3–2 = Reserved Bit 1 = Recalibrate drive 1 Bit 0 = Recalibrate drive 0	INT 0Eh INT 13h

40:3Fh	1 Byte	Diskette motor status, where:
		
		Bit 7 = 1 Current operation is a write or format
		      0 Current operation is a read or verify
		Bit 6 = Reserved
		Bits 5–4 = Drive select states where:
		    00 Drive 0 select
		    01 Drive 1 select
		    10 Reserved
		    11 Reserved
		Bits 3–2 = Reserved
		Bit 1 = 1 Drive 1 motor is on
		Bit 0 = 1 Drive 0 motor is on
			INT 08h
			INT 0Eh
			INT 13h

40:40h	1 Byte	Diskette motor time–out count	INT 0Eh INT 13h

continued

BIOS Data Area, Continued

Location	Length	Description	BIOS Service

40:41h	1 Byte	Diskette status return code, where:
		
		Bit 7 = 1 Drive not ready
		Bit 6 = 1 Seek error occurred
		Bit 5 = 1 Diskette controller failed
		Bits 4–0 = ERROR CODES, where:
		    01h Illegal function request
		    02h Address mark not found
		    03h Write protect error
		    04h Sector not found
		    06h Diskette change line active
		    08h DMA overrun on operation
		    09h Data boundary error (64K)
		    0CH Media type not found
		    10h Uncorrectable ECC or CRC error
		    20h General controller failure
		    40h Seek operation failed
		    80h Timeout
			INT 0Eh
			INT 13h

40:42h	7 Bytes	Diskette controller status bytes	INT 13h INT 0Eh
40:49h	1 Byte	Video mode setting	INT 10h
40:4Ah	1 Word	Number of columns on screen	INT 10h
40:4Ch	1 Word	Current page size (in bytes)	INT 10h
40:4Eh	1 Word	Current page address	INT 10h
40:50h	8 Words	Cursor position on each page. Two bytes/page. First byte of each pair is column; second byte is row. 0,0 is upper left corner of screen.	INT 10h
40:60h	1 Word	Cursor type defined as 6845–compatible starting and ending scan lines. High byte is starting scan line; low is ending line.	INT 10h
40:62h	1 Byte	Current display page	INT 10h
40:63h	1 Word	6845–compatible I/O port number for current mode, where: 03B4h = Monochrome 03D4h = Color	INT 10h
40:65h	1 Byte	Current mode select register	INT 10h
40:66h	1 Byte	Current palette value	INT 10h
40:67h	1 Word	Address offset of option ROM	* **

* BIOS Service varies depending on which option ROM is installed.
** Also used by POST for return from RESET and by XT for cassette data.

continued

Location	Length	Description	BIOS Service
40:69h	1 Word	Address segment of option ROM	*
40:6Bh	1 Byte	Last interrupt that occurred	POST
40:6Ch	1 Word	Least significant timer count	INT 08h INT 1Ah
40:6Eh	1 Word	Most significant timer count	INT 08h INT 1Ah
40:70h	1 Byte	24–hour rollover flag	INT 08h INT 1Ah
40:71h	1 Byte	Ctrl–Break flag	INT 09h
40:72h	1 Word	Reset flag, where: 1234h = Bypass memory test 4321h = Preserve memory 64h = Burn–in mode	INT 09h POST
40:74h	1 Byte	Status from last fixed disk operation, where: 00h = No error 01h = Invalid function request 02h = Address mark not found 04h = Sector not found 05h = Reset failed 07h = Drive parameter activity failed 08h = DMA overrun on operation 09h = Data boundary error 0Ah = Bad sector flag detected 0Bh = Bad track detected 0Dh = Invalid number of sectors on format 0Eh = Control data address mark detected 0Fh = DMA arbitration level out of range 10h = Uncorrectable ECC or CRC error 11h = ECC corrected data error 20h = General controller failure 40h = Seek operation failed 80h = Timeout AAh = Drive not ready BBh = Undefined error occurred CCh = Write fault on selected drive EOh = Status error/error register is 0 FFh = Sense operation failed	INT 13h INT 76h
40:75h	1 Byte	Number of fixed disk drives	INT 13h INT 19h INT 76h
40:76h	1 Byte	Fixed disk control byte	INT 13h INT 76h

* BIOS Service varies depending on which option ROM is installed.

continued

Location	Length	Description	BIOS Service
40:77h	1 Byte	Fixed disk port offset	INT 13h INT 76h
40:78h	2 Words	Printer time–out table (ports 0–3)	INT 17h
40:7Ch	2 Words	Serial time–out table (ports 0–3)	INT 14h
40:80h	1 Word	Offset to start of keyboard buffer (from segment 40h)	INT 09h
40:82h	1 Word	Offset to end of keyboard buffer (from segment 40h)	INT 09h

40:8Bh	1 Byte	Diskette data rate information
		
		Bits 7–6 = Last data rate set by controller, where:
		      00 500 KBS
		      01 300 KBS
		      10 250 KBS
		      11 Reserved
		Bits 5–4 = Last diskette drive step rate selected
		Bits 3–2 = Data transfer rate at operation start,
		      where:
		      00 500 KBS
		      01 300 KBS
		      10 250 KBS
		Bits 1–0 = Reserved
			INT 0Eh
			INT 13h

40:8Ch	1 Byte	Fixed disk status register (copy)	INT 13h INT 76h
40:8Dh	1 Byte	Fixed disk error register (copy)	INT 13h INT 76h
40:8Eh	1 Byte	Fixed disk interrupt flag	INT 13h INT 76h
40:8Fh	1 Byte	Diskette controller information, where: Bit 7 = Reserved Bit 6 = 1 Drive determined for drive 1 Bit 5 = 1 Drive 1 is multirate Bit 4 = 1 Drive 1 supports change line Bit 3 = Reserved Bit 2 = 1 Drive determined for drive 0 Bit 1 = 1 Drive 0 is multirate Bit 0 = 1 Drive 0 supports change line	INT 0Eh INT 13h

continued

Location	Length	Description	BIOS Service

40:90h	1 Word	Media type of both drives:
		(One byte per drive: drive 0 at 40:90h, drive 1 at 40:91h)
		
		Bits 7–6 = Data transfer rate, where:
		       00 500 KBS
		       01 300 KBS
		       10 250 KBS
		Bit 5 = 1 Double stepping required
		          (360K media/1.2MB drive)
		Bit 4 = 1 Known media in drive
		Bit 3 = Reserved
		Bits 2–0 = Definitions on return to user application:
		     111 720K media in 720K drive or 1.44MB
		           media in 1.44MB drive
		     101 Known 1.2MB media in 1.2MB drive
		     100 Known 360K media in 1.2MB drive
		     011 Known 360K media in 360K drive
		     010 Trying 1.2MB media in 1.2MB drive
		     001 Trying 360K media in 1.2MB drive
		     000 Trying 360K media in 360K drive
			INT 0Eh
			INT 13h

40:92h	1 Word	Diskette media work area. Each entry is first diskette media work area value tried. One byte per drive. Drive 0 at 92h, Drive 1 at 93h.	INT 0Eh INT 13h
40:94h	1 Word	Current track number for both drives. One byte per drive. Drive 0 at 94h, drive 1 at 95h.	INT 0Eh INT 13h
40:96h	1 Byte	Keyboard status byte: Bit 7 = 1 Read ID in progress Bit 6 = 1 Last code was first ID Bit 5 = 1 Forced Num Lock Bit 4 = 1 101/102 keyboard used Bit 3 = 1 Right Alt active Bit 2 = 1 Right Ctrl active Bit 1 = 1 Last code was E0h Bit 0 = 1 Last code was E1h	INT 09h INT 16h
40:97h	1 Byte	Status byte: Bit 7 = Error flag for keyboard command Bit 6 = LED update in progress Bit 5 = RESEND received from keyboard Bit 4 = ACK received from keyboard Bit 3 = Reserved Bit 2 = Caps Lock LED status Bit 1 = Num Lock LED status Bit 0 = Scroll Lock LED status	INT 09h

continued

Location	Length	Description	BIOS Service
40:98h	1 Word	User wait flag offset address	INT 08h INT 15h INT 1Ah
40:9Ah	1 Word	User wait flag segment address	INT 15h
40:9Ch	1 Word	Wait count (low word)	INT 08h INT 15h INT 1Ah
40:9Eh	1 Word	More significant wait count (high word)	INT 08h INT 15h INT 1Ah
40:A0h	1 Byte	Wait active flag, where: Bit 7 = 1 Wait time elapsed Bits 6–1 = Reserved Bit 0 = 1 INT 15h, AH = 86h occurred	INT 08h INT 15h INT 1Ah
40:B0h–40:B5h	3 Words	Reserved	
40:100h	1 Byte	Print screen status byte	INT 05h

Extended BIOS Data Area

ROM BIOS uses the top 1K of system RAM as an extended BIOS data area to store data needed by the Phoenix Advanced Mouse and Password Support firmware.

Location	Length	Description
EDA:00h	1 Byte	Size of EDA in K
EDA:22h	1 Word	Pointing device device driver far call offset
EDA:24h	1 Word	Pointing device device driver far call segment
EDA:26h	1 Byte	Pointing device flag (first byte) Bit 7 = 1 Command in progress Bit 6 = 1 Resend Bit 5 = 1 Acknowledge Bit 4 = 1 Error Bit 3 = 0 Reserved Bits 2–0 = Index count
EDA:27h	1 Byte	Pointing device flag (second byte) Bit 7 = Device driver far call flag Bits 6–3 = 0 Reserved Bits 2–0 = Package size
EDA:28h	1 Byte	Pointing device data
EDA:29h	1 Byte	Pointing device data
EDA:2AH	1 Byte	Pointing device data
EDA:2Bh	1 Byte	Pointing device data
EDA:2Ch	1 Byte	Pointing device data
EDA:2Dh	1 Byte	Pointing device data
EDA:2Eh	1 Byte	Pointing device data
EDA:30h– EDA:38h		Reserved
EDA:39h	1 Word	Initial count for fail–safe timer

4

Chapter 4
CMOS RAM Data

Overview

Description

The IBM PC/AT specification included a Motorola MC146818A Real Time Clock chip. This chip or equivalent circuitry has remained a fundamental element in the ISA specification. The MC146818A includes 64 bytes of battery–backed non–volatile CMOS RAM that the ROM BIOS uses for storing system configuration, system diagnostic, and other information, as well as the time and date.

The 64 bytes of CMOS RAM in the MC146818A eliminates the need for DIP switches on the system board and allows the system time and date to be maintained automatically, even when the system is powered down.

Now, manufacturers of XT systems routinely enhance the XT specification by adding a real–time clock chip with CMOS RAM. Manufacturers of ISA systems often include more than 64 bytes of CMOS RAM, adding an extended CMOS RAM data area. EISA systems require at least 4096 bytes of additional CMOS RAM to store EISA–specific configuration data.

In this chapter

This chapter provides data definitions for standard and extended CMOS RAM and describes the EISA CMOS RAM area.

Standard or Extended CMOS RAM Data Definitions

Introduction

The standard and extended CMOS RAM data areas are accessed through I/O ports 0070h and 0071h. The standard data area is defined by the ISA specification; the extended data area varies among ROM BIOS implementations.

The following tables describe the standard 64–byte CMOS RAM data area. They present the CMOS RAM data definitions for

- Real–time clock information
- Real–time clock status registers
- System configuration information

Real–time clock data definitions

Location	Size	Description
00h	1 Byte	Current second in binary coded decimal (BCD)
01h	1 Byte	Seconds alarm in BCD
02h	1 Byte	Current minute in BCD
03h	1 Byte	Minutes alarm in BCD
04h	1 Byte	Current hour in BCD
05h	1 Byte	Hour alarm in BCD
06h	1 Byte	Current day of week in BCD
07h	1 Byte	Current day of the month in BCD
08h	1 Byte	Current month in BCD
09h	1 Byte	Current year in BCD (00–99)

continued

Real–time clock status registers data definitions

Location	Size	Description
0Ah	1 Byte	Status register A, where: Bit 7 = 1 Update in progress Bits 6–4 = Divider that identifies the time–based frequency Bits 3–0 = Rate–selection bits that define output frequency and periodic interrupt rate

0Bh	1 Byte	Status register B, where:
		
		Bit 7 = 0 Run
		       = 1 Halt
		Bit 6 = 1 Enable periodic interrupt
		Bit 5 = 1 Enable alarm interrupt
		Bit 4 = 1 Enable update–ended interrupt
		Bit 3 = 1 Enable square wave interrupt
		Bit 2 = 1 Calendar is in binary format
		       = 0 Calendar is in BCD format
		Bit 1 = 1 24–hour mode
		       = 0 12–hour mode
		Bit 0 = 1 Enable Daylight Savings Time

0Ch Read only*	1 Byte	Status register C, where: Bit 7 = Interrupt Request Flag (IRQF) Bit 6 = Periodic Interrupt Flag (PF) Bit 5 = Alarm Interrupt Flag (AF) Bit 4 = Update Interrupt Flag (UF) Bits 3–0 = Reserved
0Dh Read only*	1 Byte	Status register D, where: Bit 7 = 1 Real–time clock has power Bits 6–0 = Reserved

* A read to the MC146818 Real Time Clock clears these status flags.

continued

System configuration data definitions

Location	Size	Description
0Eh	1 Byte	Diagnostic status, where: Bit 7 = 1 Real–time clock lost power Bit 6 = 1 CMOS RAM checksum is bad Bit 5 = 1 Invalid configuration information found at POST Bit 4 = 1 Memory size compare error at POST Bit 3 = 1 Fixed disk/adapter fails initialization Bit 2 = 1 CMOS RAM time found invalid Bit 1 = 1 Adapters do not match configuration (EISA) Bit 0 = 1 Timeout reading an adapter ID (EISA)
0Fh	1 Byte	Shutdown code, where: 00h = Normal execution of POST 01h = Chip set initialization for real mode entry 04h = Jump to bootstrap code 05h = Issue an EOI, flush keyboard, and JMP to Dword pointer at 40:67h 06h = JMP to Dword pointer at 40:67h without EOI 07h = Return to INT 15h, Function AH = 87h Block Move 08h = Return to POST memory test 09h = Return to INT 15h, Function AH = 87h Block Move 0Ah = JMP to Dword pointer at 40:67h without EOI 0Bh = Return IRETS through 40:67h. 0Ch = Return via Dword pointer at 40:67h
10h	1 Byte	Type of diskette drives, where: Bits 7–4 = Drive type of drive 0 Bits 3–0 = Drive type of drive 1 　　0000　　 = No drive 　　0001　　 = 360K drive 　　0010　　 = 1.2MB drive 　　0011　　 = 720K 　　0100　　 = 1.44MB 　　0101–1111 = Reserved
11h	1 Byte	Reserved
12h	1 Byte	Type of fixed disk drive (0 and 1), where: Bits 7–4 = Drive 0 Bits 3–0 = Drive 1 If either of the nibbles equals 0Fh, then bytes 19h and 1Ah are valid.
13h	1 Byte	Reserved

continued

Standard or Extended CMOS RAM Data Definitions, Continued

System configuration data definitions, cont'd

Location	Size	Description
14h	1 Byte	Equipment byte, where: Bits 7–6 = Diskette drives installed, where: 00h = 1 diskette drive installed 01h = 2 diskette drives installed 02h–03h = Reserved Bits 5–4 = Primary display, where: 00h = Adapter card with option ROM installed at segment C000h 01h = 40–column color 02h = 80–column color 03h = Monochrome Bits 3–2 = Reserved Bit 1 = Math coprocessor installed (non–Weitek) Bit 0 = Diskette drive available for boot
15h	1 Byte	Base memory in 1K multiples, low byte
16h	1 Byte	Base memory in 1K multiples, high byte
17h	1 Byte	Extended memory in 1K multiples, low byte
18h	1 Byte	Extended memory in 1K multiples, high byte
19h	1 Byte	Extended drive type (16–49) of first fixed disk
1Ah	1 Byte	Extended drive type (16–49) of second fixed disk
1Bh–27h	13 Bytes	Reserved
2Eh	1 Byte	High byte of the checksum for the contents of 10h–2Dh
2Fh	1 Byte	Low byte of the checksum for the contents of 10h–2Dh
30h	1 Byte	Extended memory size in kilobytes as reported by POST, low byte
31h	1 Byte	Extended memory size in kilobytes as reported by POST, high byte
32h	1 Byte	Century in BCD
33h–3Fh	13 Bytes	Reserved

EISA CMOS RAM Data

EISA system configurations require at least 4K of extended CMOS RAM. This memory is used to store adapter card data. The EISA specification provides for a maximum of 15 physical adapter cards and a maximum of 64 devices.

EISA CMOS RAM is accessed via INT 15h Function AH = D8h Access EISA System Information. EISA extended CMOS RAM is accessed by the subfunctions of this function and should be the only method used to access extended CMOS RAM in an EISA system.

INT 15h Function AH = D8h Access EISA System Information is described in detail in Chapter 14.

5

Chapter 5
ROM BIOS Data

Overview

Introduction

In addition to service routines, ROM BIOS contains tabular data that is used to initialize devices and to ensure IBM compatibility. This section describes this data.

In this chapter

The following topics are presented in this chapter:

- Compatibility Segment
- System Configuration Table
- Diskette Parameters Table
- ISA and EISA Fixed Disk Parameters Table
- XT Fixed Disk Parameters Table
- Baud Rate Initialization Table

Compatibility Segment

Description

The Compatibility Segment (COMPAS) provides jump vectors and tables that ensure that calls to service routines and table information are located at the memory addresses used by IBM. The COMPAS module references addresses from FE000h to FFFFFh in system ROM.

COMPAS structure

The COMPAS module is structured as shown in the following table.

Address	Length	Description
FE000h	5Bh	Reserved space
FE05Bh	03h	JMP to POST entry point
FE05Eh	265h	Reserved space
FE2C3h	03h	JMP to INT 02h Nonmaskable Interrupt Service routine
FE2C6h	138h	Reserved space
FE3FEh	03h	JMP to INT 13h Fixed Disk Service routine
FE401h	02F0h	Fixed Disk Parameters table
FE6F1h	01h	Reserved space
FE6F2h	03h	JMP to INT 19h Bootstrap Loader routine
FE6F5h	1Bh	System Configuration table
FE710h	19h	Reserved space
FE729h	10h	Baud Rate Initialization table
FE739h	03h	JMP to INT 14h Serial Communications Service routine
FE73Ch	0F2h	Reserved space
FE82Eh	03h	JMP to INT 16h Keyboard Service routine
FE831h	156h	Reserved space
FE987h	03h	JMP to INT 09h Keyboard Service routine
FE98Ah	2CFh	Reserved space
FEC59h	03h	JMP to INT 13h Diskette Service routine
FEC5Ch	2FB	Reserved space
FEF57h	03h	JMP to INT 0Eh Diskette Interrupt Service routine

continued

COMPAS structure, cont'd

Address	Length	Description
FEF5Ah	6Dh	Reserved space
FEFC7h	0Bh	Diskette Parameters table (pointed to by 1Eh)
FEFD2h	03h	JMP to INT 17h Parallel Printer Service routine
FEFD5h	90h	Reserved space
FF065h	03h	JMP to INT 10h Video Service routine
FF068h	3Ch	Reserved space
FF0A4h	58h	Video Parameters table (pointed to by INT 1Dh)
FF0FCh	745h	Reserved space
FF841h	03h	JMP to INT 12h Memory Size Service routine
FF844h	09h	Reserved space
FF84Dh	03h	JMP to INT 11h Equipment Check Service routine
FF850h	09h	Reserved space
FF859h	03h	JMP to INT 15h System Services routine
FF85Ch	212h	Reserved space
FFA6Eh	400h	Font tables for video graphics and text modes
FFE6Eh	03h	JMP to INT 1Ah Time-of-Day routine
FFE71h	34h	Reserved space
FFEA5h	03h	JMP to INT 08h System Timer routine
FFEA8h	4Bh	Reserved space
FFEF3h	30h	Table of vector offsets for initialization of INTs 08h–1Fh
FFF23h	10h	Table of vector offsets for initialization of INTs 70h–77h
FFF33h	21h	Reserved space
FFF54h	03h	JMP to INT 05h Print Screen Service routine
FFF57h	82h	Reserved space
FFFD9h	04h	EISA identification string
FFFDDh	13h	Reserved space
FFFF0h	05h	JMP to power-up entry point

continued

COMPAS structure, cont'd

Address	Length	Description
FFFF5h	08h	ASCII date of ROM BIOS version release
FFFFDh	01h	Unused space
FFFFEh	01h	System model ID (0FCh = AT compatible)
FFFFFh	01h	Reserved

System Configuration Table

Description

The System Configuration table (F000:E6F5h) contains basic information about the computer system in which ROM BIOS is operating. The table can be copied into CMOS RAM with the INT 15h DSR Function AH = C0h.

Offset	Length	Description
00h	2 Bytes	Length of table (not including this length word)
02h	1 Byte	Model byte, where: PC = FFh PC XT = FEh PC XT = FBh PCjr = FDh AT = FCh XT–286 = FCh PC Convertible = F9h
03h	1 Byte	Submodel byte, where: PC = Undefined PC XT = 00h or 01h PCjr = Undefined AT = 00h AT = 01h XT–286 = 02h PC Convertible = Undefined Unknown system board = FFh
04h	1 Byte	BIOS revision level (always 0)
05h	1 Byte	Feature information byte 1, where: Bit 7 = 1 Fixed disk BIOS uses DMA channel 3 Bit 6 = 1 Second Intel 8259A, or equivalent device is present (cascaded IRQ) Bit 5 = 1 Real–time clock is present Bit 4 = 1 Keyboard intercept (INT 15h, Function 4Fh) called by keyboard interrupt service (INT 09h) Bit 2 = 1 Extended BIOS data area is allocated Bit 1 = 0 ISA–type I/O channel is implemented Bit 0 = 0 Reserved
06h	1 Byte	Feature information byte 2 (reserved, zeros)
07h	1 Byte	Feature information byte 3 (reserved, zeros)
08h	1 Byte	Feature information byte 4 (reserved, zeros)
09h	1 Byte	Feature information byte 5 (reserved, zeros)

continued

Model and submodel bytes

The model and submodel bytes in the System Configuration table identify the type of system that the ROM BIOS is operating on. The following model/submodel byte combinations may appear in the table.

Model Byte Value	Submodel Byte Value	Machine
F9h	None	PC Convertible
FBh	00h, 01h	XT
FCh	00h, 01h	AT
FCh	02h	PC/XT–286
FDh	None	PCjr
FEh	None	XT
FFh	None	PC

Diskette Parameters Table

Description

The BIOS includes a table of parameters for manipulating diskette drives through the associated controller. This 11–byte table is located in system ROM at location F000:EFC7h and is pointed to by the INT 1Eh vector. Default values in the table can be modified as needed.

Table structure

The Diskette Parameters table is structured as follows.

Offset	Description
00h	First data byte of the diskette specify command, where: Bits 7–4 = Step rate time: Fh (1 ms), Eh (2ms), Dh (3 ms), and so on. The table below shows valid bit settings for the various media/drive combinations. **Media Type**　**Drive Type**　**Default Value** 360K　360K　DFh 360K　1.2MB　DFh 1.2MB　1.2MB　DFh 720K　720K　AFh 720K　1.44MB　AFh 1.44MB　1.44MB　AFh 720K　1.2MB　DFh Bits 3–0 = Head unload time in 32–ms increments from 0 to 240 ms. Default is 0Fh (240 ms).
01h	Second data byte of the diskette specify command, where: Bits 7–1 = Head load time in 4–ms increments from 2 to 256 ms. Default is 01h. Bit 0　　= Non–DMA mode flag The heads are loaded at the same time as the motor is started, but the motor delay is much longer so the head load time delay is not really needed. The non–DMA mode flag is always set to zero to indicate that DMA is being used.
02h	Motor turn–off delay. The amount of time in timer ticks that the diskette device service routine waits before turning off an inactive diskette drive motor. Timer ticks occur 18.2 times per second and the routine waits about two seconds. The default value for this field is 25h.

continued

Table structure, cont'd

Offset	Description
03h	Bytes per sector. This field is encoded in the following way to match the encoding used by the diskette controller: 00h = 128 bytes per sector 01h = 256 bytes per sector 02h = 512 bytes per sector (default value) 03h = 1024 bytes per sector
04h	The number of sectors per track. The range of values is 08h = 8 sectors per track (320K drive) 09h = 9 sectors per track (360K/720K 3.50– and 5.25–inch drives) 15h = 15 sectors per track (5.25–inch 1.2MB drive) 18h = 18 sectors per track (3.50–inch drives)
05h	Gap length. The length of the gap between sectors. 1Bh = 1.2MB medium in a 1.2MB drive, or a 1.44MB medium in a 1.44MB drive 2Ah = All other media/drive combinations
06h	Data length. Since the bytes per sector field is nonzero, this field is meaningless and is set to FFh.
07h	Gap length for format. The length of the gap between sectors to maintain when formatting. 50h = 360K and 720K media 54h = 1.2MB media 6Ch = 1.44MB media
08h	Fill byte for format. The default is F6h.
09h	Head settle time. The amount of time in milliseconds the diskette DSR must wait for the heads to settle after doing a seek operation. Value of this field is 0Fh.
0Ah	Motor start time. The amount of time in eighths of a second that the diskette DSR must wait for the motor to come up to speed before doing an I/O operation. Most drives have a motor start time of one second; therefore, the default value is 08h for most operations. Read and Verify operations are exceptions. Their default values are either 04h or 05h.

ISA and EISA Fixed Disk Parameters Table

Description

The ROM BIOS is designed to support up to 49 fixed disk drive types. A Fixed Disk Parameters table containing 47 different combinations of drive parameters is located in system ROM at memory location F000:E401h. Manufacturers can change the default drive descriptions. They can also build the system so that the system user can define two additional drive types during system configuration.

At system initialization, ROM BIOS sets the INT 41h vector to point to the Fixed Disk Parameters table entry associated with drive 0. If fixed disk drive 1 is installed, INT 46h is initialized to point to its corresponding entry in the table.

Table structure

The drive descriptions are ordered as follows in the Fixed Disk Drive Parameters table. The drive type number and product names do not actually appear in the table, but have been added to show popular drive types having particular sets of characteristics. See "ISA and EISA table entry format" later in this chapter for a description of the table entry format.

No.	Drive Type	Cylinders	Heads	Write Precomp	Landing Zone	Sectors
1	IBM 5.25" 10MB	306	4	128	305	17
2	IBM 5.25" 20MB Seagate ST–225 CDC Wren II 9415–5–25 * Miniscribe 8438F	615	4	300	615	17
3	IBM 5.25" 30MB	615	6	300	615	17
4	IBM 5.25" 62MB	940	8	512	940	17
5	IBM 5.25" 46MB	940	6	512	940	17
6	IBM 5.25" 20MB Miniscribe MS 8425 Tandon TM 262 *** Tandon TM 702AT ***	615	4	–1	615	17
7	IBM 5.25" 30MB	462	8	256	511	17

* OEMs may have to disable drive connector J1 Pin 2 when used on AT compatibles.

continued

Table structure, cont'd

No.	Drive Type	Cylinders	Heads	Write Precomp	Landing Zone	Sectors
8	IBM 5.25" 30MB Seagate ST–4038 *** CDC Wren II 9415–5–38 * *** Tandon TM 703AT ***	733	5	–1	733	17
9	IBM 5.25" 112MB Priam IDED 130 *	900	15	–1	901	17
10	IBM 5.25" 20MB Priam IDED 75, 100, 120, 150, 160, 230, 330 *	820	3	–1	820	17
11	IBM 5.25" 35MB Priam IDED 40, 45, 45H Priam ID45T–S, ID45T–Q *	855	5	–1	855	17
12	IBM 5.25" 49MB	855	7	–1	855	17
13	IBM 5.25" 20MB	306	8	128	319	17
14	IBM 5.25" 42MB	733	7	–1	733	17
15	Reserved					
16	IBM 5.25" 20MB	612	4	0	663	17
17	IBM 5.25" 40MB	977	5	300	977	17
18	IBM 5.25" 56MB Priam ID 60, 62 *	977	7	–1	977	17
19	IBM 5.25" 59MB	1024	7	512	1023	17
20	IBM 5.25" 30MB	733	5	300	732	17
21	IBM 5.25" 42MB	733	7	300	732	17
22	IBM 5.25" 30MB	733	5	300	733	17
23	IBM 5.25" 10MB	306	4	0	336	17
24	Reserved					
25	NEC 5126 20MB	615	4	0	615	17

*   OEMs may have to disable drive connector J1 Pin 2 when used on AT compatibles.
*** Values for Write Precomp of –1, 0, or the last track are assumed to be equivalent.

continued

Table structure, cont'd

No.	Drive Type	Cylinders	Heads	Write Precomp	Landing Zone	Sectors
26	Micropolis 1323 *** Rodime 5040	1024	4	−1	1023	17
27	Micropolis 1323A *** Seagate ST–4077R Miniscribe 3053/6053 Priam IDED 45, 45H **	1024	5	−1	1023	17
28	Micropolis 1325 *** Miniscribe 6085 Maxtor XT–1085 ***	1024	8	−1	1023	17
29		512	8	256	512	17
30	Syquest SQ312RD ** Miniscribe MS 8212 ***	615	2	615	615	17
31	CDC Wren II 9420–5–51 **	989	5	0	989	17
32		1020	15	−1	1024	17
33		615	4	−1	615	26
34		820	6	−1	820	26
35	Seagate ST–4096 Seagate ST–4144 Seagate ST–4144R	1024	9	1024	1024	17
36	Miniscribe MS 6053 Microscience HH1050	1024	5	512	1024	17
37		1024	5	512	1024	26
38	NEC 67MB	823	10	256	824	17
39	NEC D5126H 20MB	615	4	128	664	17
40	IBM 5.25" 40MB NEC D5146H	615	8	128	664	17
41	IBM 5.25" 114MB	917	15	−1	918	17
42	IBM 5.25" 127MB Priam IDED 130 **	1023	15	−1	1024	17

** Remove jumper W3.
*** Values for Write Precomp of −1, 0, or the last track are assumed to be equivalent.

continued

Table structure, cont'd

No.	Drive Type	Cylinders	Heads	Write Precomp	Landing Zone	Sectors
43	NEC	823	10	512	823	17
44	Seagate ST–251 40MB	820	6	–1	820	17
45		1024	5	–1	1023	17
46	CDC Wren II (1) 9415–5–86	925	9	–1	925	17
47		699	7	256	700	17
48	Configurable by End User					
49	Configurable by End User ****					

**** This drive type is configurable by end users when PS/2–style password option is not used.

If a Fixed Disk Parameters table entry contains –1 as the entry for the beginning write precompensation cylinder, then there is no write precompensation for the fixed disk drive type. If the write precompensation is 0, then there is write precompensation for all cylinders on the drive.

continued

ISA and EISA table entry format

Each 16–byte entry in the ISA and EISA Fixed Disk Parameters table has the following format.

Offset	Length	Description
00h	2 Bytes	Maximum number of cylinders
02h	1 Byte	Maximum number of heads
03h	2 Bytes	Reserved (set to zeros)
05h	2 Bytes	Starting cylinder for write precompensation
07h	1 Byte	Reserved (set to zero)
08h	1 Byte	Control byte, where: Bit 7 = 1 Disable retries Bit 6 = 1 Disable retries Bit 5 = 1 Defect map present at max, cylinder + 1 Bit 4 = 0 Reserved Bit 3 = 1 More than 8 heads Bits 2–0 = 0 Reserved
09h	3 Bytes	Reserved (set to zeros)
0Ch	2 Bytes	Landing zone
0Eh	1 Byte	Number of sectors per track
0Fh	1 Byte	Reserved (set to zero)

XT Fixed Disk Parameters Table

Description

The XT Fixed Disk Parameters table defines the types of fixed disk drives that can be used in an XT system. As part of system configuration, the INT 41h vector points to the Fixed Disk Parameter table entry associated with drive 0. To maintain compatibility, the Fixed Disk Parameters table is based at F000:E401h.

XT fixed disk drive type table

There are four fixed disk drive types supported by the XT–compatible Fixed Disk Service. The parameters for each of these XT–compatible drive types are shown in the following table. See "XT table entry format" on the next page for a description of the table entry format.

Parameter	Type 0	Type 1	Type 2	Type 3
Maximum cylinders	306	375	306	306
Maximum heads	2	8	6	2*
Reduced write current cylinder	306	375	128	306
Write precompensation cylinder	0	0	256	0
ECC data burst length	11	11	11	11
Control byte	0	5	5	5
Standard timeout	12	12	12	12
Format drive timeout	180	180	180	180
Check drive timeout	40	40	40	40

* Maximum number of heads can vary; for example, IBM specifies 4 for a Type 3 fixed disk drive.

continued

XT table entry format

Each 16–byte entry in the XT Fixed Disk Parameters table has the following format.

Offset	Length	Description
00h	2 Bytes	Maximum number of cylinders
02h	1 Byte	Maximum number of heads
03h	2 Bytes	Starting reduced write current cylinder
05h	2 Bytes	Starting write precompensation cylinder
07h	1 Byte	Maximum ECC burst length
08h	1 Byte	Control byte, where: Bit 7 = 1 Disable fixed disk retries Bit 6 = 1 Disable ECC retries Bits 5–3 = 1 Reserved Bits 2–0 = Drive option
09h	1 Byte	Standard time–out value
0Ch	1 Bytes	Time–out value for format drive command
0Eh	1 Byte	Time–out value for check drive command
0Fh	4 Byte	Reserved (set to zeros)

Baud Rate Initialization Table

ROM BIOS provides a Baud Rate Initialization table for serial port operations. This table is located at memory location F000:E729h and is structured as follows.

Baud Rate	Divisor
110	0417h
150	0300h
300	0180h
600	00C0h
1200	0060h
2400	0030h
4800	0018h
9600	000Ch

Chapter 6
I/O Ports

Overview

Description

The Intel 80x86 architecture includes a 64K I/O memory space for accessing external devices. The 8086/8088 and 80286 I/O spaces can be divided into 8–bit or 16–bit ports. The 80386 and 80486 allow combinations of 8–, 16– or 32–bit ports.

The XT specification divides the I/O address space into two parts. The address range 000h–01FFh is used to address peripheral devices on the system board; the address range 0200h–02FFh is used to address devices connected to the XT expansion slots.

In the ISA and EISA specifications, the boundary between system-board addresses and expansion–slot addresses is at 0100h, rather than 0200h, providing 256 more I/O addresses than the XT for the expansion slots. While 01F0h–01F8h is reserved for the fixed–disk adapter, most manufacturers of expansion boards avoid using the 0100h–0200h range to maintain XT compatibility.

In this chapter

This chapter contains tables listing the I/O ports used by the ROM BIOS. The I/O ports for MDA and CGA video adapters are described separately because of the complexity of video I/O mapping.

I/O Port List

I/O Address	Read/Write Status	Description
0000h	R/W	DMA channel 0 address byte 0 (low), then byte 1
0001h	R/W	DMA channel 0 word count byte 0 (low), then byte 1
0002h	R/W	DMA channel 1 address byte 0 (low), then byte 1
0003h	R/W	DMA channel 1 word count byte 0 (low), then byte 1
0004h	R/W	DMA channel 2 address byte 0 (low), then byte 1
0005h	R/W	DMA channel 2 word count byte 0 (low), then byte 1
0006h	R/W	DMA channel 3 address byte 0 (low), then byte 1
0007h	R/W	DMA channel 3 word count byte 0 (low), the byte 1
0008h	R	DMA channel 0–3, status register, where: Bit 7 = 1 Channel 3 request Bit 6 = 1 Channel 2 request Bit 5 = 1 Channel 1 request Bit 4 = 1 Channel 0 request Bit 3 = 1 Terminal count on channel 3 Bit 2 = 1 Terminal count on channel 2 Bit 1 = 1 Terminal count on channel 1 Bit 0 = 1 Terminal count on channel 0

0008h	W	DMA channel 0–3, command register, where:
		
		Bit 7 = 1 DACK sense active high
		       0 DACK sense active low
		Bit 6 = 1 DREQ sense active low
		       0 DREQ sense active high
		Bit 5 = 1 Extended write selection
		       0 Late write selection
		Bit 4 = 1 Rotating priority
		       0 Fixed priority
		Bit 3 = 1 Compressed timing
		       0 Normal timing
		Bit 2 = 0 Enable controller
		Bit 1 = 1 Enable memory–to–memory

0009h	W	DMA write request register

000Ah	R/W	DMA channel 0–3, mask register, where:
		
		Bits 7–3 = 0 Reserved
		Bit 2 = 0 Clear mask bit
		      1 Set mask bit
		Bits 1–0 = 00 Channel 0 select
		         01 Channel 1 select
		         10 Channel 2 select
		         11 Channel 3 select

continued

I/O Address	Read/Write Status	Description

000Bh	W	DMA channel 0–3, mode register, where:
		
		Bits 7–6 = 00 Demand mode
		          01 Single mode
		          10 Block mode
		          11 Cascade mode
		Bit 5 = 0 Address increment select
		          1 Address decrement select
		Bit 4 = 0 Autoinitialization disable
		          1 Autoinitialization enable
		Bits 3–2 = 00 Verify operation
		          01 Write to memory
		          10 Read from memory
		          11 Reserved
		Bits 1–0 = 00 Channel 0 select
		          01 Channel 1 select
		          10 Channel 2 select
		          11 Channel 3 select

000Ch	W	DMA clear byte pointer flip–flop
000Dh	R	DMA read temporary register
000Dh	W	DMA master clear
000Eh	W	DMA clear mask register
000Fh	W	DMA write mask register
I/O addresses 0020h–0021h are the master Programmable Interrupt Controller addresses.		

0020h	W	Programmable Interrupt Controller — Initialization Command Word 1 (ICW1) (Bit 4 is one), where:
		
		Bits 7–5 = 000 Only used in 80/85 mode
		Bit 4 = 1 ICW1 is being issued
		Bit 3 = 0 Edge triggered mode
		          1 Level triggered mode
		Bit 2 = 0 Successive interrupt vectors are separated by eight bytes
		          1 Successive interrupt vectors are separated by four bytes
		Bit 1 = 0 Cascade mode
		          1 Single mode — no ICW3 needed
		Bit 0 = 0 No ICW4 needed
		          1 ICW4 needed

continued

I/O Address	Read/Write Status	Description
0021h	W	ICW2, ICW3, and optionally ICW4 in sequential order after ICW1 written to Port 0020h
		ICW2, where:
		Bits 7–3 = Address lines A0–A3 of base vector address for interrupt controller
		Bits 2–0 = 000 Reserved
		ICW3 for the master controller (0021h), where:
		Bits 7–0 = 0 Slave controller not attached to corresponding interrupt pin
		1 Slave controller attached to corresponding interrupt pin
		ICW3 for the slave controller (00A1h), where:
		Bits 7–3 = 0 Reserved
		Bits 2–0 = 1 Slave ID
		ICW4, where:
		Bits 7–5 = 000 Reserved
		Bit 4 = 0 No special fully–nested mode
		1 Special fully–nested mode
		Bits 3–2 = 00 Nonbuffered mode
		01 Nonbuffered mode
		10 Buffered mode/slave
		11 Buffered mode/master
		Bit 1 = 0 Normal EOI
		1 Auto EOI
		Bit 0 = 0 8085 mode
		1 8086/8088 mode
0021h	R/W	PIC, master interrupt mask register (OCW1), where:
		Bit 7 = 0 Enable parallel printer interrupt
		Bit 6 = 0 Enable diskette interrupt
		Bit 5 = 0 Enable fixed disk interrupt
		Bit 4 = 0 Enable serial port 1 interrupt
		Bit 3 = 0 Enable serial port 2 interrupt
		Bit 2 = 0 Enable video interrupt
		Bit 1 = 0 Enable keyboard/pointing device/RTC interrupt
		Bit 0 = 0 Enable timer interrupt

continued

I/O Address	Read/Write Status	Description
0021h	W	PIC, OCW2 (Bit 4 is zero, Bit 3 is zero), where: Bits 7–5 = 000 Rotate in automatic EOI mode (clear) 001 Nonspecific EOI 010 No operation 011 Specific EOI 100 Rotate in automatic EOI mode (set) 101 Rotate on nonspecific EOI command 110 Set priority command 111 Rotate on specific EOI command Bit 4 = 0 Reserved Bit 3 = 0 Reserved Bits 2–0 = Interrupt request to which the command applies
0020h	R	Programmable Interrupt Controller (PIC) — Interrupt request/in–service registers programmed by Operation Command Word 3 (OCW3): Interrupt request register, where: Bits 7–0 = 0 No active request for the corresponding interrupt line 1 Active request for the corresponding interrupt line Interrupt in–service register, where: Bits 7–0 = 0 The corresponding interrupt line is not currently being serviced 1 The corresponding interrupt line is currently being serviced
0020h	W	PIC, OCW3 (Bit 4 is zero, Bit 3 is one), where: Bit 7 = 0 Reserved Bits 6–5 = 00 No operation 01 No operation 10 Reset special mask 11 Set special mask Bit 4 = 0 Reserved Bit 3 = 1 Reserved Bit 2 = 0 No poll command 1 Poll command Bits 1–0 = 00 No operation 01 No operation 10 Read interrupt request register on next read at Port 0020h 11 Read interrupt in–service register on next read at Port 0020h
0040h	R/W	Programmable Interrupt Timer — read/write counter 0, keyboard controller channel 0
0041h	R/W	Programmable Interrupt Timer, channel 1

continued

I/O Address	Read/Write Status	Description
0042h	R/W	Programmable Interrupt Timer — miscellaneous register, channel 2
0043h	W	PIT mode port, control word register for counters 0 and 2, where: Bits 7–6 = 00 Counter 0 select 01 Counter 1 select 10 Counter 2 select Bits 5–4 = 00 Counter latch command 01 Read/write counter bits 0–7 only 10 Read/write counter bits 8–15 only 11 Read/write counter bits 0–7 first, then bits 8–15 Bits 3–0 = 000 Mode 0 select 001 Mode 1 select — programmable 1 shot X10 Mode 2 select — rate generator X11 Mode 3 select — square wave generator 100 Mode 4 select — software–triggered strobe 101 Mode 5 select — hardware–triggered strobe Bit 0 = 0 Binary counter 16 bits 1 Binary coded decimal counter
0044h	W	Programmable Interrupt Timer, miscellaneous register (EISA)
0047h	W	Programmable Interrupt Timer, control word register for counter 0 (EISA), where: Bits 7–6 = 00 Counter 0 select 01 Reserved 10 Reserved 11 Reserved Bits 5–4 = 00 Counter latch command select counter 0 01 Read/write counter bits 0–7 only 10 Reserved 11 Reserved
0048h	R/W	Used by Programmable Interrupt Timer
0060h	W	Keyboard controller data port or keyboard input buffer (ISA, EISA)
0060h	R	Keyboard or keyboard controller data output buffer (via Programmable Peripheral Interface on XT)

continued

I/O Address	Read/Write Status	Description
0061h	R	Port B control register (ISA, EISA), where: Bit 7 = Parity check Bit 6 = Channel check Bit 5 = Timer 2 output Bit 4 = Toggles with each refresh request Bit 3 = Channel check enable Bit 2 = Parity check enable Bit 1 = Speaker data enable Bit 0 = Timer 2 gate to speaker enable
0061h	W	Port B (ISA, EISA), where: Bits 7–4 = Reserved Bit 3 = Channel check enable Bit 2 = Parity check enable Bit 1 = Speaker data enable Bit 0 = Timer 2 gate to speaker enable
0061h	W	Programmable Peripheral Interface output register (XT only), where: Bit 7 = 1 Clear keyboard Bit 6 = 0 Hold keyboard clock low Bit 5 = 0 I/O check enable Bit 4 = 0 RAM parity check enable Bit 3 = 0 Read low switches Bit 2 = Reserved Bit 1 = 1 Speaker data enable Bit 0 = 1 Timer 2 gate to speaker enable
0062h	R/W	Programmable Peripheral Interface input register (XT only), where: Bit 7 = 1 RAM parity check Bit 6 = 1 I/O channel check Bit 5 = 1 Timer channel 2 out Bit 4 = Reserved Bit 3 = 1 System board RAM size type 1 Bit 2 = 1 System board RAM size type 0 Bit 1 = 1 Coprocessor installed Bit 0 = 1 Loop in POST

continued

I/O Address	Read/Write Status	Description

0063h	R/W	Programmable Peripheral Interface Command mode register (XT only), where:
		
		Bits 7–6 = Number of diskette drives, where:
		    00 1 drive
		    01 2 drives
		    10 3 drives
		    11 4 drives
		Bits 5–4 = Type of display at power–on, where:
		    00 Reserved
		    01 40x25 color (mono mode)
		    10 80x25 color (mono mode)
		    11 MDA (80x25)
		Bits 3–2 = Memory on system board (256K chips), where:
		    00 256K
		    01 512K
		    10 576K
		    11 640K
		Bits 3–2 = Memory on system board (64K chips), where:
		    00 64K
		    01 128K
		    10 192K
		    11 256K
		Bits 1–0 = Reserved

0064h	R	Keyboard controller read status (ISA, EISA), where: Bit 7 = 1 Parity error on transmission from keyboard Bit 6 = 1 Receive timeout Bit 5 = 1 Transmit timeout Bit 4 = 0 Keyboard inhibit Bit 3 = 1 Command 0 Data Bit 2 = System flag status Bit 1 = 1 Input buffer full Bit 0 = 1 Output buffer full
0064h	W	Keyboard controller input buffer (ISA, EISA)
0070h	R	CMOS RAM index register port (ISA, EISA), where: Bit 7 = 1 NMI disabled Bits 6–0 = 0 CMOS RAM index
0071h	R/W	CMOS RAM data register port (ISA, EISA)
0080h	R/W	Extra page register (temporary storage)
0080h	R	Manufacturing diagnostics port (ISA, EISA)
0081h	R/W	DMA channel 2 address byte 2
0082h	R/W	DMA channel 3 address byte 3

continued

I/O Address	Read/Write Status	Description
0083h	R/W	DMA channel 1 address byte 2
0084h	R/W	Extra page register
0085h	R/W	Extra page register
0086h	R/W	Extra page register
0087h	R/W	DMA channel 0 address byte 2
0088h	R/W	Extra page register
0089h	R/W	DMA channel 6 address byte 2
008Ah	R/W	DMA channel 7 address byte 2
008Bh	R/W	DMA channel 5 address byte 2
008Ch	R/W	Extra page register
008Dh	R/W	Extra page register
008Eh	R/W	Extra page register
008Fh	R/W	DMA refresh page register
00A0h	R/W	NMI mask register (XT)
In ISA and EISA systems, I/O addresses 00A0h–00A1h are the slave Programmable Interrupt Controller addresses. Except as noted, bit definitions are the same as those for addresses 0020h–0021h.		
00A0h	R/W	Programmable Interrupt Controller 2
00A1h	R/W	Interrupt Controller 2 mask (OCW1), where: Bit 7 = 0 Reserved Bit 6 = 0 Enable fixed disk interrupt Bit 5 = 0 Enable coprocessor exception interrupt Bit 4 = 0 Enable mouse interrupt Bit 3 = 0 Reserved Bit 2 = 0 Reserved Bit 1 = 0 Enable redirect cascade Bit 0 = 0 Enable real–time clock interrupt
00C0h	R/W	DMA, channel 4 memory address bytes 1 and 0 (low) (ISA, EISA)
00C2h	R/W	DMA channel 4 transfer count bytes 1 and 0 (low) (ISA, EISA)
00C4h	R/W	DMA channel 5 memory address bytes 1 and 0 (low) (ISA, EISA)
00C6h	R/W	DMA, channel 5 transfer count bytes 1 and 0 (low) (ISA, EISA)

continued

I/O Address	Read/Write Status	Description
00C8h	R/W	DMA channel 6 memory address bytes 1 and 0 (low) (ISA, EISA)
00CAh	R/W	DMA channel 6 transfer count bytes 1 and 0 (low) (ISA, EISA)
00CCh	R/W	DMA channel 7 memory address byte 0 (low), then byte 1 (ISA, EISA)
00CEh	R/W	DMA channel 7 transfer count byte 0 (low), then byte 1 (ISA, EISA)
00D0h	R	DMA channel 4–7 status register (ISA, EISA), where: Bit 7 = 1 Channel 7 request Bit 6 = 1 Channel 6 request Bit 5 = 1 Channel 5 request Bit 4 = 1 Channel 4 request Bit 3 = 1 Terminal count on channel 7 Bit 2 = 1 Terminal count on channel 6 Bit 1 = 1 Terminal count on channel 5 Bit 0 = 1 Terminal count on channel 4

00D0h	W	DMA channel 4–7 command register (ISA, EISA), where:
		
		Bit 7 = 1 DACK sense active high
		     0 DACK sense active low
		Bit 6 = 1 DREQ sense active low
		     0 DREQ sense active high
		Bit 5 = 1 Extended write selection
		     0 Late write selection
		Bit 4 = 1 Rotating priority
		     0 Fixed priority
		Bit 3 = 1 Compressed timing
		     0 Normal timing
		Bit 2 = 0 Enable controller
		Bit 1 = 1 Enable memory–to–memory transfer

00D2h	W	DMA channel 4–7 write request register (ISA, EISA)

00D4h	W	DMA channel 4–7 write single mask register bit (ISA, EISA), where:
		
		Bits 7–3 = 0 Reserved
		Bit 2 = 0 Clear mask bit
		     1 Set mask bit
		Bits 1–0 = 00 Channel 4 select
		     01 Channel 5 select
		     10 Channel 6 select
		     11 Channel 7 select

continued

I/O Address	Read/Write Status	Description

00D6h	W	DMA channel 4–7 mode register (ISA, EISA), where:
		
		Bits 7–6 = 00 Demand mode
		          01 Single mode
		          10 Block mode
		          11 Cascade mode
		Bit 5 = 0 Address increment select
		          1 Address decrement select
		Bit 4 = 0 Autoinitialization disable
		          1 Autoinitialization enable
		Bits 3–2 = 00 Verify operation
		          01 Write to memory
		          10 Read from memory
		          11 Reserved
		Bits 1–0 = 00 Channel 4 select
		          01 Channel 5 select
		          10 Channel 6 select
		          11 Channel 7 select

00D8h	W	DMA channel 4–7 clear byte pointer flip–flop (ISA, EISA)
00DAh	R	DMA channel 4–7 read temporary register (ISA, EISA)
00DAh	W	DMA channel 4–7 master clear (ISA, EISA)
00DCh	W	DMA channel 4–7 clear mask register (ISA, EISA)
00DEh	W	DMA channel 4–7 write mask register (ISA, EISA)
00F0h		Math coprocessor clear busy latch
00F1h		Math coprocessor reset
00F2h–00FFh	R/W	Math coprocessor
In ISA and EISA systems, I/O addresses in the 0170h–0177h range are secondary fixed disk addresses. See addresses 01F0h–01F7h for bit definitions.		
0170h	R/W	Fixed disk 1 data register
0171h	R	Fixed disk 1 error register
0171h	W	Write precompensation register
0172h	R/W	Fixed disk 1 sector count
0173h	R/W	Fixed disk 1 sector number
0174h	R/W	Fixed disk 1 cylinder low
0175h	R/W	Fixed disk 1 cylinder high
0176h	R/W	Fixed disk 1 drive/head register

continued

I/O Address	Read/Write Status	Description
0177h	R	Fixed disk 1 status register
0177h	W	Command register

In ISA and EISA systems, I/O addresses in the 01F0h–01F7h range are the primary fixed disk addresses. Bit settings also apply to addresses 0170h–0177h.

I/O Address	Read/Write Status	Description
01F0h	R/W	Fixed disk 0 data register base port

01F1h	R	Fixed disk 0 error register, where:
		
		Diagnostic mode:
		
		Bits 7–3 = Reserved
		Bits 2–0 = Diagnostic mode errors
		       001 No errors
		       010 Controller error
		       011 Sector buffer error
		       100 ECC device error
		       101 Control processor error
		
		Operation mode:
		
		Bit 7 = 1 Bad block detected
		         0 Block OK
		Bit 6 = 1 Uncorrectable ECC error
		         0 No error
		Bit 5 = Reserved
		Bit 4 = 1 ID found
		         0 ID not found
		Bit 3 = Reserved
		Bit 2 = 1 Command completed
		         0 Command aborted
		Bit 1 = 1 Track 000 not found
		         0 Track 000 found
		Bit 0 = 1 DAM not found
		         0 DAM found (CP–3022 always 0)

01F1h	W	Write precompensation register
01F2h	R/W	Fixed disk 0 sector count
01F3h	R/W	Fixed disk 0 sector number
01F4h	R/W	Fixed disk 0 cylinder low
01F5h	R/W	Fixed disk 0 cylinder high

continued

I/O Address	Read/Write Status	Description

01F6h	R/W	Fixed disk 0 drive/head register, where:
		
		Bit 7 = 1
		Bit 6 = 0
		Bit 5 = 1
		Bit 4 = Drive select
		    0 First disk drive
		    1 Second disk drive
		Bits 3–0 = Head select bits

01F7h	R	Fixed disk 0 status register, where: Bit 7 = 1 Controller is executing a command Bit 6 = 1 Drive is ready Bit 5 = 1 Write fault Bit 4 = 1 Seek complete Bit 3 = 1 Sector buffer requires servicing Bit 2 = 1 Disk data read successfully corrected Bit 1 = Index — set to 1 each disk revolution Bit 0 = 1 Previous command ended in an error
01F7h	W	Command register
0200h–020Fh	R/W	Game control ports
0201h	R/W	Game port I/O data
0210h–0217h	R/W	Expansion unit (XT)
In ISA and EISA systems, I/O addresses in the 0278h–027Ah range are Parallel 3 addresses. See addresses 03BCh–03BEh (Parallel 1) for bit definitions.		
0278h	W	Parallel 3, data port
0279h	R/W	Parallel 3, status port
027Ah	R/W	Parallel 3, control port
02E1h		GPIB (adapter 0)
02E2h		Data acquisition (adapter 0)
02E3h		Data acquisition (adapter 0)
I/O addresses in the 02F8h–02FFh range are Serial 2 addresses. See addresses 03F8h–03FFh (Serial 1) for bit definitions.		
02F8h	W	Serial 2, transmitter holding register
02F8h	R	Serial 2, receiver buffer register
02F8h	R/W	Serial 2, divisor latch, low byte when DLAB = 1
02F9h	R/W	Serial 2, divisor latch, high byte when DLAB = 1

continued

I/O Address	Read/Write Status	Description
02F9h	R/W	Serial 2, interrupt enable register when DLAB = 0
02FAh	R	Serial 2, interrupt identification register
02FBh	R/W	Serial 2, line control register
02FCh	R/W	Serial 2, modem control register
02FDh	R	Serial 2, line status register
02FEh	R	Serial 2, modem status register
02FFh	R/W	Serial 2, scratch register
0300h–031Fh	R/W	Prototype card
0348h–0357h		DCA 3278
0360h–036Fh		PC Network

I/O addresses in the 0372h–0377h range are secondary diskette controller addresses. See addresses 03F2–03F7h for bit definitions.

I/O Address	Read/Write Status	Description
0372h	W	Diskette controller digital output register
0374h	R	Diskette controller status register
0375h	R/W	Diskette controller data register
0376h	R/W	Fixed disk controller data register
0377h	R	Diskette digital input register
0377h	W	Select register for diskette data transfer rate

I/O addresses in the 0378h–037Ah range are Parallel 2 addresses. See addresses 03BCh–03BEh (Parallel 1) for bit definitions.

I/O Address	Read/Write Status	Description
0378h	R/W	Parallel 2, data port
0379h	R/W	Parallel 2, status port
037Ah	R/W	Parallel 2, control port
0380h–038fh		SDLC and BSC communications
0390h–0393h		Cluster (adapter 0)
03A0h–03AFh		BSC communications (primary)
03B0h–03B3h*	R/W	Miscellaneous video registers
03B4h*	R/W	MDA CRTC index register

* For more information on video I/O ports, see the *Video I/O Port Lists* at the end of this chapter.

continued

I/O Address	Read/Write Status	Description
03B5h*	R/W	MDA CRTC data registers
03B8h*	R/W	MDA mode control register
I/O addresses in the 03BCh–03BEh range are Parallel 1 addresses. Bit settings also apply to Parallel 2 and Parallel 3.		
03BCh	R/W	Parallel 1 data port
03BDh	R/W	Parallel 1, status port, where: Bit 7 = 0 Busy Bit 6 = 0 Acknowledge Bit 5 = 1 Out of paper Bit 4 = 1 Printer is selected Bit 3 = 0 Error Bit 2 = 0 IRQ has occurred Bits 1–0 = Reserved
03BEh	R/W	Parallel 1, control port, where: Bits 7–5 = Reserved Bit 4 = 1 Enable IRQ Bit 3 = 1 Select printer Bit 2 = 0 Initialize printer Bit 1 = 1 Automatic line feed Bit 0 = 1 Strobe

03BFh*	R/W	Hercules configuration switch register, where:
		
		Bits 7–2 = Unused
		Bit 1 = 0 Disables upper 32K of graphics mode buffer
		      1 Enables upper 32K of graphics mode buffer at B800h:0000h
		Bit 0 = 0 Prevents graphics mode
		      1 Allows graphics mode

03C2h*	R	CGA input status register 0
03C3h*	R/W	Video subsystem enable
03C4h*	R/W	CGA sequencer index register
03C5h*	R/W	Other CGA sequencer registers
03CAh*	R/W	CGA Graphics 2 position register
03CAh*	R	CGA feature control register
03D4h*	W	Video CRTC index register
03D5h*	W	Other video CRTC registers

* For more information on video I/O ports, see the *Video I/O Port Lists* at the end of this chapter.

continued

I/O Address	Read/Write Status	Description
03D8h*	R/W	CGA mode control register
03D9h*	R/W	CGA palette register
I/O addresses in the 3F2h–03F7h range are primary diskette controller addresses. Bit settings also apply to addresses 0372h–0377h.		
03F2h	W	Diskette controller digital output register, where: Bit 7 = 0 Reserved Bit 6 = 0 Reserved Bit 5 = 1 Drive 1 motor enable Bit 4 = 1 Drive 0 motor enable Bit 3 = 1 Diskette DMA enable Bit 2 = 0 Controller reset Bit 1 = 0 Reserved Bit 0 = 0 Drive 0 select = 1 Drive 1 select
03F4h	R	Diskette controller status register, where: Bit 7 = 1 Data register is ready Bit 6 = 1 Transfer is from controller to system = 0 Transfer is from system to controller Bit 5 = 1 Non–DMA mode Bit 4 = 1 Diskette controller busy Bits 3–2 = Reserved Bit 1 = 1 Drive 1 busy Bit 0 = 0 Drive 0 busy
03F5h	R/W	Diskette controller data register

03F6h	R	Fixed disk control port, where:
		
		Bits 7–4 = Reserved
		Bit 3 = 0 Reduce write current
		      1 Head select 3 enable
		Bit 2 = 1 Disk reset enable
		      0 Disk reset disable
		Bit 1 = 0 Disk initialization enable
		      1 Disk initialization disable
		Bit 0 = Reserved

03F7h	R	Diskette digital input register, where: Bit 7 = 1 Diskette change Bit 6 = 1 Write gate Bit 5 = Head select 3/reduced write current Bit 4 = Head select 2 Bit 3 = Head select 1 Bit 2 = Head select 0 Bit 1 = Drive 1 select Bit 0 = Drive 0 select (Bits 6–0 apply to the currently–selected fixed disk drive)

* For more information on video I/O ports, see the *Video I/O Port Lists* at the end of this chapter.

continued

I/O Address	Read/Write Status	Description
03F7h	W	Select register for diskette data transfer rate, where: Bits 7–2 = Reserved Bits 1–0 = 00 500 Kbs mode 01 300 Kbs mode 10 250 Kbs mode 11 Reserved
		The I/O addresses in the 03BCh–03BEh range are the Serial 1 addresses. Bit settings also apply to Serial 2.
03F8h	W	Serial 1, transmitter holding register, which contains the character to be sent. Bit 0, the least significant bit, is sent first. Bits 7–0 = Data bits 7–0, respectively, when Divisor Latch Access Bit (DLAB) = 0
03F8h	R	Serial 1, receiver buffer register, which contains the received character. Bit 0, the least significant bit, is sent first. Bits 7–0 = Data bits 7–0, respectively, when DLAB = 0
03F8h	R/W	Serial 1, divisor latch, low byte when DLAB = 1, where: Bits 7–0 = Bits 7–0 of divisor
03F9h	R/W	Serial 1, divisor latch, high byte, when DLAB = 1, where: Bits 7–0 = Bits 15–8 of divisor
03F9h	R/W	Serial 1, interrupt enable register when DLAB = 0, where: Bits 7–4 = 0 Reserved Bit 3 = 1 Modem–status interrupt enable Bit 2 = 1 Receiver–line–status interrupt enable Bit 1 = 1 Transmitter–holding–register empty interrupt enable Bit 0 = 1 Received–data–available interrupt enable

continued

I/O Address	Read/Write Status	Description

03FAh	R	Serial 1, interrupt identification register. Information about a pending interrupt is stored here. When the ID register is addressed, the highest priority interrupt is held, and no other interrupts are acknowledged until the CPU services that interrupt.
		
		Bits 7–3 = 0 Reserved
		Bits 2–1 = Identify the pending interrupt with the highest priority:
		    11 Receiver line status interrupt; priority = highest
		    10 Received data available register interrupt; priority = second
		    01 Transmitter holding register empty interrupt; priority = third
		    00 Modem status interrupt; priority = fourth
		Bit 0 = 0 Interrupt pending; contents of register can be used as a pointer to the appropriate interrupt service routine.
		    1 No interrupt pending

03FBh	R/W	Serial 1, line control register, where:
		
		Bit 7 = 1 Divisor latch access bit (DLAB)
		    = 0 Receiver buffer, transmitter holding, or interrupt enable registers access
		Bit 6 = 1 Set break enable. Serial output is forced to spacing state and remains there
		Bit 5 = Stick parity
		Bit 4 = Even parity select
		Bit 3 = Parity enable
		    1 Even number of ones are sent and checked in the data word bits and parity bit
		    0 Odd number of ones are sent and checked
		Bit 2 = Number of stop bits
		    0 One stop bit
		    1 Zero stop bits
		Bits 1–0 = 00 Word length is 5 bits
		    01 Word length is 6 bits
		    10 Word length is 7 bits
		    11 Word length is 8 bits

continued

I/O Address	Read/Write Status	Description
03FCh	R/W	Serial 1, modem control register, where: Bits 7–5 = 0 Reserved Bit 4 = 1 Loopback mode for diagnostic testing of serial port. Output of transmitter shift register is looped back to receiver shift register input. In this mode, transmitted data is received immediately so that the CPU can verify the transmit data/receive data serial port paths. Bit 3 = 1 Auxiliary user–designated output 2 Bit 2 = 1 Auxiliary user–designated output 1 Bit 1 = 1 Force request–to–send active Bit 0 = 1 Force data–terminal–ready active
03FDh	R	Serial 1, line status register, where: Bit 7 = 0 Reserved Bit 6 = 1 Transmitter shift and holding registers empty Bit 5 = 1 Transmitter holding register empty. Controller is ready to accept a new character to send. Bit 4 = 1 Break interrupt. The received data input is held in the zero bit state longer than the time of start bit + data bits + parity bit + stop bits. Bit 3 = 1 Framing error. The stop bit that follows the last parity or data bit is a zero bit. Bit 2 = 1 Parity error. Character has wrong even or odd parity. Bit 1 = 1 Overrun error. A character was sent to the receiver buffer before the previous character in the buffer could be read. This destroys the previous character. Bit 0 = 1 Data ready. A complete incoming character has been received and sent to the receiver buffer register.
03FEh	R	Serial 1, modem status register, where: Bit 7 = 1 Data carrier detect Bit 6 = 1 Ring indicator Bit 5 = 1 Data set ready Bit 4 = 1 Clear to send Bit 3 = 1 Delta data carrier detect Bit 2 = 1 Trailing edge ring indicator Bit 1 = 1 Delta data set ready Bit 0 = 1 Delta clear to send
03FFh	R/W	Serial 1, scratch register
I/O addresses in the range 0401h–04D6h are used by EISA systems only.		
0401h	R/W	DMA channel 0 word count byte 2 (high)
0403h	R/W	DMA channel 1 word count byte 2 (high)

continued

I/O Address	Read/Write Status	Description
0405h	R/W	DMA channel 2 word count byte 2 (high)
0407h	R/W	DMA channel 3 word count byte 2 (high)
040Ah	W	Extended DMA chaining mode register, channels 0–3, where: Bits 7–5 = 0 Reserved Bit 4　　 = 0 Generates IRQ 13 　　　　　　1 Generates terminal count Bit 3　　 = 0 Do not start chaining 　　　　　　1 Programming complete Bit 2　　 = 0 Disable buffer chaining mode (default) 　　　　 = 1 Enable buffer chaining mode Bits 1–0 = DMA channel select
040Ah	R	Channel interrupt (IRQ 13) status register, where: Bits 7–5 = Interrupt on channels 7–5 Bit 4　　 = Reserved Bits 3–0 = Interrupt on channels 3–0
040Bh	W	DMA extended mode register for channels 0–3, where: Bit 7　　 = 0 Enable stop register Bit 6　　 = 0 Terminal count is an output for this channel 　　　　　　(default) 　　　　　　1 Terminal count is an input for this channel Bits 5–4 = DMA cycle timing 　　　　　　00　ISA-compatible (default) 　　　　　　01　Type A timing mode 　　　　　　10　Type B timing mode 　　　　　　11　Burst DMA mode Bits 3–2 = Address mode 　　　　　　00　8–bit I/O, count by bytes (default) 　　　　　　01　16–bit I/O, count by words, 　　　　　　　　address-shifted 　　　　　　10　32–bit I/O, count by bytes 　　　　　　11　16–bit I/O, count by bytes Bits 1–0 = DMA channel select
0461h	R/W	Extended NMI status/control register, where: Bit 7　　 = 1 NMI pending from fail–safe timer (read only) Bit 6　　 = 1 NMI pending from bus timeout NMI status 　　　　　　(read only) Bit 5　　 = 1 NMI pending (read only) Bit 4　　 = Reserved Bit 3　　 = 1 Bus timeout NMI enable (read/write) Bit 2　　 = 1 Fail–safe NMI enable (read/write) Bit 1　　 = 1 NMI I/O port enable (read/write) Bit 0　　 = RSTDRV. Bus reset (read/write) 　　　　　　0 Normal bus reset operation 　　　　　　1 Reset bus asserted

continued

I/O Address	Read/Write Status	Description
0462h	W	Software NMI register. Writing to this register causes an NMI if NMIs are enabled.
0464h	R	Bus master status latch register (slots 1–8). Identifies the last bus master that had control of the bus, where: Bit 7　= 0 Slot 8 had control last Bit 6　= 0 Slot 7 had control last Bit 5　= 0 Slot 6 had control last Bit 4　= 0 Slot 5 had control last Bit 3　= 0 Slot 4 had control last Bit 2　= 0 Slot 3 had control last Bit 1　= 0 Slot 2 had control last Bit 0　= 0 Slot 1 had control last
0465h	R	Bus master status latch register (slots 9–16), where: Bit 7　= 0 Slot 16 had control last Bit 6　= 0 Slot 15 had control last Bit 5　= 0 Slot 14 had control last Bit 4　= 0 Slot 13 had control last Bit 3　= 0 Slot 12 had control last Bit 2　= 0 Slot 11 had control last Bit 1　= 0 Slot 10 had control last Bit 0　= 0 Slot 9 had control last
0481h	R/W	DMA channel 2 address byte 3 (high)
0482h	R/W	DMA channel 3 address byte 3 (high)
0483h	R/W	DMA channel 1 address byte 3 (high)
0487h	R/W	DMA channel 0 address byte 3 (high)
0489h	R/W	DMA channel 6 address byte 3 (high)
048Ah	R/W	DMA channel 7 address byte 3 (high)
048Bh	R/W	DMA channel 5 address byte 3 (high)
04C6h	R/W	DMA channel 5 word count byte 2 (high)
04CAh	R/W	DMA channel 6 word count byte 2 (high)
04CEh	R/W	DMA channel 7 word count byte 2 (high)
04D0h	W	IRQ 0–7 interrupt edge/level registers, where: Bit 7　= 1 IRQ 7 is level sensitive Bit 6　= 1 IRQ 6 is level sensitive Bit 5　= 1 IRQ 5 is level sensitive Bit 4　= 1 IRQ 4 is level sensitive Bit 3　= 1 IRQ 3 is level sensitive Bits 2–0 = Reserved

continued

I/O Address	Read/Write Status	Description
04D1h	W	IRQ 8–15 interrupt edge/level registers, where: Bit 7 = 1 IRQ 15 is level sensitive Bit 6 = 1 IRQ 14 is level sensitive Bit 5 = Reserved Bit 4 = 1 IRQ 12 is level sensitive Bit 3 = 1 IRQ 11 is level sensitive Bit 2 = 1 IRQ 10 is level sensitive Bit 1 = 1 IRQ 9 is level sensitive Bit 0 = Reserved
04D4h	R	Chaining mode status register, where: Bits 7–5 = 1 Channels 7–5 enable Bit 4 = Reserved Bits 3–0 = 1 Channels 3–0 enable

04D4h	W	Extended DMA chaining mode register, channels 4–7, where:
		
		Bits 7–5 = 0 Reserved
		Bit 4 = 0 Generates IRQ 13
		       1 Generates terminal count
		Bit 3 = 0 Do not start chaining
		       1 Programming complete
		Bit 2 = 0 Disable buffer chaining mode (default)
		    = 1 Enable buffer chaining mode
		Bits 1–0 = DMA channel select

04D6h	W	DMA extended mode register for channels 4–7. Bit settings are the same as those for channels 0–3 (see address 040Bh).
06E2–06E3h	R/W	Data aquisition (adapter 1)
0790h–0793h	R/W	Cluster (adapter 1)
0800h–08FFh	R/W	I/O port access registers for extended CMOS RAM or SRAM (256 bytes at a time)
0AE2h–0AE3h	R/W	Cluster (adapter 2)
0B90h–0B93h	R/W	Cluster (adapter 2)
0C00h	R/W	Page register to write to SRAM or I/O
0C80h–0C83h	R/W	System board ID registers
1390h–1393h	R/W	Cluster (adapter 3)
2390h–2393h	R/W	Cluster (adapter 4)
3220h–3227h	R/W	Serial Port 3 (see description for addresses 03F8h–03FFh for details).

continued

I/O Address	Read/Write Status	Description
3228h–322Fh	R/W	Serial Port 4 (see description for addresses 03F8h–03FFh for details).
42E1h	R/W	GPIB (adapter 2)
62E1h	R/W	GPIB (adapter 3)
82E1h	R/W	GPIB (adapter 4)
A2E1h	R/W	GPIB (adapter 5)
AFFFh	R/W	Plane 0–3 system latch (video register)
C2E1h	R/W	GPIB (adapter 6)
E2E1h	R/W	GPIB (adapter 7)

Video I/O Port Lists

MDA I/O ports

The 6845 CRTC's index register is mapped to I/O port 03B4h. The index value written to port 03B4h controls the register that appears at port 03B5h. The 6845 mode control register is accessed directly via I/O port 03B8h.

I/O Address	Read/Write	Index	Description
03B4h	W	—	CRTC index register
03B5h	W	00h	Horizontal total
03B5h	W	01h	Horizontal displayed
03B5h	W	02h	Horizontal sync position
03B5h	W	03h	Horizontal sync pulse width
03B5h	W	04h	Vertical total
03B5h	W	05h	Vertical displayed
03B5h	W	06h	Vertical sync position
03B5h	W	07h	Vertical sync pulse width
03B5h	W	08h	Interlace mode
03B5h	W	09h	Maximum scan lines
03B5h	W	0Ah	Cursor start
03B5h	W	0Bh	Cursor end
03B5h	W	0Ch	Start address (high)
03B5h	W	0Dh	Start address (low)
03B5h	W	0Eh	Cursor location (high)
03B5h	W	0Fh	Cursor location (low)
03B5h	W	10h	Light pen (high)
03B5h	W	11h	Light pen (low)
03B8h	W	—	Mode control register
03BAh	R	—	CRT status register

continued

CGA I/O ports

The 6845 CRTC's index register is mapped to I/O port 03D4h. The value written to this port controls the register that appears at port 03D5h. Mode control and palette registers are accessed via ports 03D8h and 03D9h.

I/O Address	Read/Write	Index	Description
03D4h	W	—	CRTC index register
03D5h	W	00h	Horizontal total
03D5h	W	01h	Horizontal displayed
03D5h	W	02h	Horizontal sync position
03D5h	W	03h	Horizontal sync pulse width
03D5h	W	04h	Vertical total
03D5h	W	05h	Vertical displayed
03D5h	W	06h	Vertical sync position
03D5h	W	07h	Vertical sync pulse width
03D5h	W	08h	Interlace mode
03D5h	W	09h	Maximum scan lines
03D5h	W	0Ah	Cursor start
03D5h	W	0Bh	Cursor end
03D5h	W	0Ch	Start address (high)
03D5h	W	0Dh	Start address (low)
03D5h	W	0Eh	Cursor location (high)
03D5h	W	0Fh	Cursor location (low)
03D5h	W	10h	Light pen (high)
03D5h	W	11h	Light pen (low)
03D8h	W	—	Mode control register
03D9h	W	—	Palette register
03DAh	R	—	CRT status register
03DBh	W	—	Clear light pen latch
03DCh	W	—	Preset light pen latch

Chapter 7
Power-On Self Test

Overview

Description

Before a computer can be used, all the components must be tested and initialized, and the operating system must be bootstrapped into memory. This process, generally known as the power-on self test (POST), is under the control of the BIOS. This chapter describes the ROM BIOS POST process.

Initiating POST

There are three methods of starting the POST program. The BIOS responds differently in each case.

Method	ROM BIOS Response
Apply power to system (that is, turn system on)	The BIOS jumps to the entry point indicated by the processor reset vector (FFFF:0000h). POST executes all of its tests and initializations, and then invokes the INT 19h Bootstrap Loader DSR.

continued

Initiating POST, cont'd

Method	ROM BIOS Response
Reset system via optional hardware reset	The BIOS jumps to the entry point indicated by the processor reset vector (FFFF:0000h). POST executes all of its tests and initializations, and then invokes the INT 19h Bootstrap Loader DSR.
Press <Ctrl> <Alt> <Del> (warm boot)	The INT 09h keyboard hardware interrupt service routine transfers control to POST. POST does not test or initialize the system memory above 64K, but does perform all of its other tests and initializations. Then it invokes the INT 19h Bootstrap Loader DSR.

Microprocessor reset vector location

To maintain compatibility with IBM, the microprocessor reset vector points to system ROM address FFFF:0000h. This vector is also mapped by external address selection logic to point to FFFFFFFF:0000h on an 80386 microprocessor.

System RAM areas used by POST

The data definitions that POST uses are stored in system RAM at locations 40:12h, 40:15h, 40:67h, 40:6Bh, and 40:72h, but it initializes everything in 40:0h. See Chapter 3 for descriptions of these data areas.

In this chapter

This chapter presents the following information:

- Standard Tests and Initializations
- Initialization of Option ROMs
- Reentry into POST
- Error Handling
- System Boot Procedure

Standard Tests and Initializations

Introduction

POST tests, and then initializes, the following basic system components:

- hardware devices found on the system board
- system configuration data stored on the system board
- hardware devices that exist on add-in boards

Testing order of system components

POST verifies that system components, if installed, function properly before proceeding with other tests. POST tests system components in this order:

1. Microprocessor
2. CMOS RAM
3. ROM BIOS routines (checksum)
4. Any chip sets used in the system
5. Programmable timer counter #1
6. DMA controller and page registers
7. Base 64K of system RAM
8. Serial and parallel port peripherals
9. Programmable interrupt controller (PIC)
10. Keyboard controller
11. CMOS configuration data
12. Video controller, including video option ROMs
13. Real-time clock
14. Microprocessor shutdown
15. Programmable timer counter #2
16. Test I/O NMI and fail-safe timer NMI (EISA)
17. Keyboard
18. Mouse (if present and connected through the 8042 controller)
19. System RAM above the 64K boundary
20. Fixed disk and diskette controllers
21. Shadow RAM areas
22. Other option ROMs
23. Cache controller (if present)
24. Cache on the 80486 chip
25. Expansion box
26. Cassette

Initialization of Option ROMs

Introduction

Option ROMs included in a system contain functions that extend the ROM BIOS. Option ROM routines often replace existing ROM BIOS routines (for example, the support for an ESDI fixed disk or VGA video adapter).

When POST detects an option ROM, it allows the device to initialize itself and any associated hardware.

Search for option ROMs

POST searches for option ROMs over the predefined address ranges shown below.

Address Range	Description
C0000h–C7FFFh	Video Expansion ROM
	POST searches the address range C0000h–C7FFFh for a video ROM. This search proceeds in 2K increments.
C8000h–DFFFFh	General Expansion ROM
	POST searches the address range C8000h–DFFFFh for a general expansion ROM. This search proceeds in 2K increments.
E0000h	System Expansion ROM
	POST searches for an expansion ROM at E0000h. If no device exists, the search is ended. Any expansion ROM at this address must occupy the entire 64K.

continued

Setup of option ROM space

For POST to detect an option ROM, the first two words of the device's address space must be defined as follows:

Expansion ROM Byte	Value
0	55h
1	AAh
2	ROM length in 512K blocks
3	Entry point for ROM initialization

POST calculates the checksum of the area indicated by byte 2 of the option ROM. If the checksum is zero, it makes a far call to the expansion ROM's initialization code, which must begin at byte 3.

Introduction

Some computer operations require that the microprocessor be reset. For example, this occurs when the device must return to real mode from protected mode. If POST is executing when the microprocessor resets itself, then the proper reentry must be made. To find the correct point at which to begin execution, POST reads CMOS RAM location 0Fh. This one–byte location contains the microprocessor shutdown code that indicates where POST should continue execution.

POST shutdown codes

The following are the microprocessor shutdown codes that the POST can find at CMOS RAM location 0Fh:

00h	=	Normal execution of POST
01h	=	Chip set initialization for real mode reentry
04h	=	Jump to bootstrap code
05h	=	Issue an EOI and JMP to Dword pointer at 40:67h
06h	=	JMP to Dword pointer at 40:67h without EOI
07h	=	Return to INT 15h, Function AH = 87h Block Move
08h	=	Return to POST memory test
09h	=	Return to INT 15h, Function AH = 87h Block Move
0Ah	=	JMP to Dword pointer at 40:67h without EOI
0Bh	=	Return IRETS through 40:67h

If POST finds a shutdown code of 00h at CMOS RAM location 0Fh, it performs its complete suite of tests and initializations. POST also executes its complete suite of tests and initializations if it finds any code other than the one listed above.

Error Reporting

POST reports test or initialization failures through:

- Beep codes
- System failure messages
- Boot failure messages
- Informational messages

If the test of the system-board hardware fails, there is a fatal error and the POST program generates a beep code. If an adapter board test fails, the POST program displays an error message. See Appendices A and B for a listing of the POST messages.

System Boot Procedure

Introduction

Once POST completes its test and initialization procedures, it boots the system using INT 19h as follows:

- The POST program searches disk drive A:, then drive C: for a bootable disk.
- If the POST program finds a bootable disk, it reads the boot sector and writes its contents to 0000:7C00h in system memory. It then jumps to the address where execution begins.
- If neither drive A: nor C: contains a disk with a boot sector, POST issues an INT 18h, which reports the problem and waits for a keystroke to call INT 19h again.

Special use of INT 18h

The IBM BIOS uses INT 18h to point to a ROM-resident BASIC interpreter. Manufacturers of PC compatibles include BASIC on disk instead, and use INT 18h to display the message NO BOOT DEVICE AVAILABLE. The system user must then press F1 to have POST retry the boot procedure.

INT 18h can be vectored to a "no boot routine." An example of such a routine would be one that allows a system to be booted over a network.

Chapter 8
Nonmaskable Interrupt Service

Overview

Description

The microprocessor provides the nonmaskable interrupt (NMI) for use by hardware devices. NMIs interrupt the microprocessor immediately and cannot be disabled except by the logic contained on the system board. Some NMIs indicate serious hardware problems such as system or I/O board memory failures. Other NMIs are used as synchronizing signals between the microprocessor and system devices.

When its NMI pin is activated by one of these interrupt requests, the microprocessor invokes the ROM BIOS INT 02h Nonmaskable Interrupt ISR. Since the interrupt is handled by a software routine, the microprocessor does not generate an interrupt acknowledge cycle. If the microprocessor receives an NMI while servicing a previous one, it completes servicing the first interrupt before servicing the second.

continued

NMI service routines

This chapter describes two service routines that handle NMIs:

- INT 02h Nonmaskable Interrupt ISR processes NMIs for parity errors.
- INT 75h Math Coprocessor Exception ISR handles external math coprocessor exceptions in ISA and EISA systems.

In this chapter

This chapter covers the following topics:

- NMI Handling
- NMI Handling in EISA Systems
- External Math Coprocessor Exceptions
- INT 02h Nonmaskable Interrupt ISR
- INT 75h Math Coprocessor Exception ISR

NMI Handling

BIOS Nonmaskable Interrupt ISR

When the system hardware activates the NMI pin on the microprocessor, the BIOS INT 02h Nonmaskable Interrupt Service ISR is invoked.

The BIOS Nonmaskable Interrupt Service determines the reason for the NMI and takes appropriate action. In general, this involves displaying a run-time error message, and giving the user the option to shut off the NMI, reboot the system, or continue.

NMIs can only be cleared by a system reboot. The BIOS supports NMI clearing by warm (Ctrl–Alt–Del) reboot or cold reboot (system reset button or power switch).

Disabling NMIs

Programs running on an ISA or EISA systems can disable the NMIs by setting bit 7 of the CMOS RAM address register at I/O port 70h. Although the ROM BIOS POST may require that NMIs be disabled for some tests, the programmer should not permanently disable these interrupts. Permanently disabling NMIs prevents the microprocessor from recognizing serious hardware faults that may occur.

Clearing NMIs

The ROM BIOS allows programs to continue execution after an NMI has occurred. This practice may result in unpredictable results, however, and should only be used to continue a process while testing for the NMI source.

BIOS run-time error messages

The messages that may accompany NMIs, along with their possible causes and proposed solutions, are described in Appendix A for ISA and EISA systems, and Appendix B for XT systems.

Parity errors

Parity errors in system memory cause system hardware to activate the 80x86 processor's NMI pin. The two types of memory parity errors are system board memory failure and I/O board memory failure.

NMI Handling in EISA Systems

Bus time–out errors

Time–out errors cause the system hardware to set the processor's NMI pin. Bus master bus time–out errors cause NMI time–out errors.

When a bus master device uses the bus longer that 8 microseconds, an NMI and an error message is generated (see *PhoenixBIOS Run–Time Messages* in Appendix A of this book).

Fail–safe timer timeout

Timer 2, counter 0 of the Programmable Interrupt Timer implements a fail–safe timer in EISA systems. This timer generates an NMI signal at regular intervals, preventing the system from being tied up in a tight loop. The operating system should reset timer 2 counter 0 at regular intervals to prevent it from causing an NMI under normal operating conditions.

A message may be generated if the fail–safe timer detects a tight loop (see *PhoenixBIOS Run–Time Messages* in Appendix A of this book).

Assertion of IOCHK signal

An IOCHK is an NMI signal generated by an adapter card. When an adapter card receives a hardware signal, or reaches a point when it cannot operate, it may generate an IOCHK to the BIOS. The BIOS generates an NMI and an error message (see *PhoenixBIOS Run–Time Messages* in Appendix A of this book).

System software–generated NMI

System software can generate an NMI at any time by turning on bit 7 of I/O port 0462h. This procedure causes the BIOS to halt processing and alert the operator.

External Math Coprocessor Exceptions

Introduction

XT systems that include an 8087 chip indicate math coprocessor exceptions by generating an INT 02h.

ISA and EISA systems that include 80287, 80387SX, or 80387DX chips indicate math coprocessor exceptions by setting IRQ 13. IRQ 13 invokes INT 75h, the BIOS Math Coprocessor Exception ISR. INT 75h revectors IRQ 13 to INT 02h for XT compatibility.

Exception handling routines

Routines that handle external math coprocessor exceptions intercept INT 75h. The exception handling routine determines if the NMI was generated by the external math coprocessor. If so, the routine processes the exception, returning via an IRET. If not, the routine transfers control to the BIOS INT 75h ISR, which redirects external math coprocessor exceptions to the INT 02h Nonmaskable Interrupt ISR.

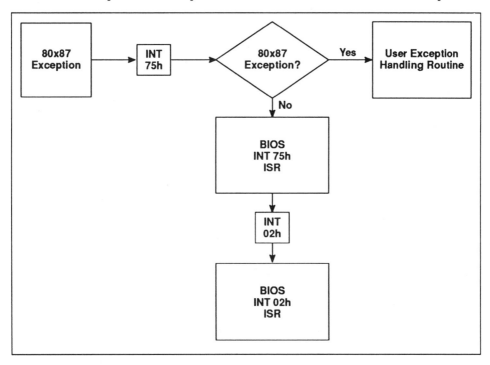

INT 02h Nonmaskable Interrupt ISR

Description

The INT 02H Nonmaskable Interrupt ISR determines the reason for an NMI and takes appropriate action. In general, this involves displaying a run–time error message and halting the microprocessor.

I/O port usage

The INT 02h ISR references I/O ports 61h, 70h–71h, 80h, and A0h. See Chapter 6 for descriptions of these ports.

Parity error messages

The INT 02h ISR displays error messages for NMIs caused by parity errors. See *PhoenixBIOS Run–Time Messages* in Appendix A (ISA and EISA systems) and *Phoenix XT BIOS Run–Time Messages* in Appendix B (XT Systems) for descriptions of these messages, their possible causes, and suggested solutions.

INT 75h Math Coprocessor Exception ISR

Description

The INT 75h Math Coprocessor Exception ISR automatically clears the math coprocessor busy latch, sends a nonspecific EOI to both the master and slave PICs, and executes INT 02h.

Chapter 9
Keyboard Services

Overview

Description

The ROM BIOS contains two keyboard–related services:

- The INT 09h Keyboard ISR, which processes the system scan codes from the keyboard in XT systems and from the keyboard controller in ISA and EISA systems. These scan codes are used for manipulating data, executing internal functions, and updating key states.
- The INT 16h Keyboard DSR, which allows system and application software to read and write to the keystroke buffer and to return the status of keyboard status flags.

In this chapter

The chapter covers the following topics:

- Theory of Operation
- Character Code Tables
- INT 09h Keyboard ISR
- INT 16h Keyboard DSR
- Keyboard Services functions

Theory of Operation

Introduction

The keyboard generates a key's make code each time that key is pressed, and it generates the key's break code each time the key is released. The byte associated with a key's break code is identical to the one associated with its make code except that bit 7 is set.

In and of itself, a key's make or break code has no direct meaning to an operating system or application software. The keyboard make and break codes generated by a U.S keyboard, for example, are identical to the keyboard codes generated by a German, French, or Italian keyboard.

Keyboard codes are converted into ASCII characters or other meaningful data through a series of transformations controlled by system software. The number of transformations involved depends directly on the kind of PC in use.

XT keyboards and the 8255A–5 controller

In XT systems, keyboard make and break codes are converted from serial to parallel form by an Intel 8255A–5 (or compatible) keyboard controller. The 8255A–5 then generates an interrupt request (IRQ 1), which invokes the ROM BIOS INT 09h Keyboard ISR.

The 8042 controller

In ISA and EISA systems, keyboard make and break codes are converted from serial to parallel form by an Intel 8042 (or compatible) keyboard controller.

Like its XT counterpart, the 8042 generates IRQ 1, which invokes the ROM BIOS INT 09h Keyboard ISR. Because of hardware differences between XT and AT keyboards, however, firmware resident in the 8042 controller must perform the additional step of converting AT key codes into system scan codes, values that are backward–compatible with those generated by XT keyboards.

continued

ROM BIOS INT 09h processing

The ROM BIOS Keyboard ISR analyzes each key code as follows:

- Codes generated by keyboard shift or toggle keys cause the Keyboard ISR to update the keyboard shift key and toggle key flags.
- Shift key combinations, such as Ctrl–Alt–Del, Ctrl–Num Lock, and Ctrl–Scroll Lock, are converted into requests for keyboard ISR internal functions, such as Reset, Pause, and Break.
- Codes that correspond to ASCII or special key values, such as, function or edit keys, are converted into two–byte character codes and are placed in a 16–word keystroke buffer. Operating systems or application software can then access the keystroke via the ROM BIOS INT16h Keyboard DSR.

Character code format

The character codes generated by the INT 09h Keyboard ISR are made up of a low order byte, called the main byte, and of a high order byte, called the auxiliary byte. The ASCII value of a keystroke, if any, is always contained in the main byte; the auxiliary byte contains the keystroke's make code or system scan code. When a key, such as a function key, edit key, or function key combination, does not have an ASCII value, the Keyboard ISR sets the main byte to 00h and the auxiliary byte to a special key value.

Typematic rate and delay

When a key is held down continuously, the keyboard hardware delays for a brief period and then sends repeat values of the key's make code to the keyboard controller chip. Upon receipt of each make code, the controller chip does its processing and generates an IRQ 1 which invokes INT 09h, the keyboard ISR.

If the make code corresponds to an alphanumeric, arrow, backspace, enter, or tab key, the keyboard ISR sends repeat character codes to the keystroke buffer until it receives the key's break code. If the make code corresponds to a special key, such as a function key or a shift/toggle key, the keyboard ISR ignores subsequent make codes from the keyboard and toggles the status of the key when it receives the key's break code.

Character Code Tables

Introduction

This chapter contains two tables of character codes for XT– and AT–compatible keyboards. The first table, "Character Codes: AH = 00h/01h", corresponds to INT 16h Function AH = 00h Read Keyboard Input and INT 16h Function AH = 01h Return Keyboard Status. The second table, "Character Codes: AH = 10h/11h", corresponds to INT 16h Function AH = 10h Read Extended Keyboard Input and INT 16h Function AH = 11h Return Extended Keyboard Status.

The tables should be read as follows:

- The data presented in each table is listed by key number and U. S. keyboard key legend. Readers who are using foreign keyboards should refer to the keyboard layout figures on the next page to see how their keyboard legend maps into key numbers.

- The columns labeled "Scan Codes" list the codes offered to the INT 09h ISR by the keyboard controller chip. In AT–compatible systems (including EISA systems) these codes are generated by the 8042 controller chip and are more commonly referred to as system scan codes. Only make code values are listed. Break codes are found by adding a value of 80h to the make code in question. Scan codes in E0–*xx*h form correspond to the 101/102–key keyboard extended keys. These keys are not present on 83– and 84–key keyboards.

- The two–byte number associated with each character code is listed in four–digit hex notation. The high order byte, which is placed by INT 16h into the AH register, is listed first. The low order byte, which is placed by INT 16h into the AL register, is listed second. The two bytes are separated with a slash. For example, the character code for the unshifted "n" key is listed on the table as 31/6E.

- Caps Lock plus any alphabetical key yields the same character code as Shift plus any key.

- Num Lock plus any numeric keypad key yields the same character code as Shift plus any numeric keypad key.

- Alt plus the decimal value for an ASCII character input from the numeric keypad yields the ASCII character. Allowable values are 0 to 255. These instances are noted with two asterisks (**) in the Alt column.

continued

83–key, 84–key, and 101/102–key keyboard numbers

The key number systems applied to 83–key XT–compatible, 84–key AT–compatible, and 101/102–key AT–compatible keyboards are shown below.

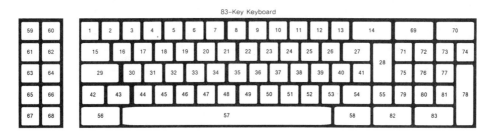

83–Key Keyboard

84–Key Keyboard

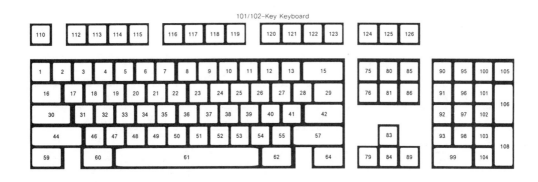

101/102–Key Keyboard

continued

Character codes AH = 00h/01h

The table below lists the character codes returned by INT 16h DSR Functions
AH = 00h Read Keyboard Input and AH = 01h Return Keyboard Status.

101/102 Key #	83 Key #	84 Key #	U.S. Keyboard Legend	Scan Codes (hex)	Character Codes AH/AL (hex)			
					Normal	Shifted	Control	Alt
1	41	1	'~	29	29/60	29/7E		
2	2	2	1!	02	02/31	02/21		78/00
3	3	3	2@	03	03/32	03/40	03/00	79/00
4	4	4	3#	04	04/33	04/23		7A/00
5	5	5	4$	05	05/34	05/24		7B/00
6	6	6	5%	06	06/35	06/25		7C/00
7	7	7	6^	07	07/36	07/5E	07/1E	7D/00
8	8	8	7&	08	08/37	08/26		7E/00
9	9	9	8*	09	09/38	09/2A		7F/00
10	10	10	9(	0A	0A/39	0A/28		80/00
11	11	11	0)	0B	0B/30	0B/29		81/00
12	12	12	-_	0C	0C/2D	0C/5F	0C/1F	82/00
13	13	13	=+	0D	0D/3D	0D/2B		83/00
15	14	15	Backspace	0E	0E/08	0E/08	0E/7F	
16	15	16	Tab	0F	0F/09	0F/00		
17	16	17	Q	10	10/71	10/51	10/11	10/00
18	17	18	W	11	11/77	11/57	11/17	11/00
19	18	19	E	12	12/65	12/45	12/05	12/00
20	19	20	R	13	13/72	13/52	13/12	13/00
21	20	21	T	14	14/74	14/54	14/14	14/00
22	21	22	Y	15	15/79	15/59	15/19	15/00
23	22	23	U	16	16/75	16/55	16/15	16/00
24	23	24	I	17	17/69	17/49	17/09	17/00
25	24	25	O	18	18/6F	18/4F	18/0F	18/00

continued

Character Code Tables, Continued

Character codes AH = 00h/01h, cont'd

101/102 Key #	83 Key #	84 Key #	U.S. Keyboard Legend	Scan Codes (hex)	Character Codes AH/AL (hex)			
					Normal	Shifted	Control	Alt
26	25	26	P	19	19/70	19/50	19/10	19/00
27	26	27	[{	1A	1A/5B	1A/7B	1A/1B	
28	27	28	] }	1B	1B/5D	1B/7D	1B/1D	
29*			\	2B	2B/5C	2B/7C	2B/1C	
30	58	64	Caps Lock	3A				
31	30	31	A	1E	1E/61	1E/41	1E/01	1E/00
32	31	32	S	1F	1F/73	1F/53	1F/13	1F/00
33	32	33	D	20	20/64	20/44	20/04	20/00
34	33	34	F	21	21/66	21/46	21/06	21/00
35	34	35	G	22	22/67	22/47	22/07	22/00
36	35	36	H	23	23/68	23/48	23/08	23/00
37	36	37	J	24	24/6A	24/4A	24/0A	24/00
38	37	38	K	25	25/6B	25/4B	25/0B	25/00
39	38	39	L	26	26/6C	26/4C	26/0C	26/00
40	39	40	; :	27	27/3B	27/3A		
41	40	41	' "	28	28/27	28/22		
42			(102–key only)	2B	2B/5C	2B/7C	2B/1C	
43	28	43	Enter ◄	1C	1C/0D	1C/0D	1C/0A	
44	42	44	L Shift	2A				
45			(102–key only)	56	56/5C	56/7C		
46	44	46	Z	2C	2C/7A	2C/5A	2C/1A	2C/00
47	45	47	X	2D	2D/78	2D/58	2D/18	2D/00
48	46	48	C	2E	2E/63	2E/43	2E/03	2E/00
49	47	49	V	2F	2F/76	2F/56	2F/16	2F/00
50	48	50	B	30	30/62	30/42	30/02	30/00

* 101–key keyboard only.

continued

Character codes AH = 00h/01h, *cont'd*

101/102 Key #	83 Key #	84 Key #	U.S. Keyboard Legend	Scan Codes (hex)	Character Codes AH/AL (hex)			
					Normal	Shifted	Control	Alt
51	49	51	N	31	31/6E	31/4E	31/0E	31/00
52	50	52	M	32	32/6D	32/4D	32/0D	32/00
53	51	53	, <	33	33/2C	33/3C		
54	52	54	. >	34	34/2E	34/3E		
55	53	55	/ ?	35	35/2F	35/3F		
57	54	57	R Shift	36				
58	29	30	L Ctrl	1D				
60	56	58	L Alt	38				
61	57	61	Space	39	39/20	39/20	39/20	39/20
62			R Alt	E0–38				
64			R Ctrl	E0–1D				
75			Insert	E0–52	52/00	52/00		
76			Delete	E0–53	53/00	53/00		
79			Left	E0–4B	4B/00	4B/00	73/00	
80			Home	E0–47	47/00	47/00	77/00	
81			End	E0–4F	4F/00	4F/00	75/00	**
83			Up	E0–48	48/00	48/00		**
84			Down	E0–50	50/00	50/00		**
85			Page Up	E0–49	49/00	49/00	84/00	
86			Page Down	E0–51	51/00	51/00	76/00	**
89			Right	E0–4D	4D/00	4D/00	74/00	**
90	69	95	Num Lock	45				**
91	71	91	7 Home	47	47/00	47/37	77/00	
92	75	92	4 Left	4B	4B/00	4B/34	73/00	
93	79	93	1 End	4F	4F/00	4F/31	75/00	**

** Alt plus the decimal value for an ASCII character input from the numeric keypad yields the ASCII character. Allowable values are 0–255.

continued

Character codes AH = 00h/01h, cont'd

101/102 Key #	83 Key #	84 Key #	U.S. Keyboard Legend	Scan Codes (hex)	Character Codes AH/AL (hex)			
					Normal	Shifted	Control	Alt
95			/	E0–35	35/2F	35/2F		**
96	72	96	8 UP	48	48/00	48/38		**
97	76	97	5	4C	4C/00	4C/35		
98	80	98	2 Down	50	50/00	50/32		
99	82	99	0 Ins	52	52/00	52/30		
100	55	106	*	37	37/2A	37/2A		
101	73	101	9 PgUp	49	49/00	49/39	84/00	
102	77	102	6 Right	4D	4D/00	4D/36	74/00	
103	81	103	3 PgDn	51	51/00	51/33	76/00	
104	83	104	. Del	53	53/00	53/2E		
105	74	107	–	4A	4A/2D	4A/2D		
106	78	108	+	4E	4E/2B	4E/2B		
108			Enter	E0–1C	1C/0D	1C/0D	1C/0A	
110	1	90	Esc	01	01/1B	01/1B	01/1B	
112	59	70	F1	3B	3B/00	54/00	5E/00	68/00
113	60	65	F2	3C	3C/00	55/00	5F/00	69/00
114	61	71	F3	3D	3D/00	56/00	60/00	6A/00
115	62	66	F4	3E	3E/00	57/00	61/00	6B/00
116	63	72	F5	3F	3F/00	58/00	62/00	6C/00
117	64	67	F6	40	40/00	59/00	63/00	6D/00
118	65	73	F7	41	41/00	5A/00	64/00	6E/00
119	66	68	F8	42	42/00	5B/00	65/00	6F/00
120	67	74	F9	43	43/00	5C/00	66/00	70/00
121	68	69	F10	44	44/00	5D/00	67/00	71/00
122			F11	57				

** Alt plus the decimal value for an ASCII character input from the numeric keypad yields the ASCII character. Allowable values are 0–255.

continued

Character codes AH = 00h/01h, cont'd

101/102 Key #	83 Key #	84 Key #	U.S. Keyboard Legend	Scan Codes (hex)	Character Codes AH/AL (hex)			
					Normal	Shifted	Control	Alt
123			F12	58				
		105	Sys Req					
124			Print Screen	E0–2A/ E0–37 E0–37			72/00	
125	70	100	Scroll Lock	46				
126			Pause	E1–1D/ 5–E1/ 9D/C5			00/00	

continued

Character codes: AH = 10h/11h

The table below lists the character codes returned by INT 16h DSR Functions AH = 10h Read Extended Keyboard Input and AH = 11h Return Extended Keyboard Status.

INT 09h places the value F0h in the low byte character code position for some Alt/character key combinations. The Return Extended Keyboard Input function strips F0h from the keyboard buffer image before returning to the caller. Keys with F0h are returned to AX with their low order byte set to 00h.

All other keys are returned to AX unmodified by this function.

101/102 Key #	U.S. Keyboard Legend	Scan Codes (hex)	Character Codes AH/AL (hex)			
			Normal	Shifted	Control	Alt
1	'~	29	29/60	29/7E		29/00
2	1!	02	02/31	02/21		78/00
3	2@	03	03/32	03/40	03/00	79/00
4	3#	04	04/33	04/23		7A/00
5	4$	05	05/34	05/24		7B/00
6	5%	06	06/35	06/25		7C/00
7	6^	07	07/36	07/5E	07/1E	7D/00
8	7&	08	08/37	08/26		7E/00
9	8*	09	09/38	09/2A		7F/00
10	9(	0A	0A/39	0A/28		80/00
11	0)	0B	0B/30	0B/29		81/00
12	-_	0C	0C/2D	0C/5F	0C/1F	82/00
13	=+	0D	0D/3D	0D/2B		83/00
15	Backspace	0E	0E/08	0E/08	0E/7F	0E/00
16	Tab	0F	0F/09	0F/00	94/00	A5/00
17	Q	10	10/71	10/51	10/11	10/00
18	W	11	11/77	11/57	11/17	11/00
19	E	12	12/65	12/45	12/05	12/00
20	R	13	13/72	13/52	13/12	13/00

continued

Character Code Tables, Continued

Character codes: AH = 10h/11h, cont'd

101/102 Key #	U.S. Keyboard Legend	Scan Codes (hex)	Normal	Shifted	Control	Alt
21	T	14	14/74	14/54	14/14	14/00
22	Y	15	15/79	15/59	15/19	15/00
23	U	16	16/75	16/55	16/15	16/00
24	I	17	17/69	17/49	17/09	17/00
25	O	18	18/6F	18/4F	18/0F	18/00
26	P	19	19/70	19/50	19/10	19/00
27	[{	1A	1A/5B	1A/7B	1A/1B	1A/00
28	] }	1B	1B/5D	1B/7D	1B/1D	1B/00
29*	I \	2B	2B/5C	2B/7C	2B/1C	2B/00
30	Caps Lock	3A				
31	A	1E	1E/61	1E/41	1E/01	1E/00
32	S	1F	1F/73	1F/53	1F/13	1F/00
33	D	20	20/64	20/44	20/04	20/00
34	F	21	21/66	21/46	21/06	21/00
35	G	22	22/67	22/47	22/07	22/00
36	H	23	23/68	23/48	23/08	23/00
37	J	24	24/6A	24/4A	24/0A	24/00
38	K	25	25/6B	25/4B	25/0B	25/00
39	L	26	26/6C	26/4C	26/0C	26/00
40	; :	27	27/3B	27/3A		27/00
41	' "	28	28/27	28/22		28/00
42	(102–key only)	2B	2B/5C	2B/7C	2B/1C	
43	Enter ⏎	1C	1C/0D	1C/0D	1C/0A	1C/00
44	L Shift	2A				
45	(102–key only)	56	56/5C	56/7C		

* 101–key keyboard only.

continued

Character codes: AH = 10h/11h, *cont'd*

101/102 Key #	U.S. Keyboard Legend	Scan Codes (hex)	Character Codes AH/AL (hex)			
			Normal	Shifted	Control	Alt
46	Z	2C	2C/7A	2C/5A	2C/1A	2C/00
47	X	2D	2D/78	2D/58	2D/18	2D/00
48	C	2E	2E/63	2E/43	2E/03	2E/00
49	V	2F	2F/76	2F/56	2F/16	2F/00
50	B	30	30/62	30/42	30/02	30/00
51	N	31	31/6E	31/4E	31/0E	31/00
52	M	32	32/6D	32/4D	32/0D	32/00
53	, <	33	33/2C	33/3C		33/00
54	. >	34	34/2E	34/3E		34/00
55	/ ?	35	35/2F	35/3F		35/00
57	R Shift	36				
58	L Ctrl	1D				
60	L Alt	38				
61	Space	39	39/20	39/20	39/20	39/20
62	R Alt	E0–38				
64	R Ctrl	E0–1D				
75	Insert	E0–52	52/E0	52/E0	92/E0	A2/00
76	Delete	E0–53	53/E0	53/E0	93/E0	A3/00
79	Left	E0–4B	4B/E0	4B/E0	73/E0	9B/00
80	Home	E0–47	47/E0	47/E0	77/E0	97/00
81	End	E0–4F	4F/E0	4F/E0	75/E0	9F/00
83	Up	E0–48	48/E0	48/E0	8D/E0	98/00
84	Down	E0–50	50/E0	50/E0	91/E0	A0/00
85	Page Up	E0–49	49/E0	49/E0	84/E0	99/00
86	Page Down	E0–51	51/E0	51/E0	76/E0	A1/00
89	Right	E0–4D	4D/E0	4D/E0	74/E0	9D/00

continued

Character codes: AH = 10h/11h, cont'd

101/102 Key #	U.S. Keyboard Legend	Scan Codes (hex)	Character Codes AH/AL (hex)			
			Normal	Shifted	Control	Alt
90	Num Lock	45				
91	7 Home	47	47/00	47/37	77/00	**
92	4 Left	4B	4B/00	4B/34	73/00	**
93	1 End	4F	4F/00	4F/31	75/00	**
95	/	E0–35	E0/2F	E0/2F	95/00	A4/00
96	8 UP	48	48/00	48/38	8D/00	**
97	5	4C	4C/00	4C/35	8F/00	**
98	2 Down	50	50/00	50/32	91/00	**
99	0 Ins	52	52/00	52/30	92/00	
100	*	37	37/2A	37/2A	96/00	37/00
101	9 PgUp	49	49/00	49/39	84/00	**
102	6 Right	4D	4D/00	4D/36	74/00	**
103	3 PgDn	51	51/00	51/33	76/00	**
014	Del	53	53/00	53/2E	93/00	
105	–	4A	4A/2D	4A/2D	8E/00	4A/00
106	+	4E	4E/2B	4E/2B	90/00	4E/00
108	Enter	E0–1C	E0/0D	E0/0D	E0/0A	A6/00
110	Esc	01	01/1B	01/1B	01/1B	01/00
112	F1	3B	3B/00	54/00	5E/00	68/00
113	F2	3C	3C/00	55/00	5F/00	69/00
114	F3	3D	3D/00	56/00	60/00	6A/00
115	F4	3E	3E/00	57/00	61/00	6B/00
116	F5	3F	3F/00	58/00	62/00	6C/00
117	F6	40	40/00	59/00	63/00	6D/00
118	F7	41	41/00	5A/00	64/00	6E/00

** Alt plus the decimal value for an ASCII character input from the numeric keypad yields the ASCII character. Allowable values are 0 to 255.

continued

Character Code Tables, Continued

Character codes: AH = 10h/11h, cont'd

101/102 Key #	U.S. Keyboard Legend	Scan Codes (hex)	Character Codes AH/AL (hex)			
			Normal	Shifted	Control	Alt
119	F8	42	42/00	5B/00	65/00	6F/00
120	F9	43	43/00	5C/00	66/00	70/00
121	F10	44	44/00	5D/00	67/00	71/00
122	F11	57	85/00	87/00	89/00	8B/00
123	F12	58	86/00	88/00	8A/00	8C/00
124	Print Screen	E0–2A/ E0–37 E0–37			72/00	
125	Scroll Lock	46				
126	Pause	E1–1D/ 45–E1/ 9D/C5			00/00	

INT 09h Keyboard ISR — Translate Scan Code

Description

The INT 09h Keyboard ISR is invoked via hardware INT 09h each time a key is pressed. It translates system scan codes into:

- Updates of the keyboard Shift key, keyboard LED, and Toggle key flags
- Requests for keyboard ISR internal functions
- Entries into the ROM BIOS keyboard buffer

INT 09h resides at address 00:24h in the Interrupt Vector table, and is initialized by the BIOS to point to system ROM address F000:E987h. The INT 09h ISR references I/O ports 60h and 64h. See Chapter 6 for a description of I/O ports.

The INT 09h ISR maintains status and buffer–control data definitions in segment 40h of the system RAM at offsets 17h–3Eh, 49h, 63h, 65h, 71h–72h, 80h, 82h, and 96h–97h. See Chapter 3 for a description of the BIOS data area of system RAM.

In ISA and EISA systems, the INT 09h ISR calls the INT 15h System Services Function 4Fh Keyboard Intercept. See Chapter 14 for a description of the BIOS System Services.

System reset (Ctrl–Alt–Del)

The INT 09h Keyboard ISR recognizes the Ctrl–Alt–Del keystroke combination as an internal request for the system RESET routine. The INT 09h ISR invokes the RESET operation with a jump call to the ROM BIOS code location (F000:E05Bh) where the routine resides.

Break (Ctrl–Break or Ctrl–Scroll Lock)

The INT 09h DSR recognizes the Ctrl–Break key combination as an internal function request for an INT 1Bh. INT 1Bh is a vector that points to a subroutine that is to be executed when the Ctrl–Break key combination is received from the keyboard. (Break and Scroll Lock are equivalent keys on some keyboards.)

During POST, INT 1Bh is initialized to point to a null subroutine. DOS revectors INT 1Bh to its own Ctrl–Break handling routine.

continued

Print Screen (Print Scrn or Shift–Print Scrn)

The INT 09h ISR invokes the INT 05h Print Screen Service DSR whenever it receives the combination of system scan codes corresponding to the left or the right Shift key and the Print Scrn key.

The system scan codes that cause the INT 09h ISR to invoke the INT 05h DSR can be generated either by pressing the Print Scrn key alone or by pressing either one of the Shift keys and the Print Scrn key.

System Request (Sys Req)

The INT 09h ISR interprets the pressing and releasing of the Sys Req key in either of two ways:

- When the key is pressed, the ISR interprets the resulting system scan code as an internal function request for the ROM BIOS INT 15h System Services DSR Function 85h, Subfunction AL = 00h, Process System Request.
- When the key is released, the INT 09h ISR interprets the resulting system scan code as an internal request for the BIOS INT 15h System Services DSR Function 85h, Subfunction AL = 01h, Terminate System Request.

Note: The Sys Req is not available on 83–key XT keyboards.

continued

Pause (Ctrl–Num Lock)

The INT 09h ISR recognizes the Ctrl–Num Lock key combination as an internal function request for the INT 09h controlled Pause state. When the INT 09h ISR puts the computer system into the Pause state, it loops until a valid key or key combination is received from the keyboard. (On a 101–key keyboard, the Pause key generates an E0h (Ctrl) E0 (Num Lock), which is recognized as a Pause state.)

To end the Pause state, bit 3 of Keyboard Shift Flags byte 2 (40:18h) must be reset to 0. The INT 09h ISR clears bit 3 of Keyboard Shift Flags byte 2 as soon as it receives either the make system scan code for any non–shift key (except for the Sys Req key) or any valid shift/toggle key combination, as shown below.

Shift Keys	** Toggle Keys **			
	Ins	Caps Lock	Scroll Lock	Num Lock
None Shift (L or R)				
Alt Alt/Shift				
Ctrl Ctrl/Shift				
Alt/Ctrl Alt/Ctrl/Shift				

LEGEND

PAUSE STATE IS ENDED (bit 3 of Keyboard Shift Flags byte 2 is reset). The scan codes normally associated with these keys do not have their usual effect on the shift and toggle flags. They are interpreted instead as a request to reset bit 3 of Keyboard Shift Flags byte 2 to zero, thus ending the Pause state.

PAUSE STATE IS NOT ENDED. The keyboard controller chip places the system scan code for (Ins) or (Shift Ins) into its internal buffer. The INT 09h ISR will act on these codes once the Pause state is ended.

PAUSE STATE IS NOT ENDED. These key combinations are treated as valid requests to change Shift/Toggle states or update LEDs. (LED updating is supported on AT–compatible keyboards only.)

PAUSE STATE IS NOT ENDED. The keys which initiate the Pause state can not be used to end the Pause state. When in the Pause state, these keys are ignored.

PAUSE STATE IS NOT ENDED. When in the Pause state, these keys are ignored.

INT 16h Keyboard DSR

Description

The INT 16h Keyboard DSR is invoked via software interrupt INT 16h, which is issued by the operating system or by application programs. It contains functions that read the ROM BIOS keyboard buffer, write to the buffer, and return the status of the keyboard service flags. Individual function codes are selected via the AH register.

INT 16h resides at address 00:58h in the Interrupt Vector table, and is initialized by the BIOS to point to system ROM address F000:E82Eh. The INT 16h DSR maintains status and buffer–control data definitions in segment 40h of the system RAM at offsets 17h, 18h, 1Ah, 1Ch, 1Eh, and 96h. See Chapter 3 for a description of the BIOS data area of system RAM.

The INT 16h Keyboard DSR references I/O ports 60h and 64h. See Chapter 6 for a description of I/O ports.

INT 16h Function 00h — Read Keyboard Input

Description

If a character code is available in the keyboard buffer, the Read Keyboard Input function reads the character code, removes it from the keyboard buffer, and returns its value in AX. The way this function processes when no character code is available depends on the kind of PC in place.

XT processing

In XT systems, if the keyboard buffer is empty, this function suspends program operation until a character code is inserted into the buffer. Programmers who wish to avoid suspending the system are advised to use Function AH = 01h Return Keyboard Status to test for the presence of a character code.

ISA and EISA processing

In ISA and EISA systems, if the keyboard buffer is empty, Function 00h invokes INT 15h Function AH = 90h Device Busy with AL = 02h Keyboard. This allows the operating system to perform another task while the keyboard loop is occurring.

Once the INT 09h Keyboard ISR places a character code in the keyboard buffer, it invokes INT 15h Function AH = 91h Interrupt Complete with AL = 02h Keyboard. The Read Keyboard Input function then reads the character code, removes it from the buffer, and returns to the caller with the character code in AX. In addition, if the keyboard LEDs do not match the current flag settings, Function AH = 00h also updates the keyboard LEDs.

Input/Output

Input: AH = 00h

Output: AH = Scan code or character ID for special character
AL = ASCII code or other translation of character.

continued

Extended key code filtering

The new and duplicate keys (the "extended keys") on 101/102–key AT–compatible keyboards generate system scan codes that are not useful to application software written to interact exclusively with the traditional 83–key XT or 84–key AT keyboards.

The INT 16h DSR Function AH = 00h acts as an 83–key/84–key keyboard filter, selectively editing the keyboard buffer contents for 83–key/84–key keyboard compatibility. When a 101–key keyboard is in place, the function does the following:

- Returns all standard 83–key/84–key keyboard character codes as is.
- Adjusts 101–key keyboard duplicate keyboard characters so that they take on the same two–byte key code as their 83–key/84–key counterparts.
- Destroys any 101–key character codes not compatible with the 83–key/84–key keyboards.

Note: The "Character Codes: AH = 00h/01h" table lists the codes returned when using the INT 16h DSR Functions AH = 00h and AH = 01h.

The 84th key

The 84th key on AT–compatible keyboards, Sys Req, is not present on 83–key XT keyboards. The absence of this 84th key is transparent to the INT 16h DSR Read Keyboard Input function; the system scan code generated by the Sys Req key is trapped by the INT 09h ISR and does not result in a character code being placed in the keyboard buffer. For a discussion of the INT 09h Sys Req key processing, see "System Request (Sys Req)" under INT 09h Keyboard ISR in this chapter.

INT 16h Function 01h — Read Keyboard Status

Description

This function checks the keyboard buffer for a two–byte character code. If a character code is waiting in the buffer, a copy of the character code is returned in AX and the Zero Flag is cleared. The buffer is not incremented to the next keystroke, and the character code remains in the buffer until it is cleared by INT 16h Function 00h.

If the keyboard buffer does not contain a character code, the Zero Flag is set.

In ISA and EISA systems, if the keyboard LEDs do not match the current flag settings, the function updates the LEDs.

Input/Output

Input:	AH	=	01h
Output:	AH	=	Scan code or character ID for special character
	AL	=	ASCII code or other translation of character.
	ZF	=	0 Character is ready
			1 No character is available

INT 16h Function 02h — Return Shift Flag Status

Description

This function returns the current shift status from SHFLGS (40:17h). In AT and EISA systems, the LED status is not updated.

Input/Output

Input: AH = 02h

Output: AL = Current shift status, where:
Bit 7 = 1 Insert active
Bit 6 = 1 Caps Lock active
Bit 5 = 1 Num Lock active
Bit 4 = 1 Scroll Lock active
Bit 3 = 1 Alt pressed
Bit 2 = 1 Ctrl pressed
Bit 1 = 1 Left Shift pressed
Bit 0 = 1 Right Shift pressed

INT 16h Function 03h —
Set Typematic Rate and Delay

Description

This function changes the typematic rate (make code per second) and the delay.

If the parameters are valid, the function transmits a Set Typematic Repeat and Delay Period command (F3h) to the keyboard controller.

Input/Output

Input: AH = 03h

AL = 05h

BH = Delay value (in milliseconds)

00h	= 250		03h	= 1000
01h	= 500		04h to FFh — Reserved	
02h	= 750			

BL = Typematic rate (in characters per second)

00h	= 30.0		11h	= 6.7
01h	= 26.7		12h	= 6.0
02h	= 24.0		13h	= 5.5
03h	= 21.8		14h	= 5.0
04h	= 20.0		15h	= 4.6
05h	= 18.5		16h	= 4.3
06h	= 17.1		17h	= 4.0
07h	= 16.0		18h	= 3.7
08h	= 15.0		19h	= 3.3
09h	= 13.3		1Ah	= 3.0
0Ah	= 12.0		1Bh	= 2.7
0Bh	= 10.9		1Ch	= 2.5
0Ch	= 10.0		1Dh	= 2.3
0Dh	= 9.2		1Eh	= 2.1
0Eh	= 8.6		1Fh	= 2.0
0Fh	= 8.0		20h to FFh — Reserved	
10h	= 7.5			

Output: None

INT 16h Function 05h — Store Key Data

Description

This function stores program–generated data into the keyboard buffer. The buffer pointer (40:1Ch) is adjusted to point to the next available location in the keyboard buffer. If the keyboard buffer is full, AL is set to indicate a keyboard buffer full error. Keyboard enhancers and other utilities can use this function to interpolate keys into the data stream viewed by application programs.

This AT–compatible function is also supported by some enhanced XT BIOSs.

Input/Output

Input:	AH	=	05h
	CL	=	ASCII character
	CH	=	Scan code
Output:	AL	=	0 No error
		=	1 Keyboard buffer full
	CF	=	0 No error
		=	1 Buffer full

INT 16h Function 10h — Read Extended Keyboard Input

Description

This function reads the next two–byte character code in the keyboard buffer and returns the value in AX. Unlike Function AH = 00h, this function does not modify character codes for 84–key keyboard compatibility.

This AT–compatible function is also supported by some enhanced XT BIOSs.

Input/Output

Input: AH = 10h

Output: AH = Scan code or character ID for special character
          AL = ASCII code or other translation of character

F0h low byte filter

INT 09h places the value F0h in the low byte character code position for some Alt/character key combinations. The INT 16h DSR Read Extended Keyboard Input function strips F0h from the keyboard buffer image before returning to the caller. Keys with F0h are returned to AX with their low order byte set to 00h. All other keys are returned to AX unmodified.

INT 16h Function 11h — Return Extended Keyboard Status

Description

This function is similar to function AH = 01h, except that it returns unique scan codes for all keys on the 101/102–key keyboard. It checks the keyboard buffer for a two–byte character code. If a character code is waiting in the buffer, a copy of the character code is returned in AX and the Zero Flag is cleared. The buffer is not incremented to the next keystroke, and the character code remains in the buffer until it is cleared by INT 16h Function 00h.

If the keyboard buffer does not contain a character code, the Zero Flag is set.

In ISA and EISA systems, if the keyboard LEDs do not match the current flag settings, the function updates the LEDs.

This AT–compatible function is also supported by some enhanced XT BIOSs.

Input/Output

Input:	AH	=	11h
Output:	AH	=	Scan code or character ID for special character (if Zero Flag is set)
	AL	=	ASCII code or other translation of character ID (Zero Flag is set)
	ZF	=	0 No key in buffer
		=	1 Key waiting

F0h low byte filter

INT 09h places the value F0h in the low byte character code position of some Alt/character combinations. The INT 16h Return Extended Keyboard Status function strips F0h from the keyboard buffer image before returning to the caller. Keys with F0h are returned to AX with their low order byte set to 00h. All other keys are returned to AX unmodified by this function.

INT 16h Function 12h — Return Extended Shift Flags

Description

This function returns the shift flag status from SHFLGS (40:17) in AL and the shift flag status from SHFLGS2 (40:18) and K101FL (40:96) in AH.

This AT–compatible function is also supported by some enhanced XT BIOSs.

Input/Output

Input:	AH	=	12h
Output:	AH	=	More keyboard shift flags, where:

Bit 7 = 1 Sys Req pressed (40:18h bit 7)
Bit 6 = 1 Caps Lock active (40:18h bit 6)
Bit 5 = 1 Num Lock active (40:18h bit 5)
Bit 4 = 1 Scroll Lock active (40:18h bit 4)
Bit 3 = 1 Right Alt active (40:96h bit 3)
Bit 2 = 1 Right Ctrl active (40:96h bit 2)
Bit 1 = 1 Left Alt active (40:18h bit 1)
Bit 0 = 1 Left Ctrl active (40:18h bit 0)

AL = Keyboard shift flags (copy of SHFLGS 40:17h), where:
Bit 7 = 1 Insert active
Bit 6 = 1 Caps Lock active
Bit 5 = 1 Num Lock active
Bit 4 = 1 Scroll Lock active
Bit 3 = 1 Alt pressed
Bit 2 = 1 Ctrl pressed
Bit 1 = 1 Left Shift pressed
Bit 0 = 1 Right Shift pressed

10

Chapter 10
Video Service

Overview

Description

The ROM BIOS Video Service allows system and application software in ISA– and EISA–compatible systems to access the video subsystem. This service is provided by the INT 10h Video Service DSR.

In this chapter

Major topics in this chapter include:

- Theory of Operation
- Video Modes
- INT 10h Video Service DSR
- Video Service functions

Theory of Operation

Introduction

The computer's video subsystem generates signals that cause the CRT's electron beam to sweep across the screen in a left to right, top to bottom pattern of horizontal lines called a raster.

The information written by the microprocessor to the video buffer is represented on the CRT screen as a pattern of illuminated dots, called pixels (picture elements). As the beam sweeps across the screen, the video subsystem turns the electron beam on and off, thus "painting" the buffer information onto the screen.

A monitor's horizontal scan frequency determines the maximum number of lines the monitor is capable of painting per second. Its vertical scan frequency determines the frames per second the monitor is capable of refreshing.

Vertical and horizontal resolution

A display's vertical resolution — the maximum number of scan lines it can display on the screen — is calculated by dividing horizontal scan frequency by vertical scan frequency.

The dots, or pixels, that appear on each horizontal scan line are generated by a crystal–driven device, called a dot clock. A display's horizontal resolution — the maximum number of dots per line — is calculated by dividing the monitor's horizontal scan frequency into the dot rate of the subsystem driving the monitor.

Monitor types

Color monitors contain three electron guns, arranged in a triangle or in a straight line, aimed at an array of pixels. Each pixel comprises three colored phosphor dots: one red, one blue, and one green. Although each gun illuminates a separate dot, the dots are so tightly focused that they appear to the eye as one color.

Monochrome monitors have only one electron gun. The color of the screen is a function of the phosphor used. In monochrome computer displays, phosphors are usually either amber, green, or white.

continued

Signal types

Computer monitors are further distinguished from each other by the kind of input signal they are designed to accept:

- Composite monitors accept a composite, analog signal in which the signals for red, green, and blue are combined by the video subsystem and separated by the monitor. Composite monochrome signals are the same except that they contain only one "color" signal. Composite signals can be sent over a single line, but the difficulty involved in accurately separating colors limits the resolution achieved on composite monitors.

- Digital RGB monitors accept signals for red, green, or blue on separate lines. The monitor does not perform color signal separation. The number of colors displayed by a digital RGB monitor is a function of the number of color lines. A digital monochrome signal is identical to its RGB counterpart except that only one "color" line is required.

- Analog RGB monitors accept signals for red, green, and blue on separate lines. The number of colors potentially displayable is infinite since the intensity of each line varies with the voltage applied to it. Video subsystems designed to drive analog color monitors must convert digital color information into analog voltages.

continued

Video data format

Each location in a video adapter's display buffer maps to a location on the monitor screen. The first byte of buffer memory maps to the top, leftmost point on the screen. As memory addresses increase, the screen location map moves from left to right and top to bottom. The BIOS writes information to the video hardware's display buffer in either of two formats: alphanumeric or graphic.

When writing alphanumeric data to the video buffer, the BIOS writes each character as a series of two bytes. The first byte contains the ASCII code for the symbol, and the second byte contains the attributes to be applied to the symbol. The video subsystem's control circuitry reads one display line of ASCII data from the video data buffer converting it into a series of pixels. Simultaneously, the video hardware translates the ASCII character's accompanying attributes into the indicated foreground and background colors.

When writing graphical data to the video data buffer, the BIOS writes the individual color value of each pixel to be painted on the CRT. It addresses the display buffer as a memory map made up of an array of bits. The video subsystem's control circuitry reads each pixel location from the buffer and generates the color and control signals necessary to write the pixel to the correct screen location with the correct color value.

Adapter types

The functions offered by a BIOS depend on the adapter. Monochrome Display Adapter (MDA) and Color Graphics Adapter (CGA) adapters rely exclusively on the video services provided in the system BIOS of ISA–compatible computers. Enhanced Graphics Adapter (EGA) and Video Graphics Array (VGA) adapters contain a dedicated ROM BIOS installed on the adapter board; therefore, they are not described in this document. Similarly, the Hercules (HGC) adapter, which is a superset of the MDA, does not contain a BIOS or use the services of the system BIOS. Applications that use Hercules graphics must contain an application–specific device driver.

continued

Adapter hardware components

When viewed on the highest functional level, all PC video adapters share the same programmable components:

- Video buffer. This block of RAM is on the adapter but is mapped into the microprocessor's address space. Each location in the video buffer maps to a location on the video screen. The video buffer address map for MDA adapters is B000:0000h–B000:0FFFh; the video buffer address map for CGA adapters is B800:0000h–B000:FFFFh.

- Cathode Ray Tube Controller (CRTC). This device generates the horizontal and vertical timing signals that control the path and duration of the electron beam sweeping the inner surface of the CRT. The CRTC also increments a video buffer address counter so that the data contained in the buffer are synchronized with the timing signals. The CRTC controls the size and location of the text mode cursor and selects the portion of the video buffer to be displayed on the screen.

- Alphanumeric character generator. This device is responsible for translating the ASCII value of a character into a matrix of dots to display on the screen. The hardware character generator references a character table under the control of the video BIOS. Depending on adapter type, this character table can reside permanently at a fixed ROM location, or it can be written (on mode set) from ROM to a fixed location in RAM.

- Attribute decoder. This component of the video adapter uses data from the video buffer to control the color and brightness of the signals produced by the video signal generator.

- Video signal generator. This device sends the signals that control what appears on the monitor's screen.

- Video mode control registers. These registers allow the video adapter to produce the indicated mode.

Video Modes

Introduction

A video mode is characterized by the screen resolution, the number of displayable colors, and the kind of data (alphanumeric or graphic) displayed.

Most PC video adapters support more than one video mode. The reason for this is largely historical: PC video adapters have evolved from low–resolution, 16–color devices to relatively high–resolution, 256–color devices. In order to maintain compatibility with software written for the previous video adapters, each successive generation of video hardware has to be made mode–compatible with its predecessors.

Establishing a video mode is a matter of programming those components of the video adapter's hardware that control the dot clock, enable or disable the character generator, and so on. Although it's possible to program these components directly, it's easier to set video modes through the video BIOS.

MDA video mode

MDA adapters support only one video mode.

Mode	Type	Resolution	Max. Colors	Scheme	Char. Box	Max. Pages	Buff. Start
7	Text	720x350	mono	80x25	9x14	1	B0000h

continued

CGA video modes

The table below lists the seven video modes supported by the CGA BIOS.

Mode	Type	Resolution	Max. Colors	Scheme	Char. Box	Max. Pages	Buff. Start
0	Text	320x200	16	40x25	8x8	4	B8000h
1	Text	320x200	16	40x25	8x8	4	B8000h
2	Text	640x200	16	80x25	8x8	4	B8000h
3	Text	640x200	16	80x25	8x8	4	B8000h
4	Graphics	320x200	4	40x25	8x8	1	B8000h
5	Graphics	320x200	4	40x25	8x8	1	B8000h
6	Graphics	640x200	2	80x25	8x8	1	B8000h

CGA video mode characteristics

The CGA video modes have the following characteristics:

- No cursor is displayed in graphics modes.
- Modes 1, 3, and 4 are the same as modes 0, 2, and 5 except that in modes 0, 2, and 5 color burst is enabled. Enabling color burst allows color information to be displayed on composite color displays.
- Digital RGB displays are not affected by enabling color burst.

Video services

The video services provided by the INT 10h Video DSR depend on the type of display and its video mode. The physical capabilities of the monitor and display adapter determine the services that the DSR can provide, and the video mode determines how the display parameters referenced by the DSR are stored in the BIOS data area of system RAM.

INT 10h Video DSR

Introduction

The INT 10h Video DSR allows programs to select the video display mode, position the cursor, write text characters to the screen, scroll the display, and so on. The ROM BIOS Video Service routines are invoked by INT 10h, whose vector resides at Interrupt Vector table address 00:40h.

Individual INT 10h DSR functions are selected via the AH register. Subfunctions are selected via the AL or the BL register. The following general rules also apply:

- The character or pixel value that is to be written is normally passed in register AL.
- Except for the AX register, all registers' contents are preserved through all function calls unless the register is used for the return value.
- The column number (x coordinate) is passed in CX for graphics modes and in DL for text modes. The row number (y coordinate) is passed in DX for graphics mode and in DH for text mode.
- Any display page value is passed in BH. Display pages are zero–based (that is, page 0 = the first page, page 1 = the second page, and so on).

The INT 10h Video DSR references control information stored in the BIOS data area of system RAM. This information is located at the following offsets of segment 40h: 10h, 49h, 66h, 4Ah–4Eh, 50h, 60h–65h and B0h. See Chapter 3 for a description of the BIOS data area.

The INT 10h Video DSR references I/O port addresses 03B4h, 03B5h, 03B8h, 03BAh, 03D4h, 03D5h, and 03D8h–03DCh. See Chapter 6 for a description of the I/O ports.

Error handling

If the number in AH is outside the legal range, no action will be taken.

INT 10h Function 00h — Set Video Mode

Description

This function sets the video mode registers for operation in any supported mode. It selects the active video mode if more than one is installed, clears the screen, positions the cursor at screen coordinates 0,0 and resets the color palette to default color values. (See the *Video Modes* heading in this chapter for a description of the video modes that the system ROM BIOS supports.)

Input/Output

Input: AH = 00h

             AL   = Video mode (00h–07h are valid values)

Output: None

Additional information

- Resetting the same video mode can be used to clear the screen.
- To avoid resetting the palette when working with colors, use Function 06h rather than Function 00h of INT 10h to clear the screen.
- The cursor is not displayed in graphics modes.
- The power–on default mode with a color monitor attached is 3.
- The power–on default mode with a monochrome monitor attached is 7.

INT 10h Function 01h — Set Cursor Type

Description

This function specifies the size of the cursor that appears in text modes. Cursor size and location within the character box is determined by the starting and ending scan lines indicated in bits 4–0 of registers CH and CL. The function stores cursor size parameters in the cursor type byte at 40:60h.

Input/Output

Input:	AH	= 01h
	CH	= Top scan line, where:

           Bit 7   = Reserved (If a value is set, then cursor blinking becomes erratic.)

           Bits 6–5 = Cursor control operation, where:
                00   Normal
                01   Cursor not displayed

           Bits 4–0 = Start line of cursor

       CL   = Bottom scan line, where:
           Bits 7–5 = Undefined
           Bits 4–0 = End line of cursor

Output: None

continued

Additional information

- Only one cursor type is available for all video pages.
- Setting bit 5 of the CH register causes the cursor to disappear completely. The cursor can also be eliminated by positioning it to a nondisplay address, such as $(x,y) = (0,25)$.
- CGA modes can display a cursor on eight lines, numbered 0 to 7, top to bottom.
- MDA mode can display a cursor on 14 lines, numbered 0 to 13, top to bottom.
- To simulate the cursor in graphics modes, use the solid block character DFh, or the blank character with a changed background color.

Default cursor settings

The default cursor settings for the video types that the ROM BIOS supports are listed below. These settings are established by INT 10h Function AH = 00h at mode set.

Type	Description
CGA	CH = 6, CL = 7
MDA	CH = 11, CL = 12

INT 10h Function 02h — Set Cursor Position

Description

This function sets the cursor position for the display page indicated in BL. It saves the position as a two–byte row–by–column table entry in the cursor coordinates byte at 40:50h. Row and column coordinates are indicated in registers DH and DL respectively.

Function AH = 02h applies to both text and graphics video modes. In text modes, if the display page selected in BH is the active display page, the screen cursor will move to the coordinates indicated in registers DH and DL. In graphics modes, the cursor is invisible but is used to define a position on the screen.

Input/Output

Input: AH = 02h
            BH = Display page number (see Function AH = 05h)
            DH = Row (0 is top row of screen)
            DL = Column (0 is leftmost column)

Output: None

Cursor positioning

Positioning the cursor to screen coordinates 0,0 places it in the upper left corner of the screen in the 80x25 text mode. Selecting coordinates 79,24 in the 80x25 text mode will allow placement of the cursor in the lower right corner of the screen. The cursor can also be placed in the lower right corner of the screen using coordinates 39,24 in the 40x25 text mode.

The cursor can be turned off by moving it to an off–screen location or by changing its coordinates to a position such as 0,25. However, if it is moved too far off–screen, the actual position of the cursor may become unpredictable.

Additional information

The display page number must be set to 0 in CGA graphics mode.

INT 10h Function 03h — Read Current Cursor Position

Description

This function reads the cursor position for the given video page from the cursor coordinates byte at 40:50h. It reads the cursor type from 40:60h and returns the current cursor position in row and column coordinates. The function is useful for determining the exact cursor type before it is changed.

Input/Output

Input:	AH	=	03h
	BH	=	Display page number (zero–based)
Output:	AX	=	00h
	CH	=	Starting cursor scan line
	CL	=	Ending cursor scan line
	DH	=	Row number
	DL	=	Column number

Additional information

A different cursor is maintained for each display page. Each of these cursors can be examined independently with Function AH = 03h, no matter which page is currently active. The number of available display pages is defined by the display mode selected.

Description

This function reads the light pen's status and position.

Input/Output

Input:	AH	= 04h
Output:	AH	= 00h Light pen switch is not active
		= 01h Light pen coordinate values
	DH,DL	= Row and column of character
	CH	= Raster line (0–199)
	CL	= Raster line (0–nnn) modes > 200 line resolution
	BX	= Pixel column (0–319,639)

Additional information

Light pens are not effective on monochrome monitors with long image–retention phosphor, and the light pen position is not accurate enough for use with high resolution devices.

Description

This function sets the active page for the video mode selected. Refer to the *Video Modes* heading in this chapter for a list of the maximum number of pages allowed for each video mode.

Input/Output

Input: AH = 05h
AL = New page number (zero–based)

Output: None

Additional information

- All page numbers are zero–based (that is, page numbers begin at page 0).
- In text modes, page numbers range from 0–7.
- Page 0, located at the beginning of display memory, is used by default in all video modes.
- Switching between pages does not alter their contents. Also, no matter which page is active (currently displayed), text can be written to any video page using INT 10h, Functions 02h, 09h, and 10h.
- In the CGA modes, no video paging is possible.
- The current cursor position is maintained by ROM BIOS for as many as eight video pages.
- An instantaneous screen change can be created by building a screen on an undisplayed page, then using Function AH = 05h to display it.

INT 10h Function 06h — Scroll Current Page Up

Description

This function employs the CH, DH, CL, and DL registers to define a screen window and allow the contents of the window to be scrolled up by the number of character rows specified in register AL. If AL = 00h, the window is also blanked.

Information appearing on the screen but lying outside the parameters of the defined window remains on the screen. Only one window can be defined at any given time.

This function operates in both text and graphics modes.

Input/Output

Input:	AH	=	06h Scroll current page up
	AL	=	Scroll distance in character rows (0 blanks entire scroll area)
	BH	=	Attribute to use on blanked lines
	CH	=	Top row (upper left corner) of window
	CL	=	Left–most column (upper left corner) of window
	DH	=	Bottom row (lower right corner) of window
	DL	=	Right–most column (lower right corner) of window
Output:	None		

Initializing a window

Setting AL = 00h initializes a window on the display screen. It blanks out the region specified by the CX and DX registers and fills the window with the attribute in the BH register.

INT 10h Function 07h — Scroll Current Page Down

Description

This function employs the CH, DH, CL, and DL registers to define a screen window and allow the contents of the window to be scrolled down by the number of character rows specified in register AL. If AL = 00h, the window is also blanked.

Information appearing on the screen but lying outside the parameters of the defined window remains on the screen. Only one window can be defined at any given time.

This function operates in both text and graphics modes.

Input/Output

Input:	AH	=	07h Scroll current page down
	AL	=	Scroll distance in character rows (0 blanks entire scroll area)
	BH	=	Attribute to use on blanked lines
	CH	=	Top row (upper left corner) of window
	CL	=	Left–most column (upper left corner) of window
	DH	=	Bottom row (lower right corner) of window
	DL	=	Right–most column (lower right corner) of window
Output:	None		

Initializing a window

Setting AL = 00h initializes a window on the display screen. It blanks out the region specified by the CX and DX registers and fills the window with the attribute in the BH register.

INT 10h Function 08h — Read Character/Attribute from Screen

Description

This function reads the character at the current cursor location. For text modes, the attribute is also returned. In graphics modes, the character matrix at the cursor position is compared to the bit patterns in the current graphics character–definition table to determine the character's ASCII value. Characters other than standard ASCII characters are returned as AL = 00h.

Input/Output

Input:	AH	=	08h
	BH	=	Display page (Refer to the *Video Modes* heading in this chapter for the maximum pages per mode.)
Output:	AH	=	Attribute (text modes only)
	AL	=	Character read

Additional information

- To read a character from any valid display page other than the active one, specify the display page number.
- Information about the screen is in screen memory and need not be stored in a program.

INT 10h Function 09h — Write Character/Attribute to Screen

Description

This function writes the character to the screen starting at the current cursor location for as many times as indicated in the CX register. The cursor is never moved.

INT 10h Functions AH = 09h and AH = 0Ah are similar. Function AH = 09h, however, should be used for all graphics modes and in all text modes where character by character control of foreground and background attributes is desired.

Input/Output

Input:	AH	=	09h
	AL	=	ASCII character to write
	BH	=	Display page (Refer to the *Video Modes* heading in this chapter for the maximum pages per mode.)
	BL	=	Character attribute (text modes)
		=	Foreground color (graphics modes)
	CX	=	Repeat count
Output:	None		

continued

Additional Information

- In text modes, the number of repeats placed into CX may exceed the number of columns remaining in a given row. Characters will wrap around from row to row. In graphics modes, the number of repeats placed into CX cannot exceed the number of columns remaining in a given row. Characters will not wrap around from row to row.

- In CGA graphics modes, the bit map used for ASCII characters 80h–FFh is stored in a table that starts at 0:7Ch. This value is stored in the vector for INT 1Fh. By resetting the vector, the bit map table location can be changed to point to a different bit map.

- Any value of AL will produce a display; this includes all control characters (for example, bell, backspace, CR, LF). These control characters are not interpreted as special characters and do not change the cursor position.

- After a character has been written, the cursor has to be explicitly moved to the next position using INT 10h Function 02h.

- To write a character without changing the attribute at the current cursor position, use INT 10h Function 0Ah.

- When this function is used to write characters in graphics mode, and bit 7 of BL is set to 1, the character is XORed with the contents of the current display. This feature can be used to write characters and then erase them.

INT 10h Function 0Ah — Write Character Only to Screen

Description

This function operates identically like INT 10h Function AH = 09h Write Character/Attribute, except that for text modes the attribute bytes corresponding to the characters remain unchanged. Use the function to write a character to the screen in text modes. Use Function AH = 09h to do this in graphics modes.

Input/Output

Input:	AH	=	0Ah
	AL	=	Character to write (ASCII codes)
	BH	=	Display page (text modes only)
	CX	=	Repeat count
Output:	None		

Additional information

- Any value of AL will produce a display; this includes all control characters (for example, bell, backspace, CR, and LF). These control characters are not interpreted as special characters and do not change the cursor position.
- After a character has been written, the cursor has to be explicitly moved to the next position using INT 10h Function 02h.
- To write a character without changing the attribute at the current cursor position, use INT 10h Function 0Ah.
- When this function is used to write characters in graphics mode, and bit 7 of BL is set to 1, the character is XORed with the contents of the current display. This feature can be used to write characters and then erase them.

INT 10h Function 0Bh — Set Color Palette

Description

This function selects colors for medium–resolution graphics modes. Depending on the value placed in BH, it will perform any of four operations.

If BH = 00h, then the value in BL sets the:

- Background and border colors for 320x200 graphics modes 4 and 5
- Border color for 320x200 text modes 0, 1, 2, and 3
- Foreground color for 640x200 graphics mode 6 and 640x480 graphics mode 11

If BH = 01h, then the value in BL sets the palette for 320x200 graphics modes 4 and 5.

Input/Output

Input: AH = 0Bh
        BH = 00h
           = If mode = 4, 5, background color is set to value in BL
           = If mode = 0, 1, 2, or 3, border color is to value in BL
           = If mode = 6 or 11, foreground color is set to value in BL
        BL = 0–31, where colors 16–31 are the intense versions of colors 0–15

        or

        BH = 01h Select palette for mode 4 or 5
        BL = 00h Palette = Green (1), Red (2), Yellow (3)
             01h Palette = Cyan (1), Magenta (2), White (3)

Output: None

Additional Information

- In CGA graphics modes, bit 4 of BL selects between normal and high intensity.
- A flashing display can be set by rapidly changing the palette.
- The background color of text is determined by the high order four bits of the attribute byte of each character.

Description

This function writes to video memory the pixel specified by the row and column numbers in DX and CX. When a video mode allows more than one page, the page number must be indicated in BH.

For all graphics modes, bit 7 of AL acts as an inverter flag. If bit 7 of AH is set, then the color value in AL is XORed with the current pixel. That pixel can be erased by writing it a second time.

Refer to the *Video Modes* heading in this chapter for the video modes, resolutions, and maximum pages per mode that ROM BIOS supports.

Input/Output

Input: AH   =   0Ch
AL   =   Color (bit 7 is XOR flag)
BH   =   Page number (for modes allowing more than one page)
CX   =   Pixel column number
DX   =   Pixel row number

Output: None

Pixel values

- In four–color graphics modes (modes 04h and 05h), pixel values range from 0–3.
- In two–color graphics modes (mode 06h), pixel values range from 0–1.

INT 10h Function 0Dh — Read Pixel

Description

This function returns the value of an addressed pixel to the low order bits of the AL register. This function can be used for collision detection in video games. It can also be used by advanced graphics programs to detect boundaries when moving a graphics object on the screen.

Refer to the *Video Modes* heading in this chapter for a listing of the video modes, resolutions, and maximum pages per mode that the ROM BIOS supports.

Input/Output

Input:	AH	=	0Dh
	BH	=	Page number (modes allowing more than one page)
	CX	=	Column number
	DX	=	Row number
Output:	AL	=	Color value of pixel read

Pixel values

Display modes 04h, 05h and 06h have valid pixel values in the ranges of 0–3, 0–3, and 0–1 respectively.

INT 10h Function 0Eh — Write Teletype to Active Page

Description

This function makes the display appear as if it were on a serial terminal. The character in AL is written to video memory to be placed in the active page at the current cursor position, and the cursor is moved to the next character location (scrolling is necessary). Screen width is a function of the video mode currently in effect.

Input/Output

Input:	AH	=	0Eh
	AL	=	Character to write
	BL	=	Foreground color (graphics modes only)
	BH	=	Active page
Output:	None		

Special characters

The four ASCII characters listed below are not displayed but are interpreted instead as control characters. All other characters, including other control characters, are interpreted as display characters.

Character	ASCII Code	Function
Bell	07h	A beep is sounded.
Backspace	08h	If the cursor is already on column 0, nothing happens. Otherwise, the cursor moves back one column.
LF	0Ah	The cursor moves down one row. If done on the last row of the screen, the display is scrolled one row.
CR	0Dh	The cursor moves to column 0 on the current row.

continued

Additional information

- When working in the active page, this function allows a character to be printed at the current cursor position. After printing the character, it moves the cursor to the right one space. It then wraps the cursor to the next line. Scrolling the screen up one line requires that the cursor be moved past the lower right corner of the screen.

- In CGA text mode, characters can be written to any legal display page, no matter which page is active.

- This function is similar to INT 10h Function 13h. However, it only prints one character at a time.

- This is the best function to use for simple output.

DOS uses the function

DOS uses Function AH = 0Eh in the console driver for writing operating system text and messages to the screen.

The function does not, however, allow the attribute of a text character to be selected. To define an attribute for a character written to the screen:

1. Write the ASCII blank character (20h) having the desired attribute to the current position using INT 10h Function AH = 09h.

2. Write the desired character using Function = 0Eh.

With this method, the application software does not have to provide for line wrapping and screen scrolling, but can allow the ROM BIOS to control these functions.

INT 10h Function 0Fh — Return Video Status

Description

This function returns current display mode information. It gives the mode, screen width in characters, and the display page number.

Refer to the *Video Modes* heading in this chapter for the maximum pages per mode that PhoenixBIOS support.

Input/Output

Input:	AH	=	0Fh
Output:	AH	=	Number of columns on screen from the screen width byte (40:4Ah)
	AL	=	Current mode from the video mode setting byte (40:49h)
	BH	=	Active display page number from the display page byte (40:62h)

Examples of use

Some ways to use this function are:

- To determine the screen width in the current screen mode before clearing the screen.
- To determine the settings of the display system at program initialization so that they can be returned to when the program terminates.
- To write terminate–and–stay–resident programs (TSRs) that pop up on the screen while another application is running. The background application may be running in a different mode than the TSR.

INT 10h Function 13h — Write String

Description

This function operates similarly to Function AH = 0Eh Write Teletype to Active Page, except that an entire string is handled with the call. The AL register contains two single–bit fields differentiated as follows:

If...	Then...
AL Bit 0 = 1	the cursor remains at the last character written.
AL Bit 0 = 0	the cursor is restored to where it was before the write string operation began.
AL Bit 1 = 1	each string character to be displayed is followed by its attribute.
AL Bit 1 = 0	carriage return, line feed, backspace, and bell are interpreted as commands rather than as printable characters. The string contains only display characters, and the attribute is taken from the BL register.

Input/Output

Input:	AH	= 13h
	ES:BP	= Pointer to start of string
	BH	= Page number (for text modes)
	BL	= Attribute for characters (graphics modes)
	CX	= Length of string (attributes don't count)
	DX	= Starting cursor position (DH = row, DL = column)
	AL	= 00h Cursor not moved. String contains characters only.
		= 01h Cursor is moved. String contains characters only.
		= 02h Cursor not moved. String contains alternating characters and attributes.
		= 03h Cursor is moved. String contains alternating characters and attributes.

Output: None

Chapter 11

Diskette Service

Overview

Description

The ROM BIOS Diskette Service performs read, write, format, initialization, and other operations for up to two internal diskette drives in an ISA-compatible system. It consists of

- the INT 0Eh Diskette ISR, which handles interrupts from the diskette drive controller, and
- the INT 13h Diskette DSR, which services software requests issued by the diskette drives.

In this chapter

This chapter discusses the following major topics:

- Theory of Operation
- INT 0Eh Diskette ISR
- INT 13h Diskette DSR
- Error Handling
- Diskette Service functions

Theory of Operation

Introduction

Diskettes remain the fundamental media for transfer of information in the micro-computing world. New software is shipped on diskettes, and despite the proliferation of networks, software in the workplace is still primarily transferred by diskette.

ROM BIOS and diskette hardware

The ROM BIOS manipulates a diskette drive through the diskette drive controller. In IBM-compatible systems the controller is a NEC 765 diskette controller chip or its equivalent.

In order to manipulate the diskette, the ROM BIOS needs to provide the controller with information about the system's diskette hardware. The information the BIOS needs is stored in a Diskette Parameters table, which is described in Chapter 5.

The Diskette Parameters table consists of eleven bytes. The first two bytes, known as the specify bytes, identify the diskette being used in the system. These bytes are used in a command block, which the BIOS sends to the controller to initiate a diskette operation. After a command has been executed, the controller sends diskette status information to the system through result bytes.

Diskette components

Diskettes systems are made up of the following basic components:

Head The head contains an electromagnet, positioned on a movable assembly just above the surface of the diskette. By pulsing the electromagnet, the head reads or writes data to or from the diskette.

Track While the head is positioned over a point on the diskette, ready to read or write, the diskette surface spins underneath it, tracing a full circle. This circle is a track. There may be 40 to 80 tracks per diskette surface, or side.

Sector Diskette systems divide each track into short arcs (usually 9, 15, or 18 per track) called sectors. Each sector usually holds 512 bytes of data. The diskette sector size can be changed with Diskette Service INT 13h, Function 05h.

continued

Diskette components illustration

The following illustration displays and explains each component of the diskette system.

Heads and surfaces

Both sides of the diskette platter surface are covered with a material that can be magnetized and is used to store information.

Diskette drives generally have two magnetic heads. One head is used for each side.

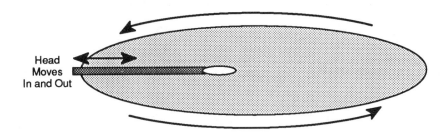

Head
Moves
In and Out

Tracks and sectors

The diskette head rapidly magnetizes areas on the diskette surface as the platter spins, representing binary zeros and ones. These areas are organized into concentric circles (tracks). There can be 40, 80, or even more tracks per diskette side.

Tracks are further subdivided into sectors. Sectors usually store 512 bytes, but the sector size can also be changed with INT 13h, Function 05h. The bytes in a sector must be organized in a prescribed manner. There can be 9, 15, 18 or more sectors per track.

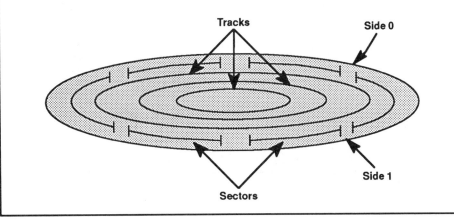

Tracks

Side 0

Side 1

Sectors

---

continued

Theory of Operation, Continued

Supported drive types

ROM BIOS supports diskette drives that utilize diskettes in all the standard IBM formats. The following table summarizes the types of diskette drives and media that it supports.

Drive Type	Diskette Capacity	Diskette Size	Tracks per Side	Sectors per Track
360K	320K	5.25 inches	40	8
360K	360K	5.25 inches	40	9
1.44MB	720K	3.5 inches	80	9
1.2MB	360K	5.25 inches	40	9
1.2MB	720K	5.25 inches	80	9
1.2MB	1.2MB	5.25 inches	80	15
1.44MB	1.44MB	3.5 inches	80	18

Note: XT computers usually support only 360K diskette drives (5.25–inch diskettes with 40 tracks per side and 9 sectors per track). However, some XTs are customized to support other drive types.

Diskette compatibility

Diskettes written on one type of 5.25-inch drive may or may not be written to or read from another. The following table shows which format of 5.25-inch media can be read from or written to which type drives. 5.25-inch diskette media can be high density (1.2MB) or double density (360K).

Media Type	If diskette was formatted on a . . .	Then it can be read from a . . .	And it can be written to by a . . .
360K	360K drive	360K drive or 1.2MB drive	360K drive
360K	1.2MB drive	1.2MB drive	1.2MB drive
1.2MB	1.2MB drive	1.2MB drive	1.2MB drive

continued

System BIOS for IBM PCs, Compatibles, and EISA Computers

Diskette compatibility, cont'd

Diskettes written on one type of 3.5-inch drive may or may not be read from or written to another such drive. The following table shows which format of 3.5-inch media can be read from or written to which type drive.

Media Type	If diskette was formatted on a ...	Then it can be read from a ...	And it can be written to by a ...
720K	720K drive	720K drive or 1.44MB drive	720K drive
1.44MB	1.44MB drive	1.44MB drive	1.44MB drive

How diskette drives are identified

Each diskette drive must be identified to the system with a unique number. There are only two valid diskette numbers: 0 for diskette drive 0 and 1 for diskette drive 1. These values must be in Register DL for most Diskette Service functions.

Data transfer rates

ROM BIOS supports the data transfer rates for diskette media that are shown in the following table. Media must be formatted using a 512-byte sector size.

Transfer Rate	Diskette Capacity	Drive Capacity	Drive Size
250 Kbs	360K	360K	5.25 inches
300 Kbs	720K	720K	5.25 inches
250 Kbs	720K	1.44MB	3.5 inches
300 Kbs	360K	1.2MB	5.25 inches
250 Kbs	720K	720K	3.5 inches
500 Kbs	1.2MB	1.2MB	5.25 inches
500 Kbs	1.44MB	1.44MB	3.5 inches
Note: Kbs = Kilobits per second			

continued

Diskette change line

Some diskette drives and controllers implement a change line that indicates if the drive door of the selected drive has been opened. The calling routine can read this signal to determine if the sector images in memory are still current. ROM BIOS checks the change line signal before each diskette I/O operation. Bit 7 of port 03F7h indicates the change line signal status. If the status bit is not set, the drive door has not been opened. If the status bit is set, the drive door has been opened. The user must then verify if the diskette has actually been changed.

Note: Diskette drives in XT systems usually don't have a change line, but some XTs may be customized to include it.

Recalibrating a diskette drive

ROM BIOS provides a service for programs that bypass their diskette operations and write directly to the diskette controller hardware. The diskette status information at location 40:3Eh contains a bit for each diskette drive that indicates if the device should be recalibrated. When ROM BIOS senses that a bit is set, it instructs the diskette controller to recalibrate the specified drive.

Diskette Service operations

The BIOS Diskette Service Read, Write, Verify, and Format functions all require data to be transferred between the diskette drive and system memory. This is always done using the DMA controller. DMA facilitates the movement of data directly from memory to I/O devices, freeing the microprocessor for other functions. The DMA controller is programmed by the BIOS before the command block is written to the diskette controller. All diskette operations use DMA controller channel 2.

The process of checking the diskette controller status, sending a byte, and waiting is repeated until all bytes in the command block are sent. Once the command block is received, the controller performs the function requested.

After the diskette controller has performed the command and transferred data, an interrupt is generated by the diskette controller. INT 0Eh, the diskette ISR, handles the interrupt, setting bit 7 of location 40:3Eh. INT 40h, the diskette DSR, monitors location 40:3Eh for up to one second, waiting for the interrupt. The interrupt indicates that one or more (a maximum of 7) result bytes may be waiting for INT 40h to read. If there is no interrupt, the time–out bit in 40:41h is set by INT 40h.

INT 0Eh Diskette ISR

Description

The INT 0Eh Diskette ISR handles interrupts from the diskette controller. The diskette controller generates an INT 0Eh to signal the completion of the last command issued by INT 13h. To maintain compatibility, the INT 0Eh entry point is located at address F000:EF57h. INT 0Eh resides at address 0:38h in the Interrupt Vector table.

The INT 0Eh Diskette ISR references control information stored in the BIOS data area of system RAM. This information is located at 40:3Eh. See Chapter 3 for a description of the BIOS data area in system RAM.

The INT 0Eh ISR references I/O port address 0020h. See Chapter 6 for a description of I/O ports.

ROM BIOS multitasking support

Each time ROM BIOS issues a diskette controller command, it also invokes INT 15h with AH = 90h Device Busy Loop. Calling INT 15h allows other tasks in the system to process while diskette I/O is in progress. However, multitasking must be implemented by the user programs, which execute in the microprocessor's real address mode.

When the diskette controller completes a command, it issues an INT 0Eh interrupt. INT 0Eh sets bit 7 of DRVSTAT (40:3Eh) and calls INT 15h with AH = 91h and AL = 01h Interrupt Complete.

INT 13h Diskette DSR

Description

The INT 13h Diskette DSR performs read, write, format, initialization, and other operations for up to two internal diskette drives. When a fixed disk is present in a system, ROM BIOS automatically redirects all INT 13h Diskette Service requests to INT 40h. This redirection is transparent to end users, however, and they should continue to invoke INT 13h for both diskette and fixed disk services.

The INT 13h Diskette DSR references control information stored in the BIOS data area of system RAM. This information is located at the following offsets of segment 40h: 10h, 3Eh–42h, 8Bh, 8Fh, and 90h–94h. See Chapter 3 for a description of the BIOS data area in system RAM.

This DSR uses the Diskette Parameters table stored in ROM for manipulating diskette drives. See Chapter 5 for a description of the ROM BIOS data area.

The DSR also references I/O port addresses 04h–5h, 0Ah–0Ch, 20h–21h, 81h, 3F2h, 3F4h–3F5h, and 3F7h. See Chapter 6 for a description of I/O ports.

Error Handling

Introduction

The INT 13h Diskette DSR returns the completion status of each of its functions via the AH register, the Carry Flag, and the BIOS data items ERRSTAT (40:41h) and FDCSTAT (40:42h).

Error codes

INT 13h stores the diskette drive status information associated with a function in ERRSTAT. If the function executed successfully, bits 4–0 of the data item are set to 00h. If the function was not successful, these bits are set to the appropriate non–zero error code.

The INT 13h error codes are listed in the table below.

Error Code	Description
00h	No error
01h	Invalid function request
02h	Address mark not found
03h	Write protect error
04h	Sector not found
06h	Diskette change line active
08h	DMA overrun on operation
09h	Data boundary error (64K boundary)
0Ch	Media type not found
10h	Uncorrectable ECC or CRC error
20h	General controller failure
40h	Seek operation failed
80h	Timeout

continued

Error Handling, Continued

Result bytes

INT 13h stores all the result bytes returned by the diskette controller in the seven–byte location FDCSTAT starting at 40:42h. Usually there are four to seven result bytes.

Functions that have executed successfully return with the following:

- AH and ERRSTAT set to 00h (i.e. error code = 00h, no error)
- Carry Flag (CF) cleared

Functions that have not executed successfully return with the following:

- Carry Flag (CF) set
- AH and ERRSTAT set to one of the error codes shown in the table on the preceding page.

Note: If the error is related to the diskette controller hardware, the contents of AH are also copied to FDCSTAT.

Description

This function resets both the diskette controller and the diskette drive. The diskette drive number (either 0 or 1) is indicated in DL.

Input/Output

Input:	AH	=	00h
	DL	=	Drive number (0 or 1)
Output:	AH	=	0 No error
		=	Diskette Service error code — also stored in ERRSTAT (40:41h)
	CF	=	0 No error
			1 Error

Function failure

Call INT13h Function 00h when a problem occurs in attempting to access the diskette subsystem with any other function. Then retry the function that failed.

The diskette subsystem will not react immediately. Instead, a reset flag will force ROM BIOS to recalibrate the diskette drive's read/write heads the next time they are used. The heads will be relocated to track 0 in order to start the next I/O operation from a known state.

Description

This function stores the error code associated with the last requested function in ERRSTAT (40:41h). If the last function executed successfully, ERRSTAT is set to 00h. If the last function was not successful, ERRSTAT is set to the appropriate non–zero error code.

The function reads the value contained in ERRSTAT and returns it in the AH register. The Carry Flag (CF) is set if the value returned in AH is non–zero. Otherwise the Carry Flag is cleared. ERRSTAT is set to 0 at the completion of this function.

Input/Output

Input:	AH	=	01h
	DL	=	Drive number (0 or 1)
Output:	AH	=	0 No error
		=	Diskette Service error code — also stored in ERRSTAT (40:41h)
	CF	=	0 No error
			1 Error

Diskette Status byte

The Diskette Status byte (ERRSTAT) is saved after each read, write, verify, or format diskette function. This allows error handling or error reporting routines that are entirely independent of diskette operation routines to be written.

Description

This function reads the number of sectors specified in AL from the drive specified in DL to the buffer specified in ES:BX.

The diskette drive head number is indicated in DH. Starting track and sector numbers are indicated in CH and CL.

Input/Output

Input:	AH	= 02h
	AL	= Number of sectors (1–18, depending on drive media type)
	CH	= Track number (0–79, depending on drive media type)
	CL	= Sector number (1–18, depending on drive media type)
	DH	= Head number (0–1)
	DL	= Drive number
	ES:BX	= Pointer to buffer
Output:	AH	= 0 No error
		= Diskette Service error code — also stored in ERRSTAT (40:41h)
	AL	= Number of sectors read/written
	CF	= 0 No error
		1 Error

Wait for device to reach proper speed

In some BIOSs, an error may be caused by the diskette drive motor being off when the request is made. The BIOS may not wait for the device to reach proper speed before trying to read. If such a situation is suspected, the calling program should reset the diskette drive (INT 13h Function 00h) and retry three times to make sure that an error actually exists.

XT **ISA**

Description

This function writes the number of sectors specified in AL from the drive specified in DL to the buffer specified in ES:BX.

The diskette drive head number is indicated in DH. Starting track and sector numbers are indicated in CH and CL.

Input/Output

Input:	AH	= 03h
	AL	= Number of sectors (1–18, depending on drive media type)
	CH	= Track number (0–79, depending on drive media type)
	CL	= Sector number (1–18, depending on drive media type)
	DH	= Head number (0–1)
	DL	= Drive number
	ES:BX	= Pointer to buffer
Output:	AH	= 0 No error
		= Diskette Service error code — also stored in ERRSTAT (40:41h)
	AL	= Number of sectors read/written
	CF	= 0 No error
		1 Error

Wait for device to reach proper speed

In some BIOSs, an error may be caused by the diskette drive motor being off when the request is made. The BIOS may not wait for the device to reach proper speed before trying to read. If such a situation is suspected, the calling program should reset the diskette drive (INT 13h Function 00h) and retry three times to make sure that an error actually exists.

INT 13h Function 04h — Verify Diskette Sectors   XT   ISA

Description

This function verifies the address fields of the number of sectors specified in AL from the drive specified in DL to the buffer specified in ES:BX.

The diskette drive head number is specified in DH. Starting track and sector numbers are specified in CH and CL. No data is transferred from the diskette in this operation. Diskette data is not compared to data in memory.

The INT13h Diskette Service function verifies diskette sectors by determining if the sectors can be found, read, and pass a Cyclic Redundancy Check (CRC).

Input/Output

Input:	AH	= 04h
	AL	= Number of sectors (1–18, depending on drive media type)
	CH	= Track number (0–79, depending on drive media type)
	CL	= Sector number (1–18, depending on drive media type)
	DH	= Head number (0–1)
	DL	= Drive number
	ES:BX	= Buffer with address field data
Output:	AH	= 0 No error
		= Diskette Service error code — also stored in ERRSTAT (40:41h)
	AL	= Number of sectors actually verified
	CF	= 0 No error
		1 Error

Determining if a readable diskette is present

INT 13h Function AH = 04h can be used to determine if a readable diskette is in the drive, although an error will occur if the diskette motor is off when this function is invoked.

The calling program should first invoke Function 00h, then invoke Function 04h. If no diskette is present, AH will contain a nonzero value and the Carry Flag will be set. The calling program should retry three times to make sure that no other error condition is occurring.

Description

This function formats a single diskette track on the drive specified in DL. The format operation consists of writing the diskette sector and track address field data on the specified track.

The number of sectors to format is specified in AL, the head number in DH, and the track number in CH. ES:BX points to a table defining the address fields for the track being formatted.

Each call to Function 05h of the Diskette Service can be verified by following it with a call to Function 04h.

Input/Output

Input:	AH	= 05h
	AL	= Number of sectors to be formatted
	CH	= Track number (starts at 0)
	DH	= Head number (0 or 1)
	DL	= Drive number (0 or 1)
	ES:BX	= Address field buffer (See "Address field table" in this chapter)
Output:	AH	= 0 No error
		= Diskette Service error code — also stored in ERRSTAT (40:41h)
	CF	= 0 No error
		1 Error

Use Function 17h or 18h first if AT system

If the diskette drive supports more than one diskette format, the calling program must invoke either Diskette Service function AH = 17h Set Diskette Type, or AH = 18h Set Media Type for Format before invoking Function 05h.

continued

Copy protection

Function 05h can be used for copy protection by doing one or more of the following:

- squeezing more sectors onto a track,
- rearranging the order of the sectors,
- leaving out a sector number,
- specifying 1 or more sectors to be an unconventional size, and/or
- adding a sector with an unconventional address mask.

Address field table

The address field table must contain one entry for each sector on the track to be formatted. Each entry consists of four bytes as defined in the table below.

Byte	Description
0	Track number
1	Head number (zero–based)
2	Sector number
3	Sector size indicator, where: 00h = 128 bytes/sector 01h = 256 bytes/sector 02h = 512 bytes/sector 03h =1024 bytes/sector

Example: address field table

For example, the address field table to format track 3, head 0 of a 9 sector/track diskette with 512-byte sectors, would be:

```
db 03, 00, 01, 02, 03, 00, 02, 02, 03, 00, 03, 02
db 03, 00, 04, 02, 03, 00, 05, 02, 03, 00, 06, 02
db 03, 00, 07, 02, 03, 00, 08, 02, 03, 00, 09, 02
```

INT 13h Function 08h — Read Drive Parameters

Description

This function returns the diskette parameters for the drive specified in DL. If successful, the Carry Flag is cleared and ERRSTAT (40:41h) is not modified.

The drive type stored in location 10h of CMOS RAM determines the parameters returned. If the drive type is not stored in CMOS RAM, all registers return a value of zero, except DL, which will contain the number of diskette drives installed. If the media type is known, the maximum media capacity is returned in BL, CH, CL, and DH. A pointer to the Diskette Parameters table is returned in ES:DI.

Input/Output

Input: AH = 08h
        DL = Drive number (0 or 1)

Output: AX = 0000h
        BH = 00h
        BL = Bits 4–7 = 0
             Bits 0–3 = Valid drive type value (See location 10h in "System configuration data definitions" section of Chapter 4)
        CH = Maximum usable track number
        CL = Maximum usable sector number
        DH = Maximum usable head number (always 1 if the CMOS RAM value is valid)
        DL = Number of diskette drives installed (0, 1, or 2)
        ES:DI= Pointer to Diskette Parameters table for the maximum media type supported on the specified drive
        CF = 0 No error
             1 Illegal parameter

Description

This function returns the drive type of the drive specified in the DL register.

Unlike most other INT 13h Diskette Service functions, the value returned in the AH register by this function is not an error code. Instead, it corresponds to one of the four indicators described in the table below:

AH Value	Meaning
0h	No drive installed
01h	Diskette drive with no change line
02h	Diskette drive with change line

Input/Output

Input:	AH	=	15h
	DL	=	Drive number (0 or 1)
Output:	AH	=	00h No drive installed
			01h Diskette drive with no change line
			02h Diskette drive with a change line
			03h Fixed disk drive installed (See Chapter 12, *Fixed Disk Service*)
	CF	=	0 No error
			1 Invalid drive number

Description

This function determines if the drive door has been opened since the last time the change line was cleared. If the drive number is not valid, the Carry Flag is set, AH is set to 01h, and control is returned to the calling program. If the specified diskette drive is not configured, AH and Diskette Status are set to 80h (timeout), CF is set, and control is returned to the calling program.

Call INT 13h Function 15h first

Calling programs should invoke INT 13h Function 15h first to determine whether the diskette drive hardware can sense when a diskette is changed. AH will be set to 02h if it can.

Diskette change line support

When INT 13h Function 16h returns with CF set, it does not necessarily mean that a diskette has been changed. It only means that the diskette drive door has been opened and closed since the last time the change line was cleared.

If the diskette drive does not implement a change line, AH and Diskette Status are set to 06h (media change), CF is cleared, and control is returned to the calling program.

Input/Output

Input:	AH	=	16h
	DL	=	Drive number (0 or 1)
Output:	AH	=	00h Diskette change line signal not active
		=	01h Invalid drive number
		=	06h Either change line not supported or diskette change line signal is active
			80h Diskette drive not ready or no drive present
	CF	=	0 No error
			1 Error

Description

This function specifies the transfer rate for the specified drives using the diskette types passed in AL. 1.44MB drives are not handled by this function. If the diskette type in AL is invalid, AH and ERRSTAT are set to 01h, CF is set, and control is returned to the calling program. If the drive number is invalid, CF is set, AH and ERRSTAT are set to 01h, and control is returned to the calling program.

Input/Output

Input:	AH	=	17h
	AL	=	01h 360K diskette in 360K drive
		=	02h 360K diskette in 1.2MB drive
		=	03h 1.2MB diskette in 1.2MB drive
		=	04h 720K diskette in 720K drive
	DL	=	Drive number (0 or 1)
Output:	AH	=	0 No error
		=	Diskette Service error code — also stored in ERRSTAT (40:41h)
	CF	=	0 No error
			1 Error

Description

This function sets the media type in preparation for a format command.

If the drive number is invalid, the Carry Flag (CF) is set and control is returned to the calling program with both AH and Diskette Status (40:41h) set to 01h. If the drive type can't be determined, AH and Diskette Status are set to 0Ch (unknown media), CF is set, and control is returned to the calling program.

If there are no problems with the values returned by this function, ROM BIOS selects a Diskette Parameters table based on the data input to this function. ES:DI points to the chosen Diskette Parameters table, AH and Diskette Status are set to 00h, CF is cleared, and control is returned to the calling program.

Input/Output

Input:	AH	=	18h
	CH	=	Maximum number of tracks
	CL	=	Sectors per track
	DL	=	Drive number (0 or 1)
Output:	AH	=	00h Track/sector combination is supported
			01h (Function is not available)
			0Ch Media unknown (CMOS RAM is not valid, drive is not configured in CMOS RAM, or diskette is not described in Diskette Parameters table)
			80h No diskette in drive
	ES:DI=		pointer to drive parameter table (only if AH equals 0)
	CF	=	0 No error
			1 Error

continued

Diskette change line support

If the drive number is valid, this function determines if the drive supports a change line. If the drive supports a change line, this function determines if there is a diskette in the drive. If there is no diskette, AH and the Diskette Status byte are set to 80h (timeout), the Carry Flag (CF) is set, and control is returned to the calling program.

Call Function 18h before Function 05h

Calling programs should invoke this function before formatting a diskette with Function 05h so that ROM BIOS can set the correct data rate for the media.

Chapter 12
Fixed Disk Service

Overview

Description

The ROM BIOS Fixed Disk Service performs read, write, format, diagnostic, initialization, and other operations for up to two fixed disk drives. This service is provided by the INT 13h Fixed Disk DSR.

In this chapter

This chapter presents the following topics:

- Theory of Operation
- INT 13h Fixed Disk DSR
- Error Handling
- Fixed Disk Service functions

Theory of Operation

Introduction

A fixed disk is an electromechanical device. The electronic part includes the read/write head(s), which are essentially electromagnets that convert rapidly pulsing digital electronic signals from the computer to semi–permanent magnetic fields on a specific location on the disk surface. There are other electronic components that control the mechanical parts. They properly align the magnetic storage and help to locate the information on the disk surface.

The mechanical part of a fixed disk drive includes a spindle and disk platters (upon which data is actually written). The motor spins the disk platter at a precisely controlled speed. The only other mechanical part is the arm, upon which the read/write heads are mounted. The arm allows the heads to move freely just above the disk surface so that the heads can be placed anywhere between the inner and outermost part of the surface. Fixed disks usually have many read/write heads and both sides of the disk platters are used. There is one read/write head positioned just above the surface of each side of the disk platter.

Disk components

A fixed disk system has the following basic components:

Head
: The head contains an electromagnet, positioned on a movable assembly just above the surface of the disk. By pulsing the electromagnet, the head reads or writes data from or to the disk platter surface.

Track
: When the head is positioned over a point on the fixed disk, ready to read or write, the disk platter surface spins underneath it, tracing a full circle. This circle is a track. There may be 40 to 150 tracks per disk surface.

Sector
: Fixed disk systems divide each track into short arcs (usually 17, 28, or 34 per track) called sectors. Each sector usually holds 512 bytes of data.

Cylinder
: Each head on the fixed disk drive (there may be many heads) traces out a separate circle (track) across the platter of the fixed disk it rides above. The combination of all of the tracks traced out by all heads at a given read/write head position forms the outline of a solid cylinder, thus such a vertical stack of tracks is called a cylinder.

continued

Fixed disk drive organization

The following illustration displays and explains each component of the fixed disk system.

Heads and surfaces

Fixed disk drives generally have several magnetic heads. One head is used for each side of each disk platter. A fixed disk can have many disk platters.

All sides of the fixed disk platter surfaces are covered with a material that can be magnetized and is used to store information.

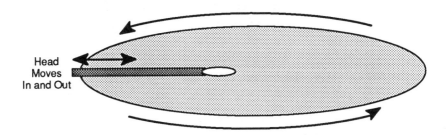

Tracks and sectors

The fixed disk head rapidly magnetizes areas on the surface of the disk platter as the platter spins, representing binary zeros and ones. These areas are organized into concentric circles (tracks). There can be 40, 80, or even more tracks per fixed disk side.

Tracks are further subdivided into sectors. Sectors usually store 512 bytes. The bytes in a sector must be organized in a prescribed manner. There can be 17, 28, 34 or more sectors per track.

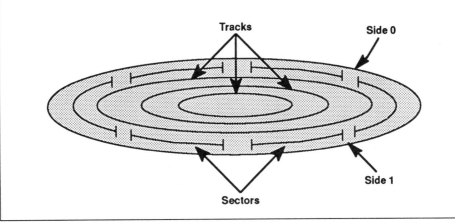

continued

Fixed disk processing

Like the Diskette Service, the BIOS Fixed Disk Service programs the fixed disk controller directly. The BIOS never writes directly from the processor to the fixed disk drive. The fixed disk controller communicates directly between the fixed disk drive, the processor, and system memory.

Fixed disk controller interfaces

The computer does not access the fixed disk directly. The computer communicates with the fixed disk controller which controls the fixed disks and often also the diskettes. The fixed disk controller uses a predetermined standard for formatting instructions and data (called an interface) for accessing the fixed disk. There are three widely used fixed disk controller standards (or interfaces):

- ST506/ST412 — standard interface
- ESDI — enhanced small device interface
- SCSI — small computer systems interface

Fixed disk data encoding methods

On the ST506 interface, the disk–generated pulses that are used to represent the actual data are passed directly to the controller. The way these pulses are arranged can make a big difference in fixed disk drive performance.

There are several methods of data encoding used by ST506 fixed disk controllers. The most frequently used methods are:

- MFM — modified frequency modulation
- RLL — run length limited
- ARLL — advanced run length limited

continued

How fixed disks are identified

Each fixed disk must be identified to the system with a unique number. There are only two valid fixed disk identification numbers — 80h and 81h:

- Fixed Disk Drive 0 = 80h
- Fixed Disk Drive 1 = 81h

These identification numbers are required arguments for many of the INT 13h fixed disk services.

ROM BIOS diskette support

When a fixed disk is installed, ROM BIOS automatically redirects all INT 13h Diskette Service requests to INT 40h. This redirecting is transparent to application programs. Application programs continue to invoke INT 13h for both diskette and fixed disk services. The BIOS decides which driver will be used by checking the drive number in the DL register. See Chapter 11 for information about the Diskette Service.

INT 13h Fixed Disk DSR

Description

The INT 13h Fixed Disk DSR reads, writes, and formats up to two fixed disk drives installed in a system. It also provides diagnostic, initialization and other operations.

The INT 13h Fixed Disk DSR references CMOS RAM data at offsets 0Eh, 12h, and 19h–1Ah. See Chapter 4 for a description of CMOS RAM data areas.

The INT 13h Fixed Disk DSR references control information stored in the BIOS data area of system RAM. This information is located at the following offsets of segment 40h: 42h, 6Ch, 72h, 74h–77h, and 8Ch–8Eh. See Chapter 3 for a description of the BIOS data area in system RAM.

The INT 13h Fixed Disk DSR references I/O port addresses 20h–21h, A0h–A1h, 170h–177h, and 1F0h–1F7h. See Chapter 6 for a description of I/O ports.

The INT 13h Fixed Disk DSR uses the Fixed Disk Parameters table, which defines the types of fixed disk drives that can be used in the system. To maintain IBM compatibility, this table is based at hex F000:E401. The address of the correct entry within the table is contained in the INT 41h vector for drive 0 and in the INT 46h vector for drive 1. For the structure and default values of the Fixed Disk Parameters table, see Chapter 5.

Error Handling

Result bytes

Upon return from each function, the Fixed Disk Service indicates the result of the operation with a numeric error code. This error code is returned in the AH register and is stored in HDSTAT (40:74h).

Functions that have executed successfully return with the following:

- AH and HDSTAT (40:74h) set to 00h (i.e. error code = 00h, no error)
- Carry Flag (CF) cleared

Functions that have not executed successfully return with the following:

- Carry Flag (CF) set
- AH and HDSTAT (40:74h) set to one of the error codes shown in the table on the following page.

If an error occurs when a function is invoked, issue a Function 00h to reset the fixed disk controller and retry the function before quitting.

Differentiating diskette from fixed disk errors

The status of the last Diskette Service operation is stored in ERRSTAT (40:41h), and the status of the last Fixed Disk Service operation is stored in HDSTAT (40:74h).

- If the error code returned in AH by this function pertains to the diskette system, then the value of ERRSTAT will be equal to the value of AH.
- If the error code in AH pertains to the fixed disk, then the value in HDSTAT will be equal to the value in AH.

continued

Error Handling, Continued

Table of error codes

The following list gives the Fixed Disk Service error codes with a brief description of each.

Error Code	Description
00h	No error
01h	Invalid function passed in AH or invalid parameter
02h	Address mark not found
04h	Sector not found
05h	Reset failed
07h	Drive parameter activity failed
09h	Data boundary error (64K boundary)
0Ah	Bad sector flag detected
0Bh	Bad cylinder detected
0Dh	Invalid number of sectors on format
0Eh	Control data address mark detected
0Fh	DMA arbitration level out of range
10h	Uncorrectable ECC or CRC error*
11h	ECC corrected data error
20h	Controller failure
40h	Seek operation failed
80h	Timeout
AAh	Drive not ready or not selected
BBh	Undefined error occurred
CCh	Write fault on selected drive
E0h	Status error/error register = 0
FFh	Sense operation failed

* ECC = Error Checking and Correcting code
CRC = Cyclic Redundancy Check code

Description

The Reset Fixed Disk System function resets the fixed disk controllers. It places the fixed disk system in a known state by reinitializing the fixed disk drive parameters and by recalibrating the read/write head positions.

The fixed disk drive number (either 80h or 81h) is specified in DL.

Note: The fixed disk is only reset if HDNUMB is greater than or equal the value in DL.

Input/Output

Input:	AH	=	00h
	DL	=	Drive number (80h or 81h)
Output:	AH	=	0 No error
		=	Fixed Disk Service error code — also stored in HDSTAT (40:74h)
	CF	=	0 No error
			1 Error

Description

The Read Disk Status function returns HDSTAT (40:74h), the status code from the last operation, in the AH register. Before returning to the calling program, this function sets HDSTAT (40:74h) and clears the Carry Flag (CF).

Input/Output

Input:	AH	=	01h
	DL	=	Drive number (80h or 81h)
Output:	AH	=	Status of last operation
	CF	=	0 No error on last operation
			1 Error

Description

This function reads the number of sectors specified in AL from the drive specified in DL to a buffer area defined by ES:BX. The fixed disk head number is indicated in DH. This function also reads the Error Correction Code (ECC) associated with that sector and if an error is detected, automatically corrects it. AH = 11h will be returned if an ECC error was corrected.

Multisector transfers are terminated after any sector that has a read error.

This function does not require a prior call to the Seek function (AH = 0Ch).

The number of sectors specified in AL must not be zero or greater than 128. Numbers greater than 128 cause a transfer of greater than 64K, and thus force a data overrun error. The ROM BIOS tests for data overrun first before transferring any data.

Input/Output

Input:	AH	=	02h
	AL	=	Number of sectors to read
	CH	=	Cylinder number (low 8 bits)
	CL	=	Cylinder/sector number, where:
			Bits 7–6 = cylinder number (high 2 bits)
			Bits 5–0 = sector number
	DH	=	Head number
	DL	=	Drive number (80h or 81h)
	ES:BX	=	Pointer to buffer
Output:	AH	=	0 No error
		=	Fixed Disk Service error code — also stored in HDSTAT (40:74h)
	CF	=	0 No error
			1 Error

Description

This function writes the number of sectors specified in AL to the drive specified in DL from a buffer area defined by ES:BX. The fixed disk head number is indicated in DH. Starting cylinder and sector number are indicated in CH and CL as shown under the Input/Output heading below.

Multisector transfers are terminated after any sector that has a write error.

This function does not require a prior call to the Seek Function (AH = 0Ch).

The number of sectors specified in AL must not be zero or greater than 128. Numbers greater than 128 cause a transfer of greater than 64K, and thus force a data overrun error. The ROM BIOS tests for data overrun first before transferring any data.

Input/Output

Input:	AH	=	03h
	AL	=	Number of sectors to write
	CH	=	Cylinder number (low 8 bits)
	CL	=	Cylinder/sector number, where:
			Bits 7–6 = cylinder number (high 2 bits)
			Bits 5–0 = sector number
	DH	=	Head number
	DL	=	Drive number (80h or 81h)
	ES:BX	=	Pointer to buffer
Output:	AH	=	0 No error
		=	Fixed Disk Service error code — also stored in HDSTAT (40:74h)
	CF	=	0 No error
			1 Error

Description

This function verifies the number of sectors specified in AL from the drive specified in DL. The cylinder and sector are specified in CX, the head number in DH.

This function does not compare data on disk with data in memory. It merely verifies that the specified sectors can be read and that the ECC/CRC is correct. This function does not cause any data to be transferred from memory to fixed disk or vice versa.

Input/Output

Input:	AH	=	04h
	AL	=	Number of sectors to verify
	CH	=	Cylinder number (low 8 bits)
	CL	=	Cylinder/sector number, where:
			Bits 7–6 = cylinder number (high 2 bits)
			Bits 5–0 = sector number
	DH	=	Head number
	DL	=	Drive number (80h or 81h)
Output:	AH	=	0 No error
		=	Fixed Disk Service error code — also stored in HDSTAT (40:74h)
	CF	=	0 No error
			1 Error

XT ISA

Description

This function formats the cylinder specified in CH and CL with the head whose number is specified in DH. The drive is specified in DL.

Input/Output

Input: AH   = 05h
CH   = Cylinder number (low 8 bits)
CL   = Cylinder/sector number, where:
Bits 7–6 = cylinder number (high 2 bits)
Bits 5–0 = sector number
DH   = Head number
DL   = Drive number (80h or 81h)
ES:BX = Pointer to address field list

Output: AH   = 0 No error
= Fixed Disk Service error code — also stored in HDSTAT (40:74h)
CF   = 0 No error
1 Error

Buffer table contents

The calling program must provide a 512–byte buffer pointed to by ES:BX. This buffer consists of the good/bad flag and sector identifier for each sector on the cylinder.

There must be one two–byte table entry for each sector on the cylinder. Table entries must be formatted as shown below:

Byte 1 = good/bad flag
00h sector is good
80h sector is bad
Byte 2 = sector number

INT 13h Function 06h — Format Bad Track

Description

This function initializes a track, writing fixed disk address fields and data sectors and setting bad sector flags. It is designed for use with an XT–type fixed disk controller.

For drive 80h, this function references the Fixed Disk Parameters table pointed to by the INT 41h vector. If successful, this function returns with AH and HDSTAT (40:74h) set to 00h.

Input/Output

Input:	AH	=	06h
	AL	=	Interleave factor
	CH	=	Cylinder number
	DH	=	Head number
	DL	=	Drive number (80h or 81h)
Output:	AH	=	0 No Error
		=	Fixed Disk Service Error Code — also stored in HDSTAT (40:74h)
	CF	=	0 No error
			1 Error

INT 13h Function 07h — Format Drive

Description

This function formats the entire fixed disk drive, starting at the cylinder number specified in CH and CL. It writes disk address fields and data sectors.

This function works only with XT–type fixed disk controllers.

Input/Output

Input:	AH	=	07h
	AL	=	Interleave factor
	CH	=	Cylinder
	DL	=	Drive number (80h or 81h)
Output:	AH	=	0 No error
		=	Fixed Disk Service error code — also stored in HDSTAT (40:74h)
	CF	=	0 No error
			1 Error

Description

This function returns parameters associated with the fixed disk drive whose number is specified in DL.

For drive 80h, the Read Disk Parameters function references the Fixed Disk Parameters table pointed to by the INT 41h vector. For drive 81h, the function references the INT 46h vector.

Input/Output

Input: AH = 08h
DL = Drive number (80h or 81h)

Output: AH = 0 No error
= Fixed Disk Service error code — also stored in HDSTAT (40:74h)
AL = 00h
CH = Maximum usable cylinder number (low 8 bits)
CL = Cylinder/sector number, where:
Bits 7–6 = Maximum usable cylinder number (high 2 bits)
Bits 5–0 = Maximum usable sector number
DH = Maximum usable head number
DL = Number of drives (zero–based, 00h if AH = 07h)
ES:DI = Address of Fixed Disk Parameters table
CF = 0 No error
1 Error

INT 13h Function 09h — Initialize Drive Parameters XT ISA

Description

This function initializes the controller associated with the fixed disk drive whose number is specified in DL.

For drive 80h, the Initialize Drive Parameters function references the Fixed Disk Parameters table pointed to by the INT 41h vector. For drive 81h, the function references the INT 46h vector.

Input/Output

Input:	AH	=	09h
	DL	=	Drive number (80h or 81h)
Output:	AH	=	0 No error
		=	Fixed Disk Service error code — also stored in HDSTAT (40:74h)
	CF	=	0 No error
			1 Error

Description

The Read Long Sector function reads the number of sectors of data specified in AL from the location specified in CH and CL, using the head specified in DH, from the fixed disk specified in DL. The data is read to the location specified in ES:BX. The function also reads the ECC (or CRC) associated with the sector(s).

Input/Output

Input:	AH	= 0Ah
	AL	= Number of sectors
	CH	= Cylinder number (low 8 bits)
	CL	= Cylinder/sector number, where:
		Bits 7–6 = Cylinder number (high 2 bits)
		Bits 5–0 = Sector number
	DH	= Head number
	DL	= Drive number (80h or 81h)
	ES:BX	= Disk transfer address
Output:	AH	= 0 No error
		= Fixed Disk Service error code — also stored in HDSTAT (40:74h)
	CF	= 0 No error
		1 Error

Description

This function writes the number of sectors specified in AL to the location on the fixed disk specified in DL from the buffer pointed to by ES:BX. The function also writes the ECC (or CRC) associated with each sector that is written.

Input/Output

Input:	AH	= 0Bh
	AL	= Number of sectors to write
	CH	= Cylinder number (low 8 bits)
	CL	= Cylinder/sector number, where:
		Bits 7–6 = cylinder number (high 2 bits)
		Bits 5–0 = sector number
	DH	= Head number
	DL	= Drive number (80h or 81h)
	ES:BX	= Disk transfer address
Output:	AH	= 0 No error
		= Fixed Disk Service error code — also stored in HDSTAT (40:74h)
	CF	= 0 No error
		1 Error

Description

This function positions the disk read/write head over the cylinder specified in CH and CL. The fixed disk drive number must be specified in DL.

Input/Output

Input:	AH	= 0Ch
	CH	= Cylinder number (low 8 bits)
	CL	= Cylinder/sector number, where:
		Bits 7–6 = Cylinder number (high 2 bits)
		Bits 5–0 = Sector number
	DH	= Head number
	DL	= Drive number (80h or 81h)
Output:	AH	= 0 No error
		= Fixed Disk Service error code — also stored in HDSTAT (40:74h)
	CF	= 0 No error
		1 Error

Additional information

The Read Disk Sectors (AH = 02h), Write Disk Sectors (AH = 03h), Read Long Sectors (AH = 0Ah), and Write Long Sectors (AH = 0Bh) functions have a seek operation implicitly built into them and do not require a prior call to this function.

Description

The Alternate Reset Fixed Disk function is identical to the Reset Diskette System and Reset Fixed Disk System functions (see AH = 00h) except that the diskette system is not reset.

The calling program must specify the fixed disk drive to reset in DL. The Alternate Reset Fixed Disk function reinitializes the fixed disk controller. It places the specified fixed disk drive in a known state by resetting the fixed disk parameters and by recalibrating the read/write head positions.

Input/Output

Input:	AH	=	0Dh
	DL	=	Drive number (80h or 81h)
Output:	AH	=	0 No error
		=	Fixed Disk Service error code — also stored in HDSTAT (40:74h)
	CF	=	0 No error
			1 Error

Description

This function reads a test buffer from the fixed disk controller into the diagnostics buffer specified in ES:BX. Data is not read from the actual physical disk drive.

Input/Output

Input:	AH	= 0Eh
	DL	= Drive number (80h or 81h)
	ES:BX	= Pointer to diagnostic buffer
Output:	AH	= 0 No error
		= Fixed Disk Service error code — also stored in HDSTAT (40:74h)
	CF	= 0 No error
		1 Error

Description

This function writes a test buffer to the controller from the diagnostics buffer specified in ES:BX. Data is not written to the actual physical disk drive.

This function should be called to initialize the sector buffer contents before formatting an XT–type fixed disk drive using INT 13h AH = 05h.

Input/Output

Input:	AH	= 0Fh
	DL	= Drive number (80h or 81h)
	ES:BX	= Pointer to diagnostic buffer
Output:	AH	= 0 No error
		= Fixed Disk Service error code — also stored in HDSTAT (40:74h)
	CF	= 0 No error
		1 Error

Description

This function determines if the drive specified in DL is ready and can process a command.

Input/Output

Input: AH = 10h
         DL = Drive number (80h or 81h)

Output: AH = 0 No error
             = Fixed Disk Service error code — also stored in HDSTAT (40:74h)
         CF = 0 No error
              1 Error

Description

This function positions head 0 over cylinder 0 of the drive specified in DL.

Input/Output

Input:	AH	=	11h
	DL	=	Drive number (80h or 81h)
Output:	AH	=	0 No error
		=	Fixed Disk Service error code — also stored in HDSTAT (40:74h)
	CF	=	0 No error
			1 Error

Description

This function causes the fixed disk controller to carry out a built–in diagnostic test on its internal sector buffer. The value in AH indicates whether the test was passed or not.

Input/Output

Input:	AH	=	12h
	DL	=	Drive number (80h or 81h)
Output:	AL	=	00h
	AH	=	0 No error
		=	Fixed Disk Service error code — also stored in HDSTAT (40:74h)
	CF	=	0 No error
			1 Invalid parameter

Description

This function causes the fixed disk controller to run internal diagnostic tests of the attached fixed disk drive. The value in AH indicates whether the test was passed or not.

Input/Output

Input:	AH	=	13h
	DL	=	Drive number (80h or 81h)
Output:	AL	=	00h
	AH	=	0 No error
		=	Fixed Disk Service error code — also stored in HDSTAT (40:74h)
	CF	=	0 No error
			1 Error

INT 13h Function 14h —
Controller Internal Diagnostic

Description

This function causes the fixed disk controller to carry out a built–in diagnostic self–test. The value in AH indicates whether the test was passed or not.

Input/Output

Input:	AH	=	14h
	DL	=	Drive Number (80h or 81h)
Output:	AL	=	00h
	AH	=	00h No error
		=	Fixed Disk Service error code — also stored in HDSTAT (40:74h)
	CF	=	0 No error
			1 Error

Description

This function returns the number of 512–byte blocks on the fixed disk if the drive specified in DL is valid.

If successful, the high word 512–byte block amount is returned in CX, and the low word amount is returned in DX. HDSTAT (40:74h), AL, and the Carry Flag (CF) are set to 00h, and control is returned to the calling program.

If unsuccessful, this function returns to the calling program with AH, AL, CX, DX, the Carry Flag (CF) and HDSTAT (40:74h) set to 00h.

Input/Output

Input:	AH	= 15h
	DL	= Drive number (80h or 81h)
Output:	AH	= 00h No drive present
		03h Drive present
	CF	= 0 No error
		1 Error
	CX:DX =	Number of 512–byte sectors

AH reports drive number validity

For drive 80h, this function references the Fixed Disk Parameters Table pointed to by the INT 41h vector. For drive 81h, it references the INT 46h vector.

Unlike most other Fixed Disk Service functions, the value stored in AH is not equal to the value stored in HDSTAT (40:74h)).

If...	Then...
AH = 00h	no drive is installed.
AH = 03h	fixed disk was accessed.

Chapter 13
Serial Communications Service

Overview

Description

The BIOS Communications Service performs RS–232C character I/O with the INT 14h Serial Communications DSR. The DSR provides a hardware–independent, interrupt–driven RS–232C serial interface with more functionality than is available from the DOS serial–port driver.

In this chapter

This chapter focuses on the Serial Communications Service. The following topics are discussed:

- Theory of Operation
- INT 14h Serial Communications DSR
- Error Handling
- Serial Communications Service functions

Theory of Operation

Description

The ROM BIOS Serial Communications Service is based on the EIA RS–232C specification and the capabilities of the National Semiconductor 8250 UART. The NS 8250 was included in the original XT specification but has been superseded by the backward–compatible NS 16450 and NS 16550 serial port controllers.

Data frames

The ROM BIOS Serial Communications Service packages each data byte into a separate frame. Each frame consists of a start bit, the data bits, an optional parity bit, and one or two stop bits.

INT 14h RS–232C compatibility

INT 14h transmits data across the RS–232C I/O path in three steps:

1. The applications program places the data byte to be sent in AL, puts Function 01h Send Character in AH, and performs an INT 14h.

2. The BIOS transfers the data in AL to the serial port specified in DX. The serial controller and the external device communicate through a series of handshaking signals, such as Data Terminal Ready (DTR) and Request To Send (RTS). When the external device signals that it is ready to begin the data transfer, the controller assembles the data frames and sends them across the I/O path.

3. The external device receives each character, removes the start, parity, and stop bits, and assembles the data bits into characters.

INT 14h Serial Communications DSR

Description

The INT 14h Serial Communications DSR provides support for sending and receiving data, and determining the status of equipment used in serial communications.

The INT 14h Serial Communications DSR references control information stored in the BIOS data area of system RAM. This information is located at the following offsets of segment 40h: 00h, 10h, and 7Ch. See Chapter 3 for a description of the BIOS data area in system RAM.

The INT 14h Serial Communications DSR references I/O port addresses 3F8h–3FFh for serial port 1 and 2F8h–2FFh for serial port 2. There are no standard I/O port addresses for serial ports 3 and 4 — the addresses referenced by the DSR for these optional serial ports are specific to each manufacturer's model. The most common I/O port addresses for serial port 3 are 3220h–3227h; the most common I/O port addresses for serial port 4 are 3228h–322Fh. See Chapter 6 for descriptions of I/O ports.

Invoking the INT 14h DSR

Software INT 14h invokes the INT 14h Serial Communications DSR. The INT 14h vector resides at address 00:50h in the Interrupt Vector table, and is initialized by the BIOS to point to system ROM address F000:E739h. DOS takes over this service and revectors the Interrupt Vector table entry.

Error Handling

Introduction

The Serial Communications Service detects two kinds of errors:

- Parameter–related errors
- Time–out errors

Parameter–related errors

Parameter–related errors do not return an error indication. Instead, the Serial Communications Service function checks the following parameter–related conditions when it receives input:

- The function number specified in AH falls within the range 0–3.
- The serial port specified in DX falls within the range 0–3.
- The serial port specified in DX exists in hardware.

If any of the conditions above are not true, the Serial Communications Service does not perform the requested function and returns with all registers preserved.

Time–out errors

A time–out error occurs when either a read or a write of a specified communications line was unable to occur.

The Serial Communications Service read and write functions test the Line Status register. When a time–out error occurs, bit 7 "time–out error" is set.

INT 14h Function 00h — Initialize Serial Adapter

Description

This function initializes the serial port with the data transmission rate, parity, stop bit, and word length parameters specified in the AL register. The function returns with the Modem Status register and the Line Status register in AL and AH, respectively. All other registers are preserved.

Input/Output

Input: AH = 00h

AL = Serial port initialization parameters, where:

Bits 7–5 = Data transmission rate, where:

000	110 bits per second
001	150 bits per second
010	300 bits per second
011	600 bits per second
100	1200 bits per second
101	2400 bits per second
110	4800 bits per second
111	9600 bits per second

Bits 4–3 = Parity, where:

00	None
01	Odd
10	None
11	Even

Bit 2 = Number of stop bits, where:

0	1 stop bit
1	2 stop bits

Bits 1–0 = Character size, where:

10	7–bit characters
11	8–bit characters

DX = Serial port number

00h — COM1
01h — COM2
02h — COM3
03h — COM4

continued

Input/Output, cont'd

Output: AH = Line Status, where:
Bit 7 = 1 Time–out error
Bit 6 = 1 Transmitter shift and holding register empty
Bit 5 = 1 Transmitter holding register empty
Bit 4 = 1 Break interrupt
Bit 3 = 1 Framing error
Bit 2 = 1 Parity error
Bit 1 = 1 Overrun error
Bit 0 = 1 Data ready

AL = Modem Status, where:
Bit 7 = 1 Data carrier detect
Bit 6 = 1 Ring indicator
Bit 5 = 1 Data set ready
Bit 4 = 1 Clear to send
Bit 3 = 1 Delta data carrier detect
Bit 2 = 1 Trailing edge ring indicator
Bit 1 = 1 Delta data set ready
Bit 0 = 1 Delta clear to send

INT 14h Function 01h — Send Character

Description

This function transmits the character supplied in AL over the communication line specified in DX. If successful, this function returns with the contents of the Line Status register in AH, Bit 7 = 0.

Input/Output

Input:	AH	=	01h
	AL	=	Character
	DX	=	Serial port number
			00h — COM1
			01h — COM2
			02h — COM3
			03h — COM4

Output: AH = Line Status register, where:

Bit 7	=	1 Time–out error
Bit 6	=	1 Transmitter shift and holding register empty
Bit 5	=	1 Transmitter holding register empty
Bit 4	=	1 Break interrupt
Bit 3	=	1 Framing error
Bit 2	=	1 Parity error
Bit 1	=	1 Overrun error
Bit 0	=	1 Data ready

INT 14h Function 02h — Receive Character

Description

This function receives one character from the serial port specified in the DX register. If successful, this function returns with the character received in the AL register and the Line Status register in AH, Bit 7 = 0.

Input/Output

Input: AH   =   02h
            DX   =   Serial port number
                    =   00h — COM1
                    =   01h — COM2
                    =   02h — COM3
                    =   03h — COM4

Output: AH   =   Line Status register, where:
                        Bit 7   =   1 Time–out error
                        Bit 6   =   1 Transmitter shift and holding register empty
                        Bit 5   =   1 Transmitter holding register empty
                        Bit 4   =   1 Break interrupt
                        Bit 3   =   1 Framing error
                        Bit 2   =   1 Parity error
                        Bit 1   =   1 Overrun error
                        Bit 0   =   1 Data ready
            AL   =   Character received

INT 14h Function 03h — Return Serial Port Status

Description

This function returns the current modem status in the AL register and the current line status in the AH register. All other registers are preserved.

Input/Output

Input: AH = 03h
        DX = Serial port number
            = 00h — COM1
            = 01h — COM2
            = 02h — COM3
            = 03h — COM4

Output: AH = Line status, where:
                Bit 7 = 1 Time–out error
                Bit 6 = 1 Transmitter shift and holding register empty
                Bit 5 = 1 Transmitter holding register empty
                Bit 4 = 1 Break interrupt
                Bit 3 = 1 Framing error
                Bit 2 = 1 Parity error
                Bit 1 = 1 Overrun error
                Bit 0 = 1 Data ready
        AL = Modem status, where:
                Bit 7 = 1 Data carrier detect
                Bit 6 = 1 Ring indicator
                Bit 5 = 1 Data set ready
                Bit 4 = 1 Clear to send
                Bit 3 = 1 Delta data carrier detect
                Bit 2 = 1 Trailing edge ring indicator
                Bit 1 = 1 Delta data set ready
                Bit 0 = 1 Delta clear to send

continued

Chapter 14
System Services

Overview

Summary

The ROM BIOS for ISA and EISA systems provides multiple services through the INT 15h System Services DSR. This service routine includes:

- Multitasking hooks. Functions AH = 80h, 81h, 82h, 85h, 90h, and 91h provide hooks for use by multitasking environments. Under DOS, the BIOS simply returns a flag indicating success or failure. Under multitasking environments, the INT 15h vector is replaced, and these function calls are intercepted and processed at the operating system level.

- Joystick support. Function 84h returns information for up to two devices attached to the game ports. This function has two subfunctions: read current switch settings and read resistive inputs.

- Wait routines. Function 83h Event Wait and Function 86h Wait, are two different wait functions. Function 86h does not return control to the calling program until a specified interval is completed. Function 83h returns control to the calling program immediately and sets an application–specified bit when the specified interval has elapsed.

continued

Summary, cont'd

- Protected mode support. Function 87h Move Block, and Function 89h Switch Protected Mode provide limited protected mode support.
- System information. Function C0h Get System Configuration Parameters Address supplies configuration information to the calling program. Function C1h Return Extended BIOS Data Area Segment Address returns the address of the extended data area if it exists. Function D8h provides access to EISA–specific system information.

INT 15h System Services DSR

Description

INT 15h invokes the BIOS's INT 15h DSR. All registers are preserved except those in which values are returned when this DSR returns the results of the INT 15h function call. Some INT 15h DSR functions, for example, 87h, 89h, and C2h, may disable interrupts during execution. The Carry Flag is set if an error occurs while the BIOS is processing a function call; it is cleared if there is no error. The INT 15h vector resides at Interrupt Vector table address 00:54h.

The INT 15h DSR functions reference several system RAM locations for counter and flag information. See Chapter 3 for a description of the BIOS data area in system RAM.

The INT 15h DSR functions use CMOS RAM locations 0Bh, 0Fh, and 30h–31h. See Chapter 4 for a description of CMOS RAM data areas.

The INT 15h AH = C0h Return System Configuration Parameters Address function references the System Configuration table and System Configuration table extension, which are located in system ROM. See Chapter 5 for a description of the ROM BIOS data area.

The INT 15h DSR functions use I/O port addresses 20h–21h, 60h, 64h, 70h–71h, A0h–A1h, and 201h. See Chapter 6 for a description of I/O ports.

Cassette functions

The cassette functions of the PCjr and older PCs are generally not supported by BIOS programs for XT, ISA, and EISA systems. The BIOS will generate an error and set the Carry Flag if a cassette function is invoked.

There are four obsolete cassette functions:

- INT 15h Function 00h — Turn Cassette Motor On
- INT 15h Function 01h — Turn Cassette Motor Off
- INT 15h Function 02h — Read Cassette
- INT 15h Function 03h — Write to Cassette

INT 15h Function 4Fh — Keyboard Intercept

Description

INT 09h ISR calls this function each time a key is pressed.

This function can be used to create alternate keyboard layouts and/or to cause the system to ignore certain keystrokes. For example, an operating system or resident utility can intercept Function 4Fh to filter the raw keyboard data stream. A new handler can be written to perform one of the following actions before returning to the calling program:

- Substitute a different scan code (by changing the value in AL)
- Return the existing scan code (returning with the Carry Flag set)
- Discard the scan code altogether (by returning with the Carry Flag cleared)

If this function is not intercepted by an alternate routine, the default BIOS routine returns to the calling program with the scan code in AL (unchanged) and the Carry Flag set.

Application programs should call INT 15h Function C0h to determine if the Keyboard Intercept function is supported by the resident BIOS.

Input/Output

Input:	AH	=	4Fh
	AL	=	Scan code
Output:	AL	=	Scan code
	CF	= 0	Scan code processed and should not be put into keyboard buffer
		1	Scan code not processed (or it has been modified) and should be put into keyboard buffer

Description

This function is used by multitasking environments to capture control of a logical device to perform a process. A multitasking environment would intercept this function and process the request as necessary. The default BIOS routine simply returns with AH set to 00h and the Carry Flag clear.

See also INT 15h, AH = 81h, 82h, 85h, 90h and 91h.

Input/Output

Input:	AH	=	80h
	BX	=	Device ID
	CX	=	Process ID
Output:	AH	=	00h Successful
	CF	=	0 Successful
	AH	=	Status (if unsuccessful)
	CF	=	1 Unsuccessful

Description

This function is used by multitasking environments to release control of a logical device for a process. A multitasking environment would intercept this function and process the request as necessary. The default BIOS routine simply returns with AH set to 00h and the Carry Flag clear.

See also INT 15h, AH = 80h, 82h, 85h, 90h and 91h.

Input/Output

Input:	AH	=	81h
	BX	=	Device ID
	CX	=	Process ID
Output:	AH	=	00h Successful
	CF	=	0 Successful
	AH	=	Status (if unsuccessful)
	CF	=	1 Unsuccessful

Description

This function is used by multitasking environments to release control of all logical devices for a process that will soon terminate. A multitasking environment would intercept this function and process the request as necessary. The default BIOS routine simply returns with AH set to 00h and the Carry Flag clear.

See also INT 15h, AH = 80h, 81h, 85h, 90h, and 91h.

Input/Output

Input:	AH	=	82h
	BX	=	Process ID
Output:	AH	=	00h Successful
	CF	=	0 Successful
	AH	=	Status (if unsuccessful)
	CF	=	1 Unsuccessful

Description

INT 15h provides two wait functions: Function 83h Set Event Wait Interval and Function 86h Wait. When INT 15h Function 83h is invoked, processing continues; when INT 15h Function 86h is invoked, processing stops until the interval is complete.

Function 83h, subfunction AL = 00h causes the BIOS to set a bit in an application–defined memory location after a specified interval passes. The calling program should ensure that the bit is cleared before invoking this function.

The real–time clock generates an interrupt after a specified amount of time, and a bit is set (bit 7 of the byte pointed to by ES:BX). The duration of a wait interval is typically a multiple of 976 microseconds.

Function 83h, subfunction AL = 01h cancels the event wait.

Subfunction:AL = 00h Set interval

This subfunction returns immediately, but causes a bit to be set after a specified elapsed time.

Input:	AH	= 83h
	AL	= 00h
	CX	= Microseconds (high byte)
	DX	= Microseconds (low byte)
	ES:BX	= Pointer to byte in calling program's memory that will have bit 7 set when the interval expires.
Output:	AH	= 00h
	AL	= A value written to CMOS RAM register B (if successful)
		= 00h Function busy
	CF	= 0 Successful
		1 Unsuccessful (already in progress)

Subfunction: AL = 01h Cancel set interval

This function cancels the event wait that is in progress.

Input:	AH	= 83h
	AL	= 01h
Output:	None	

Description

This function has two subfunctions: read current switch settings and read resistive inputs.

Subfunction: DX = 00h Read current switch settings

This subfunction returns the switch settings read from the game port in bits 4 through 7 of AL.

Input:	AH	=	84h
	DX	=	00h

Output:	AL	=	Switch settings in bits 7–4, bits 3–0 = 0
	CF	=	0 Successful
			1 Unsuccessful

Subfunction: DX = 01h Read resistive inputs

This subfunction retrieves the relative position (X and Y coordinates) of the two possible devices attached to the game port.

Input:	AH	=	84h
	DX	=	01h

Output:	AX	=	Joystick A, X–coordinate value
	BX	=	Joystick A, Y–coordinate value
	CX	=	Joystick B, X–coordinate value
	DX	=	Joystick B, Y–coordinate value
	CF	=	1 Incorrect input
			0 No error

INT 15h Function 85h — System Request Key `ISA` `EISA`

Description

This function is called by INT 09h via the SYS REQ key. When called, AL contains 00h if the SYS REQ key was pressed or 01h if it was released.

A multitasking environment would intercept this function and process the request as necessary. Normally, the default BIOS routine simply returns with AH set to 00h and the Carry Flag clear.

Input/Output

Input:	AH	=	85h
	AL	=	00h Key make
			01h Key break
Output:	AH	=	00h Successful
	CF	=	0 Successful
	AH	=	Status (if unsuccessful)
	CF	=	1 Unsuccessful

INT 15h Function 86h — Wait

Description

This function suspends the calling program for the amount of time specified in CX and DX. The values entered in CX and DX must be in microseconds. However, values entered into CX and DX will be rounded down to a multiple of 976 microseconds. The RTC, which is used by this function, is usually programmed to tick 1024 times per second, or once every 976 microseconds.

INT 15h provides two wait functions: Function 83h Set Event Wait Interval and Function 86h Wait. The difference between these two functions is that processing continues when Function 83h is invoked, but processing stops for the calling programs when Function 86h is invoked, and then resumes when the requested interval is complete.

Input/Output

Input: AH = 86h
CX = High byte of wait interval (in microseconds)
DX = Low byte of wait interval (in microseconds)

Output: CF = 0 Successful (wait performed)
1 Unsuccessful (wait not performed)

Description

This function copies a block of memory from anywhere in the system address space to anywhere else in the system address space. Memory space not normally available to real–mode programs is accessible with this function.

Input/Output

Input:	AH	= 87h
	CX	= Number of 16–bit words to be moved
	ES:SI	= Pointer to a 48–byte table allocated by the calling program
Output:	AH	= 00h Successful move
		01h RAM parity error occurred
		02h Other exception interrupt error
		03h Gate address line 20 failed
	CF	= 0 No error
		1 Error

Accessing extended memory

The Move Block function allows real–mode programs to move data to and from extended memory by using the processor's virtual–address translation mechanism. The source and destination addresses can be anywhere in the system address space — in conventional or extended memory.

A protected–mode data structure called a *descriptor* allows the processor to map logical memory to the linear address space. Descriptors are eight bytes long and are organized into global and local descriptor tables. To use this function, real–mode programs must build a global descriptor table (GDT) and provide a pointer to it before invoking this function. The BIOS uses the GDT while in protected mode to perform the block move.

When the block move is complete, the BIOS returns the processor to real mode and passes control back to the calling program.

continued

Descriptor format

The descriptor format for the 80286 is different from that of later processors. The two formats are described below:

80286 Decscriptor

Byte	Description
0–1	Bits 0–15 of the Segment Limit
2–3	Bits 0–15 of the Base Address
4	Bits 16–23 of the Base Address
5	Access Rights
6–7	Reserved (must be set to 0)

80386 and 80486 Decscriptor

Byte	Description
0–1	Bits 0–15 of the Segment Limit
2–3	Bits 0–15 of the Base Address
4	Bits 16–23 of the Base Address
5	Access Rights
6	Bits 7–4 — more Access Rights
	Bits 3–0 — upper 4 bits of Segment Limit
7	Bits 24–31 of Base Address

The Segment Limit is the length in bytes of the area addressable by this descriptor. On the 80286, one descriptor can address up to 64K; on the 80386 and 80486, a descriptor can address up to 1MB or 4GB, depending on the granularity chosen.

The Base Address is the physical address of the beginning of this segment. The Access Rights byte defines the segment type and its privilege level.

Refer to the appropriate Intel programmer's reference manuals for complete descriptions of descriptor tables.

continued

Calling Move Block

When the Move Block function is invoked, the CX register contains the count of 16–bit words to be moved. ES:SI points to a 48–byte GDT containing six 8–byte descriptors.

Two of the descriptors in the GDT specify the source and destination addresses of the block to be moved. The BIOS builds the other four descriptors.

The calling program supplies the following data in both the source and destination descriptors:

- The Segment Limit (the length in bytes of the data block to be moved)
- The Base Address of the data block
- Access Rights for each location (always 093h)

All other locations in the GDT must be zero.

continued

80286 global descriptor table

The following diagram illustrates a global descriptor table in 80286 format.

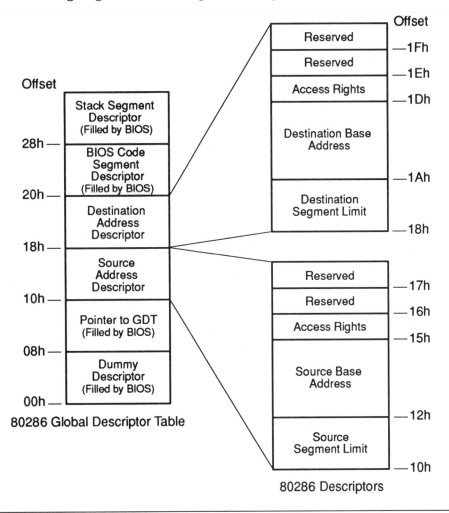

80286 Global Descriptor Table

80286 Descriptors

continued

80386 and 80486 global descriptor table

The following diagram illustrates a global descriptor table in 80386/80486 format.

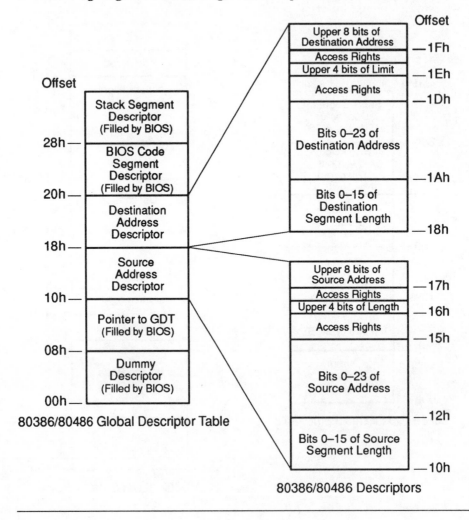

80386/80486 Global Descriptor Table

80386/80486 Descriptors

Interrupts disabled

The Move Block function is performed with interrupts disabled. This may interfere with programs that require immediate servicing of hardware interrupts.

INT 15h Function 88h —
Read Extended Memory Size

Description

The Read Extended Memory Size function reads the size of the memory address space above 100000h, from CMOS RAM locations 30h and 31h. It then stores the contents of these two bytes as a word in the AX register.

Input/Output

Input: AH = 88h

Output: AX = Number of contiguous 1K blocks of extended memory (starting at address 100000h)

INT 15h Function 89h — Switch to Protected Mode **ISA** **EISA**

Description

The Switch to Protected Mode function puts the processor into protected mode
and passes control to the code segment pointed to in the GDT (global descriptor
table) provided by the calling program.

Input/Output

Input:	AH	= 89h
	BH	= Interrupt number for IRQ 0
	BL	= Interrupt number for IRQ 8
	ES:SI	= Pointer to GDT built by application program
Output:	AH	= 00h Successful (returns in protected mode)
		FFh Unsuccessful
	CF	= 0 No error
		1 Error

Global descriptor table requirements

The global descriptor table (GDT) as described below defines the memory management environment that will be in effect upon return to the calling program.

The entry requirements are as follows:

- ES:SI points to a global descriptor table, which must be built before calling this
  function.
- The GDT entries are used by this function to initialize the interrupt descriptor
  table (IDT) register, the GDT register, and the stack segment selector (SS).
- BH must contain an index into the IDT to point to where the first eight hardware interrupts begin.
- BL must contain an index into the IDT to point to where the second eight
  hardware interrupts begin.

Refer to INT 15 Function 87h Move Block for more information on descriptors.

continued

Global descriptor table processing

All of the descriptors are initialized by the calling program except the BIOS code segment descriptor. The access rights byte is set to 09Bh, the address to F0000h, and the data segment limit to FFFFh. The DS, ES, and SS descriptors are loaded with 0018h, 0020h, and 0028h, respectively, so that the descriptors built at these GDT offsets describe the segments that these registers will reference after the BIOS returns to the calling program.

BIOS interrupt vectors do not operate in protected mode. For this reason, a program that enters protected mode must construct its own IDT. The IDT must not overlap the BIOS real mode table and must handle all interrupts while the program is in protected mode.

INT 15h Function 90h — Device Busy

Description

This function is invoked by the BIOS fixed disk, diskette, and keyboard drivers before the I/O cycle begins. A multitasking environment would intercept this function and allow other tasks to be dispatched while I/O is in progress. The default BIOS routine returns with AH set to 00h and the Carry Flag clear.

Input/Output

Input:	AH	= 90h
	AL	= Device type, where:

                              00h   Fixed disk (may time out)
                              01h   Diskette (may time out)
                              02h   Keyboard (no time out)
                              03h   Pointing device (may time out)
                              80h   Network (no time out)
                              FCh   Fixed disk reset (may time out)
                              FDh   Diskette drive motor start (may time out)
                              FEh   Printer (may time out)

	ES:BX	= Points to a request block (if AL = 80h–FFh)
Output:	CF	= 0 No wait performed — driver must perform its own wait
		= 1 Wait was performed (I/O complete or time out)

Device types

Serially reusable devices must be given device types from 00h–7Fh; reentrant devices must have types 80h–BFh; and wait only calls that have either no corresponding INT 15h Function 91h or Interrupt Complete call must have device types C0h–FFh.

Description

This function is invoked by fixed disk, diskette, and keyboard interrupt handlers to signal I/O is complete. A multitasking environment would intercept this function and allow the task requesting I/O to be reactivated. The default BIOS routine returns with AH set to 00h and the Carry Flag clear.

Input/Output

Input:	AH	= 91h
	AL	= Device type, where:
		00h Fixed disk (may time out)
		01h Diskette (may time out)
		02h Keyboard (no time out)
		03h Pointing device (may time out)
		80h Network (no time out)
		FCh Fixed disk reset (may time out)
		FDh Diskette drive motor start (may time out)
		FEh Printer (may time out)
	ES:BX	= Points to a request block (if AL = 80h–FFh)
Output:	AH	= 00h

Device types

Serially reusable devices must be given device types from 00h–7Fh; reentrant devices must have types 80h–BFh; and wait only calls that have either no corresponding INT 15h Function 91h or Interrupt Complete call must have device types C0h–FFh.

Description

This function returns a pointer in ES:BX to the System Configuration table. See Chapter 5 for a description of the ROM BIOS data area.

Input/Output

Input:	AH	= C0h
Output:	AH	= 00h Successful
		86h System model could not be determined
	CF	= 0 Successful
		1 Unsuccessful
	ES:BX	= Address of System Configuration table

INT 15h Function C1h — Return
Extended BIOS Data Area Segment Address

Description

This function returns the segment of the extended BIOS data area in ES.

This function is only supported if INT 15h Function C0h has confirmed that the extended BIOS data area exists. See Chapter 5 for a description of the ROM BIOS data area.

Input/Output

Input:　AH　=　C1h

Output:　ES　=　Extended BIOS data area segment address
　　　　　CF　=　0 Successful
　　　　　　　　 1 Unsuccessful (no EBDA, AH = 86h)

INT 15h Function C2h — Pointing Device Interface

Pointing device DSR

If the system includes support for a PS/2–compatible mouse, INT 15h is also the device service routine for pointing devices. Any type of input device that is compatible with the PS/2 8042 advanced keyboard controller interface may be used as a pointing device.

Pointing device data transmission process

INT 74h is the interrupt service routine (ISR) for PS/2–compatible pointing devices, if they are supported. When the pointing device has data to transmit to the system, it transmits the data to the 8042, and the 8042 interrupts the system on IRQ 12. The data is transmitted in a packet. The ISR (INT 74h) collects each byte of the packet and stores it in the BIOS extended data area. INT 74h also sets the appropriate flags if an acknowledge, resend, or self–test completion code is received. When all information in a packet has been collected and stored, INT 74h pushes the data onto the stack and calls the pointing device handler. The address of the pointing device handler is set using subfunction 07h.

Pointing device control

The INT 15h Pointing Device DSR controls the operation of the pointing device. It enables, resets, and disables the pointing device. It also sets the sample rate and resolution of the device, reads the device type, and sets the scale. INT 15h sends commands through the 8042 keyboard controller to perform these functions.

continued

Status Message table

The INT 15h mouse service routines return the status of the functions performed by Function C2h in register AH. The following table is referred to in the "Output" sections of the eight BIOS pointing device subfunction descriptions:

AH Value	Description
00h	No error
01h	Invalid function call
02h	Invalid input value
03h	Interface error
04h	Resend received from 8042
05h	No driver installed (i.e., Function C2h subfunction 07h has not been performed)

Subfunction: AL = 00h Enable/disable pointing device

This subfunction enables a pointing device to allow the device to be used, or disables the device so it can no longer be used.

Input:	AH	=	C2h
	AL	=	00h
	BH	=	00h Disable
			01h Enable
Output:	AH	=	00h Successful
			Status if unsuccessful (see Status Message table)
	CF	=	0 Successful
			1 Unsuccessful

continued

Subfunction: AL = 01h Reset pointing device

This subfunction resets a pointing device, stores the device ID in BH, and if successful, sets the pointing device state as follows:

- Disabled
- Sample rate will be 100 reports per second
- Resolution will be 4 counts per millimeter
- Scaling will be 1:1
- Packet size will not be changed

Input:	AH	=	C2h
	AL	=	01h
Output:	AH	=	00h Successful
		=	Status if unsuccessful (see Status Message table)
	BH	=	00h Device ID if successful
	CF	=	0 Successful
			1 Unsuccessful

Subfunction: AL = 02h Set sample rate

This subfunction sets a sample rate for the pointing device. If the rate is out of range, an invalid input condition (AH = 02h) is set and the subfunction terminates.

Input:	AH	=	C2h
	AL	=	02h
	BH	=	Sample rate, where:

00h	10 reports per second
01h	20 reports per second
02h	40 reports per second
03h	60 reports per second
04h	80 reports per second
05h	100 reports per second (default)
06h	200 reports per second

Output:	AH	=	00h Successful
		=	Status if unsuccessful (see Status Message table)
	CF	=	0 Successful
			1 Unsuccessful

continued

Subfunction: AL = 03h Set resolution

This subfunction sets the resolution of the pointing device.

Input: AH = C2h
         AL = 03h
         BH = Resolution value, where:
               00h   1 count/millimeter
               01h   2 counts/millimeter
               02h   4 counts/millimeter
               03h   8 counts/millimeter

Output: AH = 00h Successful
             = Status if unsuccessful (see Status Message table)
         CF = 0 Successful
                1 Unsuccessful

Subfunction: AL = 04h Read device type

This subfunction returns the ID byte from the pointing device in BH.

Input: AH = C2h
         AL = 04h

Output: AH = 00h Successful
             = Status if unsuccessful (see Status Message table)
         BH = 00h Device ID if successful
         CF = 0 Successful
                1 Unsuccessful

continued

Subfunction: AL = 05h Initialize pointing device interface

This subfunction initializes the pointing device.

If this subfunction completes normally, the pointing device state is:

- Disabled
- Sample rate will be 100 reports/second
- Resolution will be 4 counts/millimeter
- Scaling will be 1:1

Input:	AH	=	C2h
	AL	=	05h
	BH	=	Data package size (01h–08h, in bytes)
Output:	AH	=	00h Successful
		=	Status if unsuccessful (see Status Message table)
	CF	=	0 Successful
			1 Unsuccessful

continued

Subfunction: AL = 06h Set scaling or get status

This subfunction jumps to another subfunction based on the value in BH. If BH is out of range, this subfunction terminates and sets an invalid subfunction indicator.

Subfunction: AL = 06h, BH = 00h Return status

This subfunction reads and returns the status of the pointing device. The device sends three status bytes that are stored in registers BL, CL, and DL.

Input:	AH	=	C2h
	AL	=	06h
	BH	=	00h

Output:	AH	=	00h Successful
	BL	=	Status byte 1, where:

    Bit 7 = 0 Reserved

    Bit 6 = 0 Stream mode

           1 Remote mode

    Bit 5 = 0 Disable

           1 Enable

    Bit 4 = 0 1:1 Scaling

           1 2:1 Scaling

    Bit 3 = 0 Reserved

    Bit 2 = 1 Left button pressed

    Bit 1 = 0 Reserved

    Bit 0 = 1 Right button pressed

	CL	=	Status byte 2, where:

    00h   1 count per millimeter

    01h   2 counts per millimeter

    02h   4 counts per millimeter

    03h   8 counts per millimeter

---

continued

Subfunction: AL = 06h, BH = 00h Return status, cont'd

Output: cont'd	DL	=	Status byte 3, where:	
			0Ah	10 reports per second
			14h	20 reports per second
			28h	40 reports per second
			3Ch	60 reports per second
			50h	80 reports per second
			64h	100 reports per second
			C8h	200 reports per second
	CF	=	0 Successful	
			1 Unsuccessful	

Subfunction: AL = 06h, BH = 01h Set scaling factor to 1:1

Input:	AH	=	C2h
	AL	=	06h
	BH	=	01h
Output:	AH	=	00h Successful
		=	Status if unsuccessful (see Status Message table)
	CF	=	0 Successful
			1 Unsuccessful

Subfunction: AL = 06h, BH = 02h Set scaling factor to 2:1

Input:	AH	=	C2h
	AL	=	06h
	BH	=	02h
Output:	AH	=	00h Successful
		=	Status if unsuccessful (see Status Message table)
	CF	=	0 Successful
			1 Unsuccessful

---

continued

Subfunction: AL = 07h Set pointing device handler address

This subfunction stores the device driver address in the extended ROM BIOS data area so that the driver can be called when data is available from the pointing device.

When transferring control to the application program, the pointing device interrupt handler uses a far call. The routine in the application program should be coded as a far procedure and should not pop the parameters off the stack before returning.

When the application program is called, the following arguments are on the stack:

Word	Description
1	Status Bits 8–15 = Reserved Bit 7 = 1 Y data overflow Bit 6 = 1 X data overflow Bit 5 = 1 Y data negative Bit 4 = 1 X data negative Bit 3 = 1 Reserved Bit 2 = 0 Reserved Bit 1 = 1 Right button pressed Bit 0 = 0 Left button pressed
2	X Coordinates
3	Y Coordinates
4	Z Coordinates (always 0)

Input: AH = C2h
AL = 07h
ES:BX = Pointer to application–program's device driver

Output: AH = 00h Successful
= Status if unsuccessful (see Status Message table)
CF = 0 Successful
1 Unsuccessful

INT 15h Function C3h — Fail–Safe Timer Control

Description

This function enables or disables the EISA fail–safe timer.

The fail–safe timer ensures that a program does not turn off interrupts for too long a period. If interrupts are turned off for longer than the time period stored in WDTIC, an NMI is generated by the fail–safe timer.

Initially, the BIOS disables the fail–safe timer. The application program must enable it.

Subfunction: AL = 00h Disable fail–safe timer

This subfunction disables the fail–safe timer and clears WDTIC in the extended BIOS data area. It sets the Carry Flag if there is an invalid input.

Input: AH   = C3h
          AL   = 00h

Output: CF   = 0 No error
               1 Invalid input

Subfunction: AL = 01h Load value and enable fail–safe timer

This subfunction enables the fail–safe timer and establishes the timer count value with the value in BX. It puts the fail–safe timer in mode 0 operation, enables the fail–safe timer NMI, and places the value in BX into WDTIC in the extended BIOS data area. It sets the Carry Flag if there is an invalid input.

The fail–safe timer decrements and, at the end of the period stored in WDTIC, a fail–safe timer NMI is generated.

Input: AH   = C3h
          AL   = 01h
          BX   = Fail–safe timer

Output: CF   = 0 No error
               1 Invalid input

Description

This function is used to autoconfigure EISA controllers.

EISA extended CMOS RAM is accessed by the subfunctions of this function and should be the only method used to access extended CMOS RAM in an EISA system.

EISA extended CMOS RAM structure

EISA configuration information is stored in I/O–mapped extended CMOS RAM. Extended CMOS RAM in an EISA system must consist of at least 4K of additional CMOS RAM. This 4K of CMOS RAM is in addition to the 64 bytes of CMOS RAM storage used in ISA systems for RTC and basic system configuration data.

EISA controllers and devices

Controllers in an EISA system are referred to as EISA devices. Each device performs a function, such as serial port control, parallel port control, diskette drive control, and so on. There can be up to 64 devices. Of these, up to 16 can be physical devices, and the rest can be embedded or logical (virtual) devices.

Controllers, devices and slots

There is a close relationship between controllers, devices, and slots in EISA terminology. Controllers and devices are in fact equivalent. Slots are the actual physical locations where controllers (devices) reside in an EISA system and are used as the address for the device.

Controllers, or devices, are addressed by their physical or logical slot number. The system board is always slot 0. Other physical slots are numbered 1 through 15.

Physical controllers reside in slots and are addressed by a slot number. A controller can also be called a device.

continued

Device numbers

A physical device resides in an actual slot in the computer. Physical devices can be numbered 1 through 15. Virtual devices are numbered sequentially after the last embedded device — they must be addressed as slot 16 through 64.

Virtual devices

EISA also supports virtual (or logical) devices. A virtual device is generally a software driver that may need system resources (such as memory) but does not actually exist as a physical entity. A virtual device may also be an ISA device that is embedded on the system board.

There can be up to 50 or so virtual devices as long as the total number of physical, embedded, and virtual devices does not exceed 64.

Embedded devices

The system board may also have one or more integrated devices, which are called embedded devices. Embedded devices are addressed as additional EISA devices.

The device number for embedded devices begins with the next number after the last physical device number used. For example, if there are four adapter cards in the computer, they will be assigned device numbers 1 through 4. The first embedded device will be device number 5. All other embedded devices are numbered sequentially afterwards.

Device functions

A function is equivalent to a system component or system function. A device may have more than one function associated with it. Typical functions include the

- Memory function
- Serial function
- Parallel function
- Diskette function
- Fixed disk function

continued

Subfunction: AL = 00h Read slot information

This subfunction returns data about the EISA device in the specified slot. This function determines the number of EISA functions supported in the system and the types of functions supported by this slot.

Input:	AH	=	D8h
	AL	=	00h
	AL	=	00h (CS specifies 16–bit addressing)
	AL	=	80h (CS specifies 32–bit addressing)
	CL	=	Slot number (0–63)
Output:	AH	=	00h Successful completion
		=	80h Invalid slot number
		=	82h Extended CMOS RAM corrupted
		=	83h Empty slot specified
		=	86h Invalid BIOS routine call
		=	87h Invalid system configuration
	AL	=	Miscellaneous vendor information byte

Bit 7   = Duplicate IDs exist
Bit 6   = Product ID
Bit 5–4   = Slot type
           00 Expansion slot
           01 Embedded device
           10 Virtual device
           11 Reserved
Bits 3–0   = Duplicate ID number
           0000 If no duplicate ID
           0001 If first duplicate ID
           ⋮
           1111 If fifteenth duplicate ID

BH	=	Major revision number of the configuration utility
BL	=	Minor revision number of the configuration utility
CH	=	MSB of checksum for configuration file
CL	=	LSB of checksum for configuration file
DH	=	Number of device functions
DL	=	Combined function information
SI:DI =		Four–byte compressed vendor ID

continued

INT 15h Function D8h —
Access EISA System Information, Continued

Error conditions

The Carry Flag (CF) will be set and AH will be set to a nonzero value if there is an error.

Subfunction: AL = 01h Read function information

This subfunction returns 320 bytes of data about the specified EISA function in the specified slot. The data is in a predefined format, as shown below.

Input:	AH	= D8h
	AL	= 01h (CS specifies 16–bit addressing)
	AL	= 81h (CS specifies 32–bit addressing)
	CH	= Function number (0–n–1)
	CL	= Slot number (0–63)
	DS:SI	= Address pointer for output data
Output:	AH	= 00h Successful completion
		80h Invalid slot number
		81h Invalid function number
		82h Extended CMOS RAM corrupted
		83h Empty slot specified
		86h Invalid BIOS routine call
		87h Invalid system configuration
	DS	= Segment for return data buffer
	SI	= Offset to return data buffer (16–bit call)
	ESI	= Offset to return data buffer (32–bit call)

---

continued

Function Information table

The following table describes the 320–byte block pointed to by DS:SI. It contains the configuration information for one expansion board function.

The data fields have fixed sizes unless the free–form data bit (function information byte, bit 6) is set. If the free–form data bit equals 1, the fields following offset 073h are replaced by a free–form data field.

Offset	Size	Description
00h	2 Words	Compressed ID Byte 0 Bit 7 = Reserved Bits 6–2 = Character 1 Bits 1–0 = Character 2 Byte 1 Bits 7–5 = Character 2 Bits 4–0 = Character 3 Byte 2 Bits 7–4 = Second digit of product number Bits 3–0 = First digit of product number Byte 3 Bits 7–4 = Third digit of product number Bits 3–0 = Product revision number

continued

Function Information table, cont'd

Offset	Size	Description
04h	1 Word	ID and slot information Byte 0 Bit 7 = 0 No duplicate ID is present 1 Duplicate ID is present Bit 6 = 0 ID is readable 1 ID is not readable Bits 5–4 = Slot type 00 Expansion slot 01 Embedded slot 10 Virtual slot 11 Reserved Bits 3–0 = Duplicate configuration file names (IDs) 0000 No duplicate configuration file name 0001 First duplicate configuration file name ⋮ 1111 Fifteenth duplicate configuration file name Byte 1 Bit 7 = 0 Configuration complete 1 Configuration incomplete Bits 6–2 = Reserved Bit 1 = 0 EISA IOCHKERR not supported 1 EISA IOCHKERR supported Bit 0 = 0 EISA ENABLE not supported 1 EISA ENABLE supported
06h	1 Word	Configuration file extension revision level Byte 0 — Minor revision level Byte 1 — Major revision level
08h	13 Words	Selections Byte 0 — First selection Byte 1 — Second selection ⋮ Byte 25 — Twenty–sixth selection
022h	1 Byte	Function information Bit 7 = 0 Function is enabled 1 Function is disabled Bit 6 = Configuration extension free–form data Bit 5 = Port initialization entries follow Bit 4 = Port range entries follow Bit 3 = DMA entries follow Bit 2 = Interrupt entries follow Bit 1 = Memory entries follow Bit 0 = Type/subtype entries follow

continued

Function information table, *cont'd*

Offset	Size	Description
023h	80 Bytes	Type and subtype ASCII string (strings less than 80 characters are zero–filled) Byte 0 — First character of ASCII string Byte 1 — Second character of ASCII string ⋮ Byte 79 — Eightieth character of ASCII string
073h	63 Bytes	Memory configuration information (if function information bit 6 is not set) Byte 0 Bit 7 = 0 Last entry 1 More entries follow Bit 6 = Reserved Bit 5 = 0 Unshared memory 1 Shared memory Bits 4–3 = Memory type 00 SYS (base or extended) 01 EXP (expanded) 10 VIR (virtual) 11 OTH (other) Bit 2 = Reserved Bit 1 = 0 Not cached 1 Cached Bit 0 = 0 Read only (ROM) 1 Read/write (RAM) Byte 1 Bits 7–4 = Reserved Bits 3–2 = Decode size 00 20 01 24 10 32 11 Reserved Bits 1–0 = Data size (access size) 00 Byte 01 Word 10 Doubleword 11 Reserved Bytes 2–4 — Memory start address divided by 100h Bytes 5–6 — Memory size divided by 400h Up to eight more seven–byte entries may follow.

continued

Function information table, cont'd

Offset	Size	Description
0B2h	14 Bytes	Interrupt configuration (if function information bit 6 is not set) Byte 0 Bit 7　　= 0 Last entry 　　　　　　 1 More entries follow Bit 6　　= 0 Not shared 　　　　　　 1 Shared Bit 5　　= 0 Edge triggered 　　　　　　 1 Level triggered Bit 4　　= Reserved Bits 3–0 = Interrupt (0–F) Byte 1 — Reserved Up to six more two–byte entries may follow.
0C0h	4 Words	DMA channel description (if function information bit 6 is not set) Byte 0 Bit 7　　= 0 Last entry 　　　　　　 1 More entries follow Bit 6　　= 0 Not shared 　　　　　　 1 Shared Bits 5–3 = Reserved Bits 2–0 = DMA channel number (0–7) Byte 1 Bits 7–6 = Reserved Bits 5–4 = Data timing 　　　　　　 00 Default (ISA compatible) 　　　　　　 01 Type A 　　　　　　 10 Type B 　　　　　　 11 Type C (Burst) Bits 3–2 = Transfer size 　　　　　　 00 8–bit transfer 　　　　　　 01 16–bit transfer 　　　　　　 10 32–bit transfer 　　　　　　 11 Reserved Bits 1–0 = Reserved Up to three more two–byte entries may follow.

continued

Function information table, cont'd

Offset	Size	Description

0C8h	60 Bytes	Port I/O information
		
		Byte 0
		Bit 7 = 0 Last entry
		           1 More entries follow
		Bit 6 = 0 Not shared
		           1 Shared
		Bit 5 = Reserved
		Bits 4–0 = Number of sequential ports (minus 1)
		
		Bytes 1–2 — I/O port address
		
		Up to 19 more three–byte entries may follow.

continued

Function information table, cont'd

Offset	Size	Description
0104h	60 Bytes	Initialization data (if function information bit 6 is not set)

Byte 0 — Initialization type
Bit 7　= 0 Last entry
　　　　1 More entries follow
Bits 6–3 = Reserved
Bit 2　= Port value or mask value
　　　　0 Write to port without mask
　　　　1 Write to port using mask
Bits 1–0 = Type of access
　　　　00 Byte addressable
　　　　01 Word addressable
　　　　10 Doubleword addressable
　　　　11 Reserved

Bytes 1–2 — I/O port address

Bytes 3–10
The values of bytes 3–10 in each initialization data entry depend on the value of byte 0, bit 2.

If byte 0, bit 2 equals 0 (no mask), bytes 3–6 will have the following values based on the access type specified by byte 0, bits 0–1:

Byte 0, bits 0–1
00　Byte 3 — port value
01　Bytes 3–4 — port value
10　Bytes 3–6 — port value
11　Reserved

If byte 0, bit 2 equals 1 (use mask), bytes 3–10 will have the following values based on the access type specified by byte 0, bits 0–1.

Byte 0, bits 0–1
00　Byte 3 — port value
　　Byte 4 — port mask
01　Bytes 3–4 — port value
　　Bytes 5–6 — port mask
10　Bytes 3–6 — port value
　　Bytes 7–10 — port mask
11　Reserved

Up to seven more four–, five–, seven–, or 11–byte entries may follow.

continued

Function information table, cont'd

Offset	Size	Description
When bit 6 is set in the function information byte, the 320–byte data block has a free–form format beginning at offset 073h.		
073h	205 Bytes	Free–form data Byte 0 — Length of free–form data Byte 1 — First byte of free–form data ⋮ Byte 204 — Two hundred and fourth byte of free–form data

Subfunction: AL = 02h Clear configuration storage

This subfunction places zeros in all extended CMOS RAM data areas.

Input:	AH	= D8h
	AL	= 02h (CS specifies 16–bit addressing)
		= 82h (CS specifies 32–bit addressing)
	BH	= Configuration utility major revision level
		= Configuration utility minor revision level
Output:	AH	= 00h Successful
		84h Error writing to extended CMOS RAM
		86h Invalid BIOS routine call
		88h Configuration utility not supported

continued

Subfunction: AL = 03h Write configuration storage

This subfunction writes configuration data from a table defined by the calling program. This table is pointed to by the value in DS:SI to extended CMOS RAM.

This subfunction also updates all internal variables and generates and stores a new checksum value for extended CMOS RAM.

This subfunction must be called sequentially for each slot. This subfunction must be called once for each slot, in sequence, even for empty slots. To write configuration information for an empty slot, the calling program must call this subfunction with a pointer to a data table filled with zeros.

Note that the two–byte checksum data entry of the configuration file must be part of the input data structure pointed to by DS:SI, even though this subfunction will recalculate the checksum before returning to the calling program.

Input:	AH	= D8h
	AL	= 03h
	CX	= Length of data structure (in bytes)
	DS	= Segment of data buffer
	SI	= Offset of data buffer (16–bit call)
	ESI	= Offset of data buffer (32–bit call)
Output:	AH	= 00h Successful
		84h Error writing to extended CMOS RAM
		85h CMOS RAM is full
		86h Invalid BIOS routine call

Function Information table

The following table describes the configuration data block pointed to by DS:SI in the Write Nonvolatile Memory BIOS routine.

Each block of variable–length data fields describes an individual expansion board.

Size	Description
2 Words	**Compressed ID** Byte 0 Bit 7 = Reserved Bits 6–2 = Character 1 Bits 1–0 = Character 2 Byte 1 Bits 7–5 = Character 2 Bits 4–0 = Character 3 Byte 2 Bits 7–4 = Second digit of product number Bits 3–0 = First digit of product number Byte 3 Bits 7–4 = Third digit of product number Bits 3–0 = Product revision number

1 Word	**ID and slot information**
	
	Byte 0
	Bit 7 = 0 No duplicate ID is present
	       1 Duplicate ID is present
	Bit 6 = 0 ID is readable
	       1 ID is not readable
	Bits 5–4 = Slot type
	       00 Expansion slot
	       01 Embedded slot
	       10 Virtual slot
	       11 Reserved
	Bits 3–0 = Duplicate configuration file names (IDs)
	       0000 No duplicate configuration file name
	       0001 First duplicate configuration file name
	       ⋮
	       1111 Fifteenth duplicate configuration file name
	
	Byte 1
	Bit 7 = 0 Configuration complete
	       1 Configuration incomplete
	Bits 6–2 = Reserved
	Bit 1 = 0 EISA IOCHKERR not supported
	       1 EISA IOCHKERR supported
	Bit 0 = 0 EISA ENABLE not supported
	       1 EISA ENABLE supported

continued

Function Information table, cont'd

Size	Description
1 Word	Configuration file extension revision level Byte 0 — Minor revision level Byte 1 — Major revision level
1 Word	Function length Length does not include the length of this (function length) field, or the checksum at the end of nonvolatile memory. The function length of the last configuration data function entry equals zero.
2–27 Bytes	Selections Byte 0 — First selection Byte 1 — Second selection ⋮ Byte 25 — Twenty–sixth selection
1 Byte	Function information Bit 7 = 0 Function is enabled 1 Function is disabled Bit 6 = Configuration extension free–form data Bit 5 = Port initialization entries follow Bit 4 = Port range entries follow Bit 3 = DMA entries follow Bit 2 = Interrupt entries follow Bit 1 = Memory entries follow Bit 0 = Type/subtype entries follow
2–81 Bytes	Type and subtype ASCII string (strings less than 80 characters are zero–filled) Byte 0 — First character of ASCII string Byte 1 — Second character of ASCII string ⋮ Byte 79 — Eightieth character of ASCII string

continued

Function information table, cont'd

Size	Description

7–63 Bytes	Memory configuration information (if function information bit 6 is not set)
	
	Byte 0
	Bit 7 = 0 Last entry
	           1 More entries follow
	Bit 6 = Reserved
	Bit 5 = 0 Unshared memory
	           1 Shared memory
	Bits 4–3 = Memory type
	         00 SYS (base or extended)
	         01 EXP (expanded)
	         10 VIR (virtual)
	         11 OTH (other)
	Bit 2 = Reserved
	Bit 1 = 0 Not cached
	           1 Cached
	Bit 0 = 0 Read only (ROM)
	           1 Read/write (RAM)
	
	Byte 1
	Bits 7–4 = Reserved
	Bits 3–2 = Decode size
	         00 20
	         01 24
	         10 32
	         11 Reserved
	Bits 1–0 = Data size (access size)
	         00 Byte
	         01 Word
	         10 Doubleword
	         11 Reserved
	
	Bytes 2–4 — Memory start address divided by 100h
	
	Bytes 5–6 — Memory size divided by 400h
	
	Up to eight more seven–byte entries may follow.

2–14 Bytes	Interrupt configuration (if function information bit 6 is not set)
	
	Byte 0
	Bit 7 = 0 Last entry
	           1 More entries follow
	Bit 6 = 0 Not shared
	           1 Shared
	Bit 5 = 0 Edge triggered
	           1 Level triggered
	Bit 4 = Reserved
	Bits 3–0 = Interrupt (0–F)
	
	Byte 1 — Reserved
	
	Up to six more two–byte entries may follow.

continued

Function Information table, cont'd

Size	Description

2–8 Bytes	DMA channel description (if function information bit 6 is not set)
	
	Byte 0
	Bit 7 = 0 Last entry
	           1 More entries follow
	Bit 6 = 0 Not shared
	           1 Shared
	Bits 5–3 = Reserved
	Bits 2–0 = DMA channel number (0–7)
	
	Byte 1
	Bits 7–6 = Reserved
	Bits 5–4 = Data timing
	         00 Default (ISA compatible)
	         01 Type A
	         10 Type B
	         11 Type C (Burst)
	Bits 3–2 = Transfer size
	         00 8–bit transfer
	         01 16–bit transfer
	         10 32–bit transfer
	         11 Reserved
	Bits 1–0 = Reserved
	
	Up to three more two–byte entries may follow.

3–60 Bytes	Port I/O information
	
	Byte 0
	Bit 7 = 0 Last entry
	           1 More entries follow
	Bit 6 = 0 Not shared
	           1 Shared
	Bit 5 = Reserved
	Bits 4–0 = Number of sequential ports (minus 1)
	
	Bytes 1–2 — I/O port address
	
	Up to 19 more three–byte entries may follow.

continued

Function information table, cont'd

Size	Description
4–60 Bytes	Initialization data (if function information bit 6 is not set)
	Byte 0 — Initialization type
	Bit 7 = 0 Last entry
	1 More entries follow
	Bits 6–3 = Reserved
	Bit 2 = Port value or mask value
	0 Write to port without mask
	1 Write to port using mask
	Bits 1–0 = Type of access
	00 Byte addressable
	01 Word addressable
	10 Doubleword addressable
	11 Reserved
	Bytes 1–2 — I/O port address
	Bytes 3–10
	The values of bytes 3–10 in each initialization data entry depend on the value of byte 0, bit 2.
	If byte 0, bit 2 equals 0 (no mask), bytes 3–6 will have the following values based on the access type specified by byte 0, bits 0–1:
	Byte 0, bits 0–1
	00 Byte 3 — port value
	01 Bytes 3–4 — port value
	10 Bytes 3–6 — port value
	11 Reserved
	If byte 0, bit 2 equals 1 (use mask), bytes 3–10 will have the following values based on the access type specified by byte 0, bits 0–1.
	Byte 0, bits 0–1
	00 Byte 3 — port value
	Byte 4 — port mask
	01 Bytes 3–4 — port value
	Bytes 5–6 — port mask
	10 Bytes 3–6 — port value
	Bytes 7–10 — port mask
	11 Reserved
	Up to seven more four–, five–, seven–, or 11–byte entries may follow.
1 Word	Configuration file checksum

When bit 6 is set in the function information byte, free–form data follow the type and subtype ASCII string field.

Size	Description
2–205 Bytes	Free–form data
	Byte 0 — Length of free–form data
	Byte 1 — First byte of free–form data
	⋮
	Byte 204 — Two hundred and fourth byte of free–form data

Chapter 15
Parallel Printer Service

Overview

Description

The Parallel Printer Service provides BIOS–level support for up to three parallel printer ports through the INT 17h Parallel Printer DSR. The INT 17h vector resides at address 005Ch in the Interrupt Vector table. The BIOS initializes the INT 17h vector to address F000:EFD2h.

The INT 17h DSR makes use of information located in the BIOS data area of system RAM. See Chapter 3 for a description of the BIOS data area in system RAM.

The INT 17h DSR uses I/O ports 0278h–027Ah, 0378h–037Ah, and 03BCh–03BEh. If a system doesn't define the extended data area — for a PS/2–style mouse, for example — that space can be used to define a fourth parallel port. The system manufacturer must then specify the I/O port to be used. See Section 6 for a description of I/O ports.

In this chapter

This chapter includes the following topics:

- Theory of Operation
- Parallel Printer Service functions

Theory of Operation

Description

The 8–bit–wide parallel printer port on an XT, AT, or EISA computer is designed to drive printers that conform to the Centronics standard. While it's theoretically possible to connect any eight–bit parallel device, the parallel port's electrical specifications make it almost impossible to interface with input devices.

The parallel printer port has a 25–pin connector at the rear of the adapter. The connection with a printer is typically made with a shielded 25–conductor cable that has a 36–pin Centronics–type connector at the printer end.

Signal Name	25–Pin Connector	Description
Strobe	1	Output signal indicating the eight data lines can be read
Data bit 0–7	2–9	Five volts = logical one; zero volts = logical zero
Acknowledge	10	Input signal indicating data received
Busy	11	Input signal indicating Do Not Transmit
Paper end	12	Input signal indicating printer is out of paper
Select	13	Input signal indicating printer is on line, ready to receive
Auto feed	14	Output signal selecting the line–feed option. If the signal is low, the printer is commanded to automatically feed one line when it detects a carriage return; if the signal is high, an explicit line–feed character is required.
Fault	15	Input signal indicating an error
Initialize printer	16	Output signal resetting the printer to its default operating parameters
Select input	17	Output signal to switch the printer on and off line
Ground	18–25	Ground

continued

Initializing the parallel ports

The three standard parallel ports are each assigned three I/O ports in the XT, ISA, and EISA specifications. These three sets of I/O ports have the respective base addresses of 03BCh, 0378h, and 0278h.

During POST, the BIOS examines the three sets of I/O ports to see if printers are attached. The I/O port base addresses are examined in the following order:

- The first I/O port base address examined, 03BCh, was originally reserved for the parallel port on the IBM Monochrome Display Adapter card. If a printer is attached at 03BCh, it becomes PRT1; otherwise, PRT1 remains unassigned.
- After examining base address 03BCh, the BIOS continues to base address 0378h and examines it for an attached printer. If a printer is attached, it is assigned the next available printer number (PRT1, if another printer is not attached at 03BCh, or PRT2 if another printer is already attached at 03BCh).
- Then base address 0278h is examined for an attached printer, and the next available printer number — PRT1, PRT2, or PRT3 — is assigned.
- If the system manufacturer has added a fourth parallel port, its base address is similarly examined.

As the BIOS assigns the parallel ports, it constructs an internal table that is used by the Parallel Printer Services to route data and control signals to and from the printer(s).

INT 17h and the parallel port

The Parallel Printer Service is invoked by software interrupt 17h. This service contains three BIOS functions that interact with the parallel port. These functions are as follows:

- Function 00h, which prints the character in AL to the printer specified in DX
- Function 01h, which initializes the printer specified in DX
- Function 02h, which reads and returns the status of the printer specified in DX

The INT 17h functions reference three parallel printer I/O ports: the data port, the printer control port, and the printer status port.

continued

Error handling

Before entering any functions, the INT 17h Parallel Printer DSR ensures that DX is not out of range, that the function number is not out of range, and that the printer is at the address specified by DX.

If any of these conditions aren't met, the service returns to the calling program with all registers restored except AH. When DX is out of range or the printer does not exist, AX is not modified. When the function number is out of range, AH is returned.

INT 17h Function 00h — Print Character

Description

This function prints the character that is in the AL register to the printer specified in the DX register.

Input/Output

Input: AL = Character to print

DX = Printer number (0, 1, or 2) used as an index to the printer base port address table at 40:08h

Output: AH = Printer status, where:

Bit 7 = 1 Printer not busy

Bit 6 = 1 Acknowledgment from printer

Bit 5 = 1 Out of paper

Bit 4 = 1 Printer selected

Bit 3 = 1 I/O error

Bit 2 = Reserved

Bit 1 = Reserved

Bit 0 = 1 Time–out error

INT 17h Function 01h — Initialize Printer

Description

This function initializes the printer specified in the DX register and the printer status is returned in register AH.

Input/Output

Input: DX = Printer number (0, 1, or 2) used as an index to the printer base port address table at 40:08h

Output: AH = Printer status, where:

Bit 7	=	1	Printer not busy
Bit 6	=	1	Acknowledgment from printer
Bit 5	=	1	Out of paper
Bit 4	=	1	Printer selected
Bit 3	=	1	I/O error
Bit 2	=	Reserved	
Bit 1	=	Reserved	
Bit 0	=	1	Time–out error

INT 17h Function 02h — Read Printer Status

Description

This function reads and returns the status of the printer specified by the DX register.

Input/Output

Input: DX = Printer number (0, 1, or 2) used as an index to the printer base port address table at 40:08h

Output: AH = Printer status, where:
  Bit 7 = 1 Printer not busy
  Bit 6 = 1 Acknowledgment from printer
  Bit 5 = 1 Out of paper
  Bit 4 = 1 Printer selected
  Bit 3 = 1 I/O error
  Bit 2 = Reserved
  Bit 1 = Reserved
  Bit 0 = 1 Time–out error

Chapter 16
Time–of–Day Service

Overview

Description

This chapter describes the device and interrupt service routines that the ROM BIOS provides for accessing the time–keeping devices in an ISA–compatible system:

- The INT 1Ah Time–of–Day DSR sets and reads the system clock device and the time and date from the real–time clock device (RTC) and sets the RTC alarm.
- The INT 08h System Timer ISR maintains a clock tick count for system timing.
- The INT 1Ch Timer Tick ISR provides a vector that can be redirected to a software routine for execution on the system clock tick.
- The INT 70h Real–Time Clock ISR maintains the clock tick for tracking time delays requested by software and the RTC alarm.
- The INT 4Ah User Alarm ISR provides a vector that application programs can redirect to a routine for processing the RTC alarm.

Intel 8254 Programmable Interval Timer

ISA and EISA systems include an Intel 8254 Programmable Interval Timer (PIT), or equivalent device, that creates clock signals for system and applications software. The PIT creates a clock signal by dividing the system clock signal by an integer. After the program initializes one of the 8254's three counters, the device counts to the set value and issues an interrupt request.

Channel 0 of the 8254 is typically programmed to generate a tick 18.2 times a second. On each tick, the device invokes the INT 08h System Timer ISR, which maintains the system timer counter at system RAM locations 40:6Ch and 40:6Eh. The system time value as recorded in the counter is the number of timer ticks since midnight.

When the 8254 invokes INT 08h, the INT 08h System Timer ISR calls the INT 1Ch Timer Tick ISR. This routine points to a vector that the system or application program can redirect to a procedure. The calling program must restore all registers and return to the ROM BIOS by executing an IRET instruction. The calling program must also restore the original vector if it exits and is no longer going to hook INT 1Ch.

Motorola MC146818A Real Time Clock

In addition to the 8254, ISA and EISA systems include a Motorola MC146818A Real Time Clock, or equivalent device. This device keeps track of the system time and date. It supplies a periodic interrupt that is usually programmed to generate a tick 1024 times a second and provides an alarm function.

Note: Some manufacturers include a real–time clock in their XT systems. These enhanced XTs include all of the BIOS functions described in this chapter.

The INT 1Ah Time–of–Day DSR reads and sets the system time and the RTC time and date information stored on the MC146818A. It also sets the alarm timer.

The MC146818A invokes the INT 70h Real–Time Clock ISR at each periodic interrupt and whenever an alarm occurs.

When INT 70h is invoked for an expired alarm, it invokes the INT 4Ah User Alarm ISR. The INT 4Ah vector points to a dummy IRET that a system or application program can replace. The calling program must always return to the ROM BIOS with all registers intact. The calling program must also restore the original vector when it's exiting the ISR and is no longer going to intercept INT 4Ah.

INT 1Ah Time–of–Day DSR

Introduction

The INT 1Ah Time–of–Day DSR provides access to system time and date data, and the RTC time and alarm on the MC146818A.

System and application programs invoke the INT 1Ah Time–of–Day DSR via software interrupt INT 1Ah. Individual functions are selected via the AH register. Subfunctions are selected via the AL register. The INT 1Ah vector resides at address 00:68h in the Interrupt Vector table. ROM BIOS initializes the INT 1Ah vector to address F000:FE6Eh.

The INT 1Ah Time–of–Day DSR uses the system RAM data at locations 40:6Ch and 40:70h. See Chapter 3 for a description of the BIOS data area of system RAM.

The INT 1Ah Time–of–Day DSR uses CMOS RAM data in locations 00h–0Dh and 32h. Time and alarm data are stored in locations 00h–0Dh, while the century is stored in location 32h. See Chapter 4 for a description of CMOS RAM data areas.

To access the time–keeping information or the CMOS RAM area on the RTC, a system or application program must write the index to bits 0–6 of I/O port 70h. The contents of the CMOS RAM location can then be read or written at I/O port 71h.

INT 1Ah uses I/O ports 20h–21h, 70h–71h, and A0h–A1h (the port addresses for the Programmable Interrupt Controller). See Chapter 6 for a description of I/O ports.

Error handling

All functions of the INT 1Ah Time–of–Day DSR set the Carry Flag if an invalid function is requested. The function number remains in AH. The INT 1Ah functions handle all other errors uniquely. Refer to the descriptions of each of the functions for specific information.

INT 1Ah Function 00h —
Read System Time Counter

Description

This function reads and returns the system tick count from the system RAM locations 40:6Eh (high word) and 40:6Ch (low word). The value returned is the cumulative number of Intel 8254 PIT clock ticks since midnight.

The system tick count is defined by the frequency of the INT 08h interrupt, which usually occurs 18.2 times per second. The contents of 40:70h, the Timer Overflow Flag, are returned in AL. This value will be zero if the timer has not exceeded 24 hours.

Interrupts are disabled while reading the system RAM data memory locations to prevent a timer tick update.

Execution of this function causes the Timer Overflow Flag at 40:70h to be reset to zero. No errors are returned.

Input/Output

Input: AH = 00h

Output: AH = 00h

AL = Timer overflow value, where:

= 0 Timer count is less than 24 hours since the last power–on or system reset.

= Any value greater than 0.
The timer count is more than 24 hours since the last power–on, system reset, last system–timer time counter read, or the last time the system–timer time counter was set.

CX = High word of tick count
DX = Low word of tick count

INT 1Ah Function 01h — Set System Time Counter ISA EISA

Description

This function stores the values from CX and DX to system RAM data areas 40:6Eh (high word) and 40:6Ch (low word). This sets the INT 08h timer tick count.

Execution of this function causes the Timer Overflow Flag at 40:70h to be reset to 0. No errors are returned.

Input/Output

Input: AH = 01h
         CX = High word of tick count
         DX = Low word of tick count

Output: AH = 00h

INT 1Ah Function 02h —
Read Real–Time Clock Time

ISA   EISA

Description

This function first finds out if the real–time clock device is currently updating its clock value. If so, the Carry Flag is set, the function is not performed, and control is returned to the calling program.

If an update is not in progress, the appropriate values are read from the RTC CMOS RAM and returned to the calling program in the AL, CX, and DX registers, as specified below, with the Carry Flag cleared and AH = 00h.

Input/Output

Input:	AH	=	02h
Output:	AH	=	00h
	AL	=	Hours in BCD
	CH	=	Hours in BCD
	CL	=	Minutes in BCD
	DH	=	Seconds in BCD
	DL	=	00h No daylight saving time option
			01h Daylight saving time option
	CF	=	00h Clock operating
			01h Clock not operating

INT 1Ah Function 03h — Set Real–Time Clock Time ISA EISA

Description

This function first finds out if the RTC is currently updating its clock value. If an update is in progress, the RTC is initialized, the Carry Flag is set, the function is not performed, and control is returned to the calling program.

If a timeout occurs, the RTC is initialized and the routine continues as if an update were not in progress.

The values placed by the calling program in CX and DX are stored in their respective CMOS RAM storage locations. No errors are returned.

Input/Output

Input:	AH	=	03h
	CH	=	Hours in BCD (if time is valid)
	CL	=	Minutes in BCD
	DH	=	Seconds in BCD
	DL	=	00h No daylight saving time option
			01h Daylight saving time option
Output:	AH	=	00h
	AL	=	Value written to CMOS RAM register 0Bh
	CF	=	00h Clock operating
			01h Clock not operating

INT 1Ah Function 04h —
Read Real–Time Clock Date

Description

This function first finds out if the RTC is currently updating its clock value. If it is, the Carry Flag is set, this function is not performed, and control is returned to the calling program.

If a timeout occurs, indicating an update is in progress, the Carry Flag is set, AH is cleared, and control is returned to the calling program.

If no timeout occurs, the century, year, month, and day are extracted from CMOS RAM and returned to the calling program as indicated below. Upon return, the Carry Flag is cleared and AH is set to 00h.

Input/Output

Input:	AH	=	04h
Output:	AH	=	00h
	AL	=	Century (if no timeout has occurred)
	CH	=	Century in BCD (either 19 or 20)
	CL	=	Year in BCD
	DH	=	Month in BCD
	DL	=	Day in BCD
	ZF	=	00h
	CF	=	00h Clock operating
			01h Clock not operating

INT 1Ah Function 05h — Set Real–Time Clock Date

Description

This function first finds out if the RTC is currently updating its clock value. If so, the Carry Flag is set, this function is not performed, and control is returned to the calling program.

If a timeout occurs, which indicates that an update is in progress, the RTC is initialized and the Carry Flag is set.

The values placed in CX and DX are stored in their respective CMOS RAM storage locations. The function then returns to the calling program with the Carry Flag cleared and AH set to 00h.

Input/Output

Input: AH = 05h
        CH = Century in BCD (either 19 or 20)
        CL = Year in BCD
        DH = Month in BCD
        DL = Day in BCD

Output: AH = 00h
        AL = Value written to CMOS RAM register 0Bh
        CF = 00h
        ZF = 00h

INT 1Ah Function 06h —
Set Real–Time Clock Alarm

Description

This function sets the alarm function of the RTC. It first tests if an alarm is in progress. If so, control is returned to the calling program with the Carry Flag set and AH cleared.

If an alarm is currently not enabled, the function determines if the RTC is updating its clock value. If a timeout occurs indicating an update is in progress, the RTC is initialized. The function then sets the alarm with the values from the CH, CL, and DH registers.

The alarm interrupt will take place at the hour, minute, and second specified in CH, CL, and DH registers, respectively. Only one alarm function can be in an active state at any one time. The alarm interrupt, once set, will be activated every 24 hours until reset. If the calling program wishes to pass control to itself, it must place the address of an interrupt handling routine in the vector for INT 4Ah. The address of INT 4Ah in the Interrupt Vector table is 0:128h.

The RTC clock values defined in CH, CL, and DH are stored in their respective CMOS RAM storage locations. Unlike all other INT 1Ah DSR functions, this one clears both AH and AL.

Input/Output

Input:	AH	=	06h
	CH	=	Hours in BCD
	CL	=	Minutes in BCD
	DH	=	Seconds in BCD
Output:	AH	=	00h
	AL	=	00h
	CF	=	00h No error
			01h Alarm already set

INT 1Ah Function 07h —
Reset Real–Time Clock Alarm

Description

This function stops the RTC alarm, canceling any pending alarm request stored in the date/time location in CMOS RAM.

Input/Output

Input:	AH	=	07h
Output:	AH	=	00h
	AL	=	Value written to CMOS RAM register 0Bh
	CF	=	00h No error
			01h Error

INT 08h System Timer ISR

Description

The INT 08h System Timer ISR increments the system time count for each clock tick of the Intel 8254. It reads and writes the system time count at locations 40:6Ch (low word) and 40:6Eh (high word) in the system RAM data area. When the system time count exceeds 24 hours, then INT 08h sets the Timer Overflow Flag at location 40:70h and clears the count.

Note that multiple midnight rollovers cannot be detected because the Time Overflow Flag is set, rather than incremented.

The INT 08h System Timer ISR references the system RAM data at locations 40:3Fh–40:40h, 40:6Ch, 40:6Eh, and 40:70h. See Chapter 3 for a description of the BIOS data area of system RAM. It references I/O port addresses 20h and 40h–43h. See Chapter 6 for a description of I/O ports.

Invoking the INT 08h ISR

The INT 08h System Timer ISR is invoked via hardware IRQ 0. The INT 08h vector resides at address 00:20h in the Interrupt Vector table. ROM BIOS initializes the vector to F000:FEA5h.

Execution of INT 08h decrements the diskette drive motor count at system RAM location 40:40h. When this count reaches zero, the diskette drive motors are turned off.

Once it has serviced the clock, INT 08h issues an INT 1Ch Timer Tick ISR. This routine allows system and application programs to redirect INT 1Ch to their own routines. If not redirected, INT 1Ch returns immediately to the calling program with all registers preserved.

Description

The INT 70h Real–Time Clock ISR maintains any time delays set by INT 15h Functions 83h Set Event Wait and Function 86h Reset Wait. It decrements the specified delay count every 1/1024 second.

INT 70h is also called when the RTC alarm expires. It invokes the INT 4Ah User Alarm ISR that permits a system or application program to redirect the INT 4Ah vector to an alarm processing routine. The calling program is responsible for saving and restoring all registers and the original vector on return to the ROM BIOS. The return should be made through an IRET.

Invoking INT 70h

The INT 70h Real–Time Clock ISR is invoked via IRQ 8. The INT 70h vector resides at address 0000:1C0h in the Interrupt Vector table.

The INT 70h Real–Time Clock ISR references flag and counter information in system RAM. See Chapter 3 for a description of the BIOS data area of system RAM. It references CMOS RAM data at locations 0Bh, 0Ch, and 0Dh. See Chapter 4 for a description of CMOS RAM data areas. It references I/O port addresses 20h, 70h–71h, and A0h. See Chapter 6 for a description of I/O ports.

INT 1Ch Timer Tick ISR   ISA EISA

Once the INT 08h System Timer ISR has serviced the clock, it invokes the INT 1Ch Timer Tick ISR. This ISR points to the INT 4Ah vector that system and application programs may redirect to a routine for execution on every system clock tick.

The ROM BIOS takes no action unless the INT 1Ch vector is modified by a calling program. Programs should return control to the ROM BIOS through an IRET. They are also responsible for saving and restoring all registers and the original vector before returning to DOS. If not redirected, INT 1Ch returns immediately to the calling program with all registers preserved.

INT 4Ah Alarm ISR   ISA EISA

When the RTC alarm function is activated, the RTC will generate an interrupt request at the time that was specified when INT 1Ah Real–Time Clock Alarm Function AH = 06h was last invoked. When the alarm time occurs, INT 4Ah is invoked.

The calling program must redirect the INT 4Ah vector to an alarm processing routine before invoking INT 1Ah to set the alarm. It must also cancel the alarm and restore the 1Ah vector to its original value before returning to DOS.

Chapter 17
Single–Function Services

Overview

Description

The ROM BIOS contains services that perform only one function:

- The INT 05h Print Screen DSR allows printing the contents of the monitor's screen to the printer.
- The INT 11h Equipment Check DSR provides information about the equipment installed in the system.
- The INT 12h Memory Size DSR indicates the amount of base memory in the system.
- The INT 18h Process Boot Failure DSR displays an error message if the system boot process fails.
- The INT 19h Bootstrap Loader DSR loads the operating system (DOS) from the boot device.

INT 05h Print Screen DSR

Description

The INT 05h Print Screen DSR performs the following functions:

- Prints the contents of the entire current video screen to printer 0, the default printer
- Moves the cursor across the screen as the lines on the screen are printed
- Repositions the cursor position to its original position
- Returns all registers to their original values

INT 05h is usually invoked by the keyboard interrupt handler (INT 09h) when the Print Screen key is pressed. See Chapter 10 for a description of keyboard functions.

The INT 05h vector resides at Interrupt Vector table address 00:14h. The BIOS initializes this vector to address F000:FF54h. The INT 05h DSR uses two system RAM data definitions. The definitions are located in the BIOS data area at locations 40:84h and 40:100h. See Chapter 3 for a description of the BIOS data area in system RAM.

Interrupts are enabled while the INT 05h routine is executing.

Input/Output

Input: None

Output: None (registers are preserved)

continued

Error handling

The INT 05h Print Screen DSR recognizes four error conditions:

- Printing error
- Printer is busy
- Printer is out of paper
- Recursive print screen request

The DSR responds to these errors as follows:

- Sets location 40:100h to FFh
- Restores the contents of all registers
- Returns to the calling program

Except for recursive print–screen request errors, the DSR also returns the cursor to its original position.

INT 11h Equipment Check DSR

Description

The INT 11h Equipment Check DSR returns the contents of system RAM location 40:10h in the AX register. This location contains the system equipment list as determined by the BIOS POST routine.

The INT 11h vector resides at Interrupt Vector table address 0:44h. The BIOS initializes this vector to address F000:F84Dh.

Input/Output

Input: None

Output: AX = Contents of 40:10h, where:

Bits 15–14	= Number of printer adapters
Bits 13–12	= Reserved
Bits 11–9	= Number of RS232–C asynchronous adapters
Bit 8	= Reserved
Bits 7–6	= Number of diskette drives, (if Bit 0 = 1), where:
	00 1 diskette drive
	01 2 diskette drives
Bit 5–4	= Initial video mode, where:
	00 EGA or VGA
	01 40x25 color
	10 80x25 color
	11 80x25 black and white
Bit 3	= Reserved
Bit 2	= 1 PS/2–type pointing device installed
Bit 1	= 1 External math coprocessor installed
Bit 0	= 1 Diskette available for boot

INT 12h Memory Size DSR

Description

The INT 12h Memory Size DSR returns the contents of system RAM location 40:13h in the AX register. This location contains the amount of available base memory in kilobytes as it is determined by the BIOS POST routine. POST determines the amount of available base memory by subtracting any memory reserved for the extended BIOS data area from the total installed base memory.

The INT 12h vector resides at the Interrupt Vector table address 0:48h. The BIOS initializes the INT 12h DSR vector to address F000:F841h.

Input/Output

Input: None

Output: AX   =   Contents of 40:13h (available base memory in kilobytes)

INT 18h Process Boot Failure DSR

Description

In the original IBM PC, INT 18h was used to load the BASIC interpreter from ROM. In PC–compatible systems made by other manufacturers, BASIC is disk–based. These systems use INT 18h along with INT 19h in the boot process. INT 18h generates a message such as "No boot device available – press F1 to retry boot" if the system does not boot properly from diskette or fixed disk.

INT 19h Bootstrap Loader DSR

Description

The INT 19h Bootstrap Loader DSR attempts to load the 512–byte boot sector code for DOS from either diskette or fixed disk to address 0:7C00h. It then attempts to transfer control to that code segment. The boot code is located in the first sector of the diskette (track 0, head 0, sector 1) or in the first sector of the fixed disk (cylinder 0, head 0, sector 1).

The INT 19h vector resides at Interrupt Vector table address 0:64h. The BIOS initializes this vector to address F000:E6F2h.

Bootstrap processing

Once INT 19h has been invoked, the INT 19h Bootstrap Loader DSR executes as described below:

Stage	Description
1. Locates and loads boot code.	The boot code is located in the first sector of the diskette (track 0, head 0, sector 1) or in the first sector of the fixed disk (cylinder 0, head 0, sector 1). The Bootstrap Loader attempts to locate the boot sector and load it into memory at address 0:7C00h.
2. Checks for power–on password if support is included in the BIOS.	On those systems that *have* password protection, the INT 19h Bootstrap Loader DSR tests for the presence of a system power–on password before it attempts to transfer control to the boot code. Application programs enable or disable the power–on password via the system's password control program. Power–on passwords are not supported in most AT compatibles.
3. Gets power–on password from application program if it is enabled.	If there is password support and the power–on password is enabled, INT 19h allows the application program three opportunities to enter the password correctly. After three attempts, the system halts and must be turned off, then turned on again before INT 19h may be invoked again. The INT 19h Bootstrap Loader DSR recalculates the CRC if the power–on password has been changed. This step is ignored in most systems.
4. Processes boot code, if found.	The INT 19h Bootstrap Loader DSR transfers control to the boot code if it has been located.
5. If no boot code found, invokes INT 18h.	If INT 19h does not find the boot sector code, it invokes INT 18h. By default, INT 18h displays the message "No boot device available, press F1 to retry boot." (See INT 18h DSR handler.)

continued

INT 18h Process Boot Failure DSR

If no boot sector is found either on the diskette in drive A: or on the fixed disk, the INT 19h Bootstrap Loader DSR invokes software interrupt INT 18h. INT 18h can be vectored to a "no boot device" routine that takes over the boot process. For example, INT 18h can be vectored to a routine that would allow the system to be booted over a network.

In IBM PCs, INT 18h loads the ROM–based BASIC interpreter.

Input/Output

Input:	None
Output:	None (DL = boot drive 0 or 80)

Appendix A
ISA/EISA Error Codes and Messages

Introduction

The tables on the following pages present error and informational messages, their possible causes and proposed corrective actions. These messages include the following:

- IBM BIOS POST and Boot Messages
- PhoenixBIOS POST messages for ISA and EISA platforms
  - Error
  - Informational
  - Beep Codes
- PhoenixBIOS Run–Time Messages

IBM BIOS POST and Boot Messages

Error Number	Message	Possible Cause
101	System Board Error	System interrupt failed.
102	System Board Error	System timer failed.
103	System Board Error	System timer interrupt failed.
104	System Board Error	Protected mode operation failed.
105	System Board Error	Keyboard communication failure.
106	System Board Error	POST logic test problem.
107	System Board Error	NMI test failed.
108	System Board Error	Failed system timer test.
109	System Board Error	Problem with first 64K of RAM.
161	System Options Not Set (Run SETUP)	Possible bad battery.
162	System Options Not Set (Run SETUP)	Invalid checksum.
163	Time & Date Not Set (Run SETUP)	RTC failed.
164	Memory Size Error – (Run SETUP)	CMOS RAM checksum error.
201	Memory Error	RAM failed test.
202	Memory Address Error	RAM failed test.
203	Memory Address Error	RAM failed test.
301	Keyboard Error	Keyboard not connected.
302	System Unit Keylock Is Locked Unlock System Unit Keylock	Unlock the keyboard.
303	Keyboard Or System Unit Error	Keyboard chord or keyboard itself is bad.
304	Keyboard Or System Unit Error	Keyboard chord or keyboard itself is bad.
401	CRT Error	Monochrome monitor or video adapter bad.
501	CRT Error	Color monitor or video adapter bad.
601	Diskette Error	Diskette drive or controller bad.
602	Diskette Boot Record Error	No boot sector on diskette.
1780	Disk 0 Failure	Primary fixed disk failed.
1781	Disk 1 Failure	Secondary fixed disk failed.

continued

IBM BIOS POST and Boot Messages, Continued

Error Number	Message	Possible Cause
1782	Disk Controller Failure	Fixed disk controller failed.
1790	Disk 0 Error	Error on fixed disk number 0.
1791	Disk 1 Error	Error on fixed disk number 1.
	ROM Error	Error reading ROM BIOS code.

PhoenixBIOS ISA/EISA POST Messages

Within POST, there are three kinds of messages:

- Error messages: These messages appear when there is a failure in hardware, software, or firmware.
- Informational messages: These messages provide information to the user but require no action.
- Beep codes: This kind of warning sounds when POST errors occur and the screen is not available.

The following sections list each type of message.

continued

Error messages

Message	Possible Cause	Action
Diskette drive failure	The 0 or 1 drive failed or is missing.	Check the drive to determine the problem.
Diskette drive *x* failure where *x*=0 or *x*=1	The designated drive has either failed or is missing.	Check the designated drive to determine the problem.
Diskette read failure — press F1 to retry boot (or may also say, press F1 to retry boot, F2 for SETUP utility)	The diskette is either not formatted or is defective.	Replace the diskette with a bootable diskette and retry.
Display adapter failed; using alternate	The color/monochrome switch is set incorrectly. The primary video adapter failed.	Change the switch to the correct setting. Check the primary video adapter.
Gate A20 failure	The keyboard controller is not accepting commands, specifically, the enable and disable A20 commands.	Check the keyboard controller and the system board. Turn the power off, then back on again. If the problem persists, contact qualified service personnel.
Fixed disk configuration error	The specified configuration is not supported or doesn't match the actual hardware installed.	Correct the fixed disk configuration.
Fixed disk controller failure	The controller card has failed.	Replace the controller card.
Fixed disk failure	The fixed disk may be defective.	Try rebooting. If that doesn't work, replace the fixed disk.
Fixed disk read failure — press F1 to retry boot (or may also say press F1 to retry boot, F2 for SETUP utility)	The fixed disk may be configured incorrectly or is defective.	Check the drive type selected in SETUP. Try rebooting. If that doesn't work, replace the fixed disk.
Internal cache test failed — cache is disabled	Faulty cache memory in the 80486 processor chip.	Check the processor and the system board. Turn the power off, then back on again. If the problem persists, contact qualified service personnel.
Pointer device failure	The mouse failed.	Try rebooting. If problem persists, check the mouse, its cable and connector. (Only for PS/2–style mouse.)

continued

Error messages, cont'd

Message	Possible Cause	Action
No boot device available — press F1 to retry boot (or may also say, press F1 to retry boot, F2 for SETUP utility)	Either diskette drive A:, the fixed disk, or both the diskette and disk are defective.	Try rebooting. If problem persists, replace the diskette or the fixed disk.
No boot sector on fixed disk — press F1 to retry boot (or may also say, press F1 to retry boot, F2 for SETUP utility)	The C: drive is not formatted or is not bootable.	Format the C: drive and make it bootable.
Not a boot diskette — press F1 to retry boot (or may also say, press F1 to retry boot, F2 for SETUP utility)	The diskette in drive A: is not formatted as a bootable diskette.	Replace the diskette with a bootable diskette and try rebooting.
No timer tick interrupt	The timer chip has failed.	Check the system board. Turn the power off, then back on again. If the problem persists, contact qualified service personnel.
xxxxh Option ROM checksum failure where xxxxh is the starting address of the option ROM	The peripheral card contains a defective ROM.	Try rebooting. If the problem persists, replace the peripheral card.
Shutdown failure	Either the keyboard controller is not accepting the reset command or the associated reset logic has failed.	Check the keyboard controller and the system board. Turn the power off, then back on again. If the problem persists, contact qualified service personnel.
Time of day not set — run SETUP program	Clock not set.	Run SETUP utility.
Timer 2 failure	The timer chip has failed.	Check the system board. Turn the power off, then back on again. If the problem persists, contact qualified service personnel.
F2 to enter ROM–based SETUP	Invalid configuration information must be changed.	You must run SETUP utility and correct configuration information.

continued

Error messages, cont'd

Message	Possible Cause	Action
Invalid configuration information — please run SETUP	Display adapter is configured incorrectly. Memory size is incorrect. Wrong number of diskette drives. Other configuration errors.	Run the SETUP utility.
Keyboard clock line failure	The keyboard, the keyboard cable connection, or the keyboard controller is defective.	Make sure the keyboard cable and keyboard are connected properly. Check the keyboard controller and the system board. Turn the power off, then back on again. If the problem persists, contact qualified service personnel.
Keyboard data line failure	The keyboard controller firmware has failed.	Check the keyboard controller and the system board. Turn the power off, then back on again. If the problem persists, contact qualified service personnel.
Keyboard controller failure	The keyboard controller firmware has failed.	Check the keyboard controller and the system board. Turn the power off, then back on again. If the problem persists, contact qualified service personnel.
Keyboard stuck key failure	A key is jammed.	Locate the jammed key and fix it. Make sure the keyboard cable and keyboard are connected properly. Turn the power off, then back on again. If the problem persists, contact qualified service personnel.
Memory failure at *hex–value*, read *hex–value*, expecting *hex–value*	Circuitry associated with the memory chips has failed.	Turn the power off, then back on again. If the problem persists, contact qualified service personnel.
Unexpected interrupt in protected mode	Hardware interrupt or NMI occurred while in protected mode.	Check the timer chip or the interrupt controller on the system board.

continued

Error messages, cont'd

Message	Possible Cause	Action
Real time clock failure	The RTC or battery failed.	Run SETUP and turn the power off and on. If the problem persists, replace the battery. If the problem remains, contact qualified service personnel.
Keyboard is locked — unlock	Locked keyboard.	Unlock the keyboard.
EISA–Specific Messages		
No fail safe timer NMI	The EISA fail–safe timer is not operating correctly.	Check the system board. Turn the power off, then back on again. If the problem persists, contact qualified service personnel.
No Software Port NMI	Generating an NMI through the EISA software NMI port is not functioning.	Check the system board. Turn the power off, then back on again. If the problem persists, contact qualified service personnel.
Invalid configuration information. Please run the Configuration Utility.	System configuration stored in ISA CMOS RAM is invalid.	Run the configuration utility.
Invalid EISA configuration storage. Please run the Configuration Utility.	System configuration stored in EISA CMOS RAM is invalid.	Run the configuration utility.
Configuration error for slot *n*	There is an EISA expansion card that has not been configured by the configuration utility.	Run the configuration utility.
ID information mismatch for slot *n*	There is an EISA expansion card that has a different ID than the one it is configured for by the configuration utility.	Run the configuration utility.

continued

Informational messages

Message	Meaning
*nnn*K Base Memory	The amount of base memory that tested successfully.
*nnn*K Extended	The amount of extended memory that tested successfully.
Memory tests terminated by keystroke	This message indicates that a user pressed the spacebar while the memory tests were running and stopped the memory tests.
Press the F1 key to continue	This message indicates that an error was found during POST. Pressing the F1 key allows the system to attempt to boot.
Beginning memory test Press the SPACEBAR to terminate the memory test	A user can stop the memory tests by pressing the spacebar.
Press the F1 key to continue, F2 to run the Setup utility	This message indicates that an error was found during POST. Pressing the F1 key allows the system to attempt to boot. Pressing F2 allows users to run the ROM–based Phoenix SETUP utility to correct configuration information.

Beep codes

Beep codes are used to identify a POST error that occurs when the screen is not available. Once the screen is operating, diagnostic messages are reported to the screen. There are beep codes for both fatal and nonfatal system board errors.

Note: No beep code is sounded if a test is aborted while in progress. However, diagnostic cards can be installed that display the contents of the diagnostic port, 80h, to identify the area of failure.

continued

Explanation of test terms for beep code table

The following terms are used in the Test Performed column of the beep code table.

Pattern test — One or more particular patterns are written to a location then read back from the same location. Examples of patterns used are 55h and AAh. If the value read does not match the value written, the test is considered a failure.

Rolling ones test — Several patterns are constructed. These patterns represent a one rolling through the given location. For example, to roll a one through three bits, the following patterns would be constructed: 001, 010, 011, 100, 101, 110, and 111. The patterns are written to the location and then read back, one by one. If the value read does not match the value written, the test is considered a failure.

Rolling zeros test — Several patterns are constructed. These patterns represent a zero rolling through the given location. For example, to roll a zero through three bits, the following patterns would be constructed: 011, 001, and 000. The patterns are written to the location and then read back, one by one. If the value read does not match the value written, the test is considered a failure.

Checksum test — All of the values in a given range of locations are added together. The range includes a location which, when added to sum of the ranges, will produce a known result, such as zero (0).

Beep codes for system board errors

Beep Code	Diagnostic Code	Description	Test Performed
none	01h	CPU register test in progress or failure.	Pattern test of most of the 16-bit CPU registers. Failure will result in a system halt.
1–1–3	02h	CMOS write/read test in progress or failure.	Rolling ones test in the shutdown byte (offset 0Eh) of the CMOS RAM. Failure will result in a system halt.
1–1–4	03h	ROM BIOS checksum test in progress or failure.	The range of ROM that includes the BIOS is checksummed. Failure will result in a system halt.

continued

Beep codes for system board errors, cont'd

Beep Code	Diagnostic Code	Description	Test Performed
1–2–1	04h	Programmable interval timer 0 test in progress or failure.	Over a period of time, the current count values in timer 0 are read and accumulated by ORing them into the values read so far. It is expected that during the time period, all bits will be set. Failure will result in a system halt.
1–2–2	05h	DMA channel 0 address and count register test in progress or failure.	Rolling ones and rolling zeros test of the address and count registers of DMA channel 0. Failure will result in a system halt.
1–2–3	06h	DMA page register write/read test in progress or failure.	Pattern test of DMA page registers. Failure will result in a system halt.
1–3–1	08h	RAM refresh verification test in progress or failure.	Over a period of time, the refresh bit (bit 4) in port 60h is read and tested. The refresh bit should toggle from 0 to 1, then 1 to 0 within the time period. Failure will result in a system halt.
none	09h	First 64K RAM test in progress.	No specific test is performed — just indicates that the test is beginning (i.e., no failure).
1–3–3	0Ah	First 64K RAM chip or data line failure, multi–bit.	The first 64K of RAM is tested with a rolling ones test and a pattern test. If any of the pattern tests fail, then the BIOS reports that multiple data bits failed (see specific bit tests following). Failure results in a system halt.
1–4–2	0Dh	Parity failure first 64K RAM.	At the completion of the rolling ones and pattern tests of the first 64K, the BIOS checks the parity error bits (bits 7 and 6) of port 60h. Failure results in a system halt.
1–4–3	0Eh	Fail–safe timer failure (only used by EISA BIOS).	The EISA fail–safe timer is enabled with a time–out value. An NMI should occur within the time period. If an NMI does not occur, an error message will be displayed and POST will continue.

continued

Beep codes for system board errors, cont'd

Beep Code	Diagnostic Code	Description	Test Performed
1–4–4	0Fh	Software NMI port failure (only used by EISA BIOS).	The EISA software NMI is enabled and an NMI is forced. An NMI should occur within a specified time period. If the NMI does not occur, an error message will be displayed and POST will continue.
2–1–1 2–1–2 2–1–3 2–1–4 2–2–1 2–2–2 2–2–3 2–2–4 2–3–1 2–3–2 2–3–3 2–3–4 2–4–1 2–4–2 2–4–3 2–4–4	10h–1Fh	First 64K RAM chip or data line failure on bit x (see test description).	The first 64K of RAM is tested with a rolling ones test and a pattern test. If any of the rolling ones tests fail, then the BIOS reports the specific bit that failed. To determine the bit number from the diagnostic code, subtract 10h. For example, if 15h is displayed at the diagnostic port, bit 5 failed. Failure results in a system halt.
3–3–1	20h	Slave DMA register test in progress or failure.	Pattern test of channels 1 through 3 of the slave controller (starting port address = 2). Failure results in a system halt.
3–1–2	21h	Master DMA register test in progress or failure.	Pattern test of channels 1 through 3 of the master DMA controller (starting port address = C4h). Failure results in a system halt.
3–1–3	22h	Master interrupt mask register test in progress or failure.	Rolling ones and zeros tests of the mask register of the master programmable interrupt controller (port 21h). Failure results in a system halt.
3–1–4	23h	Slave interrupt mask register test in progress or failure.	Rolling ones and zeros tests of the mask register of the slave programmable interrupt controller (port A1h). Failure results in a system halt.
none	25h	Interrupt vector loading in progress.	No specific test is performed — just indicates that the Interrupt Vector table is being initialized (i.e., no failure).

continued

Beep codes for system board errors, cont'd

Beep Code	Diagnostic Code	Description	Test Performed
3–2–4	27h	Keyboard controller test in progress or failure.	The self–test command (AAh) is issued to the 8042 (keyboard controller) and the results are monitored. Failure results in a system halt.
none	28h	CMOS RAM power failure and checksum calculation test in progress.	The power–fail bit in CMOS RAM is tested and the lower CMOS RAM area is being checksummed. A failure does not result in a system halt.
none	29h	CMOS RAM configuration validation for video in progress.	No specific test is performed — just indicates that the configuration specified in CMOS for video is being matched against the actual installation. A failure does not result in a system halt.
3–3–4	2Bh	Screen memory test in progress or failure.	The video buffers (B0000h and B8000h) are tested with a pattern test and a rolling ones test. Failure will result in a beep code but not a system halt.
3–4–1	2Ch	Screen initialization in progress.	Until the video installation is confirmed, any calls to INT 10h Function 0 (set mode) will be prefaced with this diagnostic code. There is no expected failure from this.
3–4–2	2Dh	Screen retrace test in progress or failure.	Over a period of time, the retrace bit (bit 0) in the appropriate CRT controller status register (either port 3BAh or 3DAh) is read and tested. The retrace bit should toggle from 0 to 1, then 1 to 0 within the time period.
none	2Eh	Search for video ROM in progress.	No specific test is performed by the system BIOS — just indicates that the BIOS is about to jump to the initialization code in the video option ROM.
none	30h	Screen running with video ROM.	No specific test is performed — just indicates that a video option ROM was found and is believed to be operating.
none	31h	Monochrome monitor operable.	No specific test is performed — just indicates that the BIOS believes a monochrome monitor is installed and is operating.

continued

Beep codes for system board errors, cont'd

Beep Code	Diagnostic Code	Description	Test Performed
none	32h	Color monitor (40–column) operable.	No specific test is performed — just indicates that the BIOS believes a color monitor is installed and is operating. The mode has been set to 40–column as selected by the user in CMOS RAM.
none	33h	Color monitor (80–column) operable.	No specific test is performed — just indicates that the BIOS believes a color monitor is installed and is operating. The mode has been set to 80–column as selected by the user in CMOS RAM.
4–2–1	34h	Timer–tick interrupt test in progress or failure.	All interrupts except the timer–tick interrupt are masked off at the interrupt controllers. If a timer–tick interrupt does not occur during a specific timer period, an error message is displayed on the screen. The system does not halt.
4–2–2	35h	Shutdown test in progress or failure.	A return address is stored in 40:67h and the processor is reset via the keyboard controller. If a timer tick occurs during this time period, an error message is displayed on the screen. Other failures are hard to detect. If possible, the BIOS will continue with POST, skipping the memory tests.
4–2–3	36h	Gate A20 failure.	To test extended memory, the processor must be placed in protected mode and the A20 line must be enabled. For the memory tests, the BIOS generally uses the keyboard controller to enable A20. If the A20 line is not properly set during the memory tests, an error message is displayed on the screen and the memory tests are suspended. The system does not halt.

continued

Beep codes for system board errors, cont'd

Beep Code	Diagnostic Code	Description	Test Performed
4–2–4	37h	Unexpected interrupt in protected mode.	During the memory tests, the processor is placed in protected mode. All interrupts in the interrupt descriptor table are initialized to point to a special handler that displays a message on the screen. All hardware interrupts are masked off and interrupts are disabled. The system does not half when an unexpected interrupt occurs.
4–3–1	38h	RAM test of memory above 64K in progress or failure.	The memory above the first 64K is tested with a rolling ones test and a pattern test. All success and failure messages are displayed on the screen and POST will continue.
4–3–2	3Ah	Programmable interval timer channel 2 test in progress or failure.	Over a period of time, the current count values in timer 2 are read and accumulated by ORing them into the values read so far. It is expected that during the time period, all bits will be set. If an error is detected, an error message will be displayed on the screen and POST will continue.
4–3–4	3Bh	Real–time clock text in progress or failure.	Over a period of time, the Update–In–Progress bit of Status register A of the real–time clock is read and tested. The bit should toggle from 0 to 1 within the time period.
4–4–1	3Ch	Serial port test in progress or failure.	Pattern test of one or more of the installed serial ports. If a failure is detected, an error message will be displayed and POST will continue.
4–4–2	3Dh	Parallel port test in progress or failure.	Rolling ones test is done to one or more of the installed parallel ports. If a failure is detected, an error message will be displayed and POST will continue.
4–4–3	3Eh	Math coprocessor test in progress or failure.	An integer load and store is performed with the math coprocessor. If the values do not match, an error message will be displayed and POST will continue.

PhoenixBIOS Run–Time Messages

Run–time error messages

Run–time error messages are displayed if an error occurs after the boot procedure has successfully completed.

Message	Cause	Action
I/O card parity interrupt at *address*. Type (S)hut off NMI, (R)eboot, other keys to continue	Memory on a peripheral card has failed.	Check the memory cards installed in the system.
Memory parity interrupt at *address*. Type (S)hut off NMI, (R)eboot, other keys to continue	A memory chip(s) has failed.	Check the memory on the system board.
Unexpected HW interrupt *interrupt* at *address*. Type (R)eboot, other keys to continue	Hardware problem. Not displayed if the extended interrupt handler is not enabled.	Check all the hardware in the system.
Unexpected SW interrupt *interrupt* at *address*. Type (R)eboot, other keys to continue	Error(s) in the software program. Not displayed if the extended interrupt handler is not enabled.	Turn the machine off and then on again. If that doesn't work, check the program.
Unexpected type 02 interrupt at *xxxxx*h. Type (S)hut off NMI, (R)eboot, other keys to continue	A parity error occurred, but the source cannot be determined.	Turn the power off and on.
EISA–Specific Messages		
Unresolved memory parity error. Type (S)hut off NMI, (R)eboot, other keys to continue	There is a memory parity error caused by system memory.	Check the system board.
Fail safe timer NMI. Type (S)hut off NMI, (R)eboot, other keys to continue	Applications software package failed.	Check the program being run.
Software NMI. Type (S)hut off NMI, (R)eboot, other keys to continue	A systems software routine has generated an NMI to halt processing.	Check all programs operating in the system.
Bus Timeout NMI, Slot *n*. Type (S)hut off NMI, (R)eboot, other keys to continue	EISA bus master has caused a bus time-out NMI. The bus–master slot is designated by *n* (1–15).	Check the bus–master card.
Unresolved Bus Timeout NMI. Type (S)hut off NMI, (R)eboot, other keys to continue	Bus timeout is generated but its source is not identified.	Check all hardware in the system.

continued

Run–time error messages, cont'd

Message	Cause	Action
I/O Expansion Board NMI. Slot *n*. Type (S)hut off NMI, (R)eboot, other keys to continue	Appears if an EISA expansion board has caused an NMI. The expansion board slot is designated by *n* (1–15).	Check the expansion board.
Expansion Board was disabled. Type (S)hut off NMI, (R)eboot, other keys to continue	The NMI handler disabled an EISA expansion board, which generated an NMI error.	Check all expansion boards in the system.

Appendix B
XT BIOS Error Messages

Introduction

The tables on the following pages present error and informational messages, their possible causes and proposed corrective actions. These messages include the following:

- IBM XT BIOS POST Messages
- Phoenix XT BIOS POST Messages
  - System failure
  - Boot failure
  - Informational
  - Beep Code
- Phoenix XT BIOS Run–Time Messages

Each of these types of messages are discussed on the following pages.

IBM XT BIOS POST Messages

The following messages may be generated by the IBM XT BIOS POST routine:

Message	Possible Cause
101	System board error
201	Memory error
ROM	Error reading ROM code
1801	Expansion I/O box error
Parity Check 1	NMI parity error found in I/O adapter card
Parity Check 2	NMI parity error found in memory
?????	Unknown NMI error

Phoenix XT BIOS POST and Boot Messages

Phoenix XT BIOS POST error messages

POST and boot messages are displayed during the power–on process. Within POST, there are three kinds of messages:

- System failure messages: These messages appear when there is a failure in hardware, software, or firmware.
- Boot failure messages: These messages appear when there is a failure in the boot process.
- Informational messages: These messages provide information to a user but require no action.

The following tables list these messages and describe their possible causes and suggested corrective actions. Note that some messages may be shortened in very small versions of the XT BIOS.

System failure messages

Message	Possible Cause	Action
Bad DMS port = *hex value*	Bad system board.	Test the system board.
Disk bad	Diskette failure.	Try another diskette. If the problem persists, the drive or the controller may need replacing.
Expansion Box Bad	Adapter cards may be malfunctioning.	Test adapter cards and all plugs. Replace if necessary.
No scan code from keyboard	Keyboard may be discon-nected or malfunctioning.	Check keyboard plug and key-board. Replace if necessary.
Memory parity NMI	Memory card failed.	Replace the card.
ROM bad checksum = *hex value*	Read failed on ROM access.	Retry. If error persists, replace ROM.
Hex–value = Scancode, check keyboard	An erroneous scan code was received from the keyboard.	Key may be stuck on key-board. Keyboard connector may be bad, or keyboard controller must be replaced.
Bad RAM at *<address>* = *<xxxx>* expected = *<xxxx>*	Circuitry associated with the memory chips has failed.	Turn the power off and on. If the problem persists, contact qualified service personnel.
ROM Bad *<address>* Optional	An option ROM on a card may be defective.	Try rebooting. If the problem persists, replace the card.

continued

System failure messages, cont'd

Message	Possible Cause	Action
Stuck key scancode = *hex–value*	Key stuck on keyboard.	Loosen stuck key. Check scan code table to identify key.
Timer or Interrupt Controller Bad	Interrupt controller or timer chip inoperative.	Replace system board.
Timer chip counter 2 failed	Timer bad.	Replace system board or timer chip.

Boot failure messages

Message	Possible Cause	Action
<128 not OK, parity disabled	First 128K of RAM failed parity test.	Reboot. If message repeats, replace bad RAM chip(s).
Error. Press F1 key to continue.	A recoverable error occurred.	Press F1 to continue (there may be errors), or reboot.
Boot disk failure. Type key to retry	The disk may not be bootable.	Retry the disk. If the problem persists, try another system diskette.

Informational messages

The following messages are for information only. No action is required.

Message	Meaning
RAM test	Appears while POST is performing the RAM tests.
Hard disk wait complete	The message appears in two parts. "Hard disk wait" displays while the fixed disk is spinning to come up. "Hard disk wait complete" displays when the fixed disk is initialized and ready.
Memory space preserved	Appears in some systems after a warm reboot indicating that the values in RAM have been preserved.

Beep Code

If a power–on self test message occurs before the video monitor testing is completed, there is no way for the BIOS to write an error message to the screen. Therefore, the BIOS will sound one long beep and then one short beep to indicate a POST error, and will stop all testing at the point of the error.

Phoenix XT BIOS Run–Time Messages

Run–time message table

Run–time messages generated by a Phoenix BIOS are displayed if an error occurs after the boot procedure is complete.

Message	Cause	Action
8087 Non–Maskable Interrupt at *<address>* Type (S)hut off NMI, (R)eboot, other keys to continue	An NMI occurred on access to the math coprocessor.	Type (S)hut off NMI.
Memory Parity Non–Maskable Interrupt at *<address>* Type (S)hut off NMI, (R)eboot, other keys to continue	A memory chip(s) has failed.	Type (S)hut off NMI. This will only temporarily allow you to continue. You must replace the memory chip(s).
Unexpected HW interrupt *interrupt* at*<address>* Type (R)eboot, other keys to continue	This could be any hardware–related problem. Not displayed if the extended interrupt handler is not enabled.	Check the hardware devices for loose cables, malfunctions, and other problems.
Unexpected SW interrupt *interrupt* at *<address>* Type (R)eboot, other keys to continue	There is an error(s) in the software program. Not displayed if the extended interrupt handler is not enabled.	Turn the machine off and on. If the message displays again, check the program.
I/O Card Non–Maskable Interrupt at *<address>* Type (S)hut off NMI, (R)eboot, other keys to continue	An NMI occurred on access to an adapter card.	Turn the machine off and on. If that doesn't work, replace the adapter card.

Glossary

Access Time

The amount of time necessary to read data from or write data to a storage medium. For DRAMs, the amount of time necessary to transfer a bit between a memory cell and the bus. See *Cycle Time*.

ACK

Acknowledge. A serial–interface control signal indicating receipt of data or a command.

ALE

Address Latch Enable. A control signal from the CPU to latch the address that has been asserted onto the bus into an address latch.

ANSI

American National Standards Institute.

ASCII

American Standard Code for Information Interchange.

ASIC

Application–Specific Integrated Circuit.

continued

AT

The IBM PC/AT — an 80286–based successor to the 8088–based PC/XT micro-computer, introduced in 1984.

Base Memory

The lower 640K of DOS memory — the address range 00000h–9FFFFh. Also called Conventional Memory.

BCD

Binary–Coded Decimal.

BIOS

Basic Input/Output System.

bps

Bits per second.

Burst Mode

A synchronous data–transfer method that sends large blocks of data in an uninter-rupted burst, rather than a continual stream of smaller blocks.

Bus Latency

The time delay between a request for bus control by a bus master and the granting of control.

Bus Master

A peripheral device that uses ISA control signals (an ISA Bus Master) or EISA control signals (an EISA Bus Master) to perform bus operations independent of the host CPU.

Bus Slave

A peripheral device that uses ISA control signals (an ISA Bus Slave) or EISA control signals (an EISA Bus Slave) to interface with the bus.

Cache Memory

A small high–speed memory for temporary data storage, usually used between main memory and the CPU. In PCs, cache memory is most often an SRAM device that contains an associated "tag" memory for fast data searching.

continued

CAS

Column Address Strobe. The portion of the RAM chip–select signal that clocks the column address into an internal address latch. CAS also acts as a memory cell's output enable: when CAS is asserted, the three–state driver on the data–out pin is enabled. See *RAS*.

CGA

Color Graphics Adapter. A low–resolution text–and–graphics display device.

Checksum

A byte–oriented error–checking method used to compare a range of data. The sums of each of two data blocks is computed, ignoring any carry. The two sums are then compared; any discrepancy indicates an error. See *CRC*.

Chip Set

A small group of integrated circuits that contains the functions of many of the discrete devices in the XT, ISA, or EISA specification.

CMOS

Complimentary Metallic Oxide Semiconductor. A fabrication method for producing integrated circuits, or an integrated circuit fabricated from CMOS. Circuits in CMOS devices are smaller and consume less power than comparable circuits fabricated by other methods.

CMOS RAM

The small (usually 64–256 bytes) battery–backed memory area in ISA and EISA systems associated with the real–time clock. This non–volatile memory area is used to store the system time and date, and configuration data.

Conventional Memory

See *Base Memory*.

Coprocessor

An auxiliary processor that executes instructions in parallel with the CPU. Math coprocessors in the Intel 80x87 family perform floating–point arithmetic instructions. The 8087 and 80287 conform to IEEE standard *P754 Floating Point Arithmetic for Microprocessors* (1981); the 80387 conforms to IEEE standard 754–195, *IEEE Standard for Binary Floating–Point Arithmetic* (1985).

continued

Cycle Stealing

The method used by a DMA controller of using the bus while the CPU is performing tasks that leave the bus idle.

Cycle Time

For DRAMs, the amount of time necessary to read from or write to a memory cell. Data is read from or written to a DRAM cell in two stages: a precharge stage and an access stage. During the precharge stage, the memory cell's capacitor recovers from any previous access and then stabilizes its charge. During the access stage, the bit is transferred between the cell and the bus. DRAM cycle time is the sum of the precharge time and the access time.

CRC

Cyclic Redundancy Check. A bit–oriented error–checking method used to compare a range of data. A number is computed for each of two data blocks. The two numbers are then compared, and any discrepancy indicates an error. CRC detects errors 99.99% of the time. See *Checksum*.

CTS

Clear To Send. A serial–interface enable signal from the receiver to the transmitter.

Descriptor

An 8–byte component of the 80x86 protected–mode virtual–address translation table that contains the starting and ending segment addresses and the segment's access privileges. See GDT and LDT.

DIN

Deutsche Industrie Normenausschuss. A German standards group that originated the DIN connector — a round electrical connector commonly used in PCs to connect the keyboard to the system cabinet.

DIP

Dual Inline Package. A rectangular enclosure for an integrated circuit that has two parallel rows of terminals or lead wires.

DMA

Direct Memory Access. A method by which data is transferred between memory and peripheral devices without intervention by the CPU. The BIOS transfers data between memory and the diskette controller using DMA.

continued

Dot Pitch

The distance, measured in hundredths of a millimeter, between the colored dots on a monitor screen. Each pixel on a color monitor contains three colored dots.

DRAM

Dynamic Random–Access Memory. Random–access memory that requires periodic refreshing. DRAM cells are simple and small, usually comprising a single transistor and a capacitor. See *RAM* and *SRAM*.

DSR

1. Device Service Routine. A BIOS, DOS, or application–program routine for handling software interrupts. See *ISR*. 2. Data Set Ready. An RS–232C control signal from the modem to the terminal.

DTR

Data Terminal Ready. An RS–232C control signal from the terminal to the modem.

Edge–triggered

A method of activating a circuit by detecting a sudden change in voltage, such as the rising edge of a square wave form.

EGA

Enhanced Graphics Adapter. A medium–resolution text–and–graphics color display device that is backward compatible with MDA and CGA.

EIA

Electronic Industries Association. Promulgators of several electrical interface standards, including EIA RS–232C.

EISA

Extended Industry Standard Architecture. A 32–bit extension of ISA.

EPROM

Erasable Programmable Read–Only Memory. Read–only memory that can be erased by prolonged exposure to intense ultraviolet light. After an EPROM device has been erased, it can be reprogrammed. EPROM packages have glass windows that expose the ICs so that they can be erased.

continued

ESDI

Enhanced Small Device Interface. A high–performance, device–level, fixed–disk protocol, whose circuitry is divided between an expansion card in an ISA slot and an embedded controller on the drive housing. ESDI includes a serial command line, in addition to the usual control signals, over which 17–bit commands can be sent to the controller. ESDI disks are often cached.

Expanded Memory

Bank–switched memory accessed using the protocol defined in the Lotus–Intel– Microsoft Expanded Memory Specification (LIM EMS).

Extended Memory

The memory space in ISA and EISA systems above the DOS 1MB limit. Extended memory can only be accessed in protected–mode.

GDT

Global Descriptor Table. The table that contains the memory segment descriptors that don't reside in LDTs. Descriptors in the GDT are available to all tasks.

h, hex

Hexadecimal.

IDE

Integrated Device Electronics. A fixed–disk protocol that puts all the controller circuitry on the drive housing, eliminating the need for a separate controller card. An IDE drive is attached to the system board via a 40–conductor cable.

IDT

Interrupt Descriptor Table. A table of descriptors, similar to the GDT or an LDT. The IDT contains the 256 gate descriptors that allow an 80386 or 80486 CPU to locate exception–handling routines.

IEEE

Institute of Electrical and Electronic Engineers.

INT

Interrupt. The 80x86 assembly–language mnemonic for the interrupt instruction.

continued

Interleaving

1. A technique for increasing the efficiency of DRAM access in which main memory is divided into an even number of memory banks, with alternating banks having odd and even addresses. Sequential memory accesses alternate between the memory banks, halving the number of accesses to each bank and, in the process, reducing the time required for DRAM reads and writes. Interleaving allows the precharge cycle of one bank to overlap the access cycle of the other. See *Cycle Time*. 2. A multiprogramming technique in which the execution of sequences of instructions from one program alternate with sequences of instructions from one or more other programs.

Interrupt

A signal that stops the CPU's execution of its current task in order to service the hardware device or software program that initiated the signal.

IRET

Interrupt Return. The 80x86 assembly–language mnemonic for the instruction that returns program control from an interrupt–handling routine.

IRQ

Interrupt Request. One of the interrupt signals from a device to an interrupt controller.

ISA

Industry Standard Architecture. The specification for the PC/AT computer.

ISR

Interrupt Service Routine. A BIOS routine for handling hardware interrupts. See *DSR.*

K

Kilobytes.

Kbs

Kilobits per second.

LDT

Local Descriptor Table. A table, similar to the GDT, that contains the memory segment descriptors available to those tasks that are allowed to use the LDT.

continued

Level–sensitive

A method of activating a circuit and determining its state by its voltage level.

LSB

Least–Significant Byte, or Bit.

MB

Megabytes.

Mask

A bit pattern used to control the accessibility of specific bits in a register.

MDA

Monochrome Display Adapter. A text–only, one–color display.

Memory Relocation

A technique for redefining redundant RAM memory as extended memory. Some systems contain both ROM and RAM at the same addresses in the range A0000h–FFFFFh, with one or the other disabled. If this address range is not used for EMS or shadowing, the RAM's upper address bits can be set to effectively relocate it to the top of the system's address space.

MFM

Modified Frequency Modulation. A data encoding method that doubles the density of simple phased and frequency–modulation encoding methods by varying both the amplitude and frequency of the write signal.

MHz

Megahertz. Millions of cycles per second.

MSB

Most–Significant Byte, or Bit.

NMI

Nonmaskable Interrupt. A hardware interrupt that cannot be disabled by software. An NMI is typically used for high–priority error interrupts, such as an abort signal, a memory parity error, or a power–fail detection, and is always processed at the end of the current instruction execution.

continued

Paging

1. A statistically–based memory management technique that divides the address space into pages that share a row address. Paging anticipates that consecutive reads and writes will be to sequential addresses within a page, that the row address will stay the same, and that only new column addresses will have to be generated. See *RAS* and *CAS*. 2. An 80386/80486 method of managing physical memory. An 80386/80486 page is a 4K subdivision of a segment. Paging is used by operating system, disk I/O, and on–chip cache swapping algorithms. See *Segment*.

PEL

See *Pixel*.

PIC

Programmable Interrupt Controller. An integrated circuit that handles vectored priority interrupts for the CPU. The Intel 8259A Programmable Interrupt Controller is the standard device in the XT, ISA, and EISA specifications.

PIT

Programmable Interval Timer. An integrated circuit containing counters that can be set by software. The Intel 8254 Programmable Interval Counter is the standard device in the XT, ISA, and EISA specifications.

Pixel

Picture element. The smallest component of a composite image, such as a dot on a screen display or output from a laser printer. Also called PEL.

POST

Power–On Self Test. A series of routines in the ROM BIOS that are executed on power–up. These routines check main memory and other system parts for malfunctions, examine the bus to see what peripherals are attached, and build the Interrupt Vector table.

Protected Mode

The virtual–addressing mode of 80286, 80386, and 80486 processors. The address space above 100000h (1MB) is addressed in protected mode, using the processor's virtual–address translation mechanism.

continued

PS/2

Personal System/2. The IBM architecture that succeeded the PC/AT. Like the XT and AT, the PS/2 family of microcomputers is based on the Intel 80x86 series of microprocessors. However, IBM introduced a new bus specification, Micro Channel Architecture (MCA), with the PS/2 that is not backward compatible with the XT or AT (ISA) buses.

RAM

Random–Access Memory. Read/write memory that does not have to be accessed sequentially.

RAS

Row Address Strobe. The portion of the RAM chip–select signal that clocks the row address into an internal address latch. See *CAS*.

Real Mode

The addressing mode of 80286, 80386, and 80486 processors that corresponds to the 20–bit segment:offset addressing scheme of the 8086/8088. The real–mode address space is the megabyte between 00000h and FFFFFh.

RLL

Run–Length Limited. A self–clocking data encoding method that restricts the number of possible consecutive zeros. This technique stores data more efficiently than MFM but requires complex encoding and decoding.

ROM

Read–Only Memory. Memory whose contents are permanent.

RS–232C

A serial–communication interface standard defined by the Electronics Industries Association (EIA). Originally developed for connecting modems to computer terminals, RS–232C has been adopted as a defacto interface standard for most microcomputer serial communication.

RTC

Real–Time Clock. In the ISA specification and in some enhancements of the XT, the Motorola MC146818A battery–backed RTC chip.

continued

RTS

Request To Send. A serial–interface control signal from the transmitter to the receiver.

SCSI

Small Computer System Interface. A system–level interface that includes a peripheral bus specification for attaching multiple high–performance I/O devices to a microcomputer. SCSI allows a system bus to extend beyond the microcomputer's chassis via a 50–conductor cable.

Segment

A logical division of the linear address space used by Intel 80x86 processors. The 8086/8088 and 80286 processors compute effective addresses by adding a 16–bit offset to a 16–bit segment address. The 80386 and 80486 processors compute an effective address by adding a 32–bit offset to a 32–bit segment address.

Selector

A 16–bit component of the 80x86 protected–mode virtual address that corresponds to the segment component of the real–mode segment:offset address.

SIMM

Single Inline Memory Module. A small circuit board containing memory chips that fits into a socket on the system board.

SIP

Single Inline Package. A rectangular enclosure for an integrated circuit that has a single row of terminals or lead wires along one edge.

Shadowing

A technique for improving the speed of ROM–based code. The code is copied from ROM to high–speed RAM at the same address, the ROM is disabled, and the RAM is then write–protected.

SRAM

Static Random–Access Memory. Random–access memory that retains its state when power is not applied. SRAM cells are built from several transistors, so they are larger, more expensive to fabricate, and faster than DRAM cells. See *RAM* and *DRAM*.

ST506/412

A device–level, fixed–disk protocol introduced in the IBM XT.

continued

Task

A program or a related group of programs running on an 80386– or 80486–based system under a multitasking operating system.

UART

Universal Asynchronous Receiver/Transmitter. A serial line controller that transmits and receives serial data, performs parallel/serial conversions, and inserts and checks synchronizing control bits in the serial data stream.

VGA

Virtual Graphics Array. A high–resolution, analog, text–and–graphics color display that is backward compatible with EGA.

XMS

Extended Memory Specification. A standard developed by a four–company consortium (AST Research, Lotus Development, Intel, and Microsoft) that allows DOS applications to access the 64K of memory space between 640K and 704K (A0000h–B0000h).

XT

The IBM PC/XT — an 8088–based successor to the simpler 8088–based PC microcomputer. Introduced in 1983, the PC/XT abandoned the PC's cassette interface and added a fixed disk.

Selected Bibliography

Introduction

This bibliography has been developed to provide readers with additional sources of information related to the ROM BIOS. It is divided into sections by topic area.

The ROM BIOS

Cohen, Howard N. and John Hanel. "A Timing-Independent BIOS." *BYTE — IBM Special Edition*, Fall 1987, pp. 219–222.

Duncan, Ray. *IBM® ROM BIOS*. Redmond, WA: Microsoft Press, 1988.

Shiell, Jon. "IBM PC Family BIOS Comparison." *BYTE — IBM Special Edition*, Fall 1987, pp. 173–180.

IBM PC, Compatibles, and EISA Computers

Anderson, Brian T. and Marcy A. Puhnaty. "Serving Many Masters." *BYTE — IBM Special Edition*, Fall 1989, pp. 131–140.

Dowden, Tony. *Inside the EISA Computers*. Reading, MA: Addison–Wesley Publishing Co., Inc., 1990.

Eggebrecht, Lewis C. *Interfacing to the IBM Personal Computer, 2nd ed.* Indianapolis: Howard W. Sams and Company. 1990.

Glass, L. Brett. "Inside EISA." *BYTE*, November 1989, pp. 417–425.

IBM PC, Compatibles, and EISA Computers, cont'd

International Business Machines Corporation. *IBM Personal Computer XT and Portable Personal Computer Technical Reference*. Boca Raton, FL: International Business Machines Corporation, 1986.

International Business Machines Corporation. *IBM Personal Computer AT Technical Reference*. Boca Raton, FL: International Business Machines Corporation, 1984.

Mosley, J D. "MCA and EISA square off." *EDN*, April 12, 1990, pp. 61–68.

Newcom, Kerry. "The Micro Channel versus the AT Bus." *BYTE — IBM Special Edition*, Fall 1988, pp. 91–98.

Norton, Peter. *Inside the IBM® PC*. New York, NY: Brady Books, a division of Simon and Schuster, 1986.

Norton, Peter and Richard Wilton. *The New Peter Norton Programmer's Guide to the IBM® PC and PS/2®*. Redmond, WA: Microsoft Press, 1988.

Pappas, Chris H., and William H. Murray, III. *80386 Microprocessor Handbook*, Berkeley, CA: Osborne McGraw-Hill, 1988.

Rosch, Winn L. "The New EISA Standard: Did IBM Miss the Bus?" *PC Magazine*, June 12, 1990, pp. 315–328.

Rosch, Winn L. "A Further Look at the The New EISA Standard for the PC Bus." *PC Magazine*, June 26, 1990, pp. 349–354.

Sargent, Murray, and Richard L. Shoemaker. *The IBM PC™ from the Inside Out*. Reading, MA: Addison–Wesley Publishing Co., Inc., 1986.

White, George. "A Bus Tour." *BYTE*, September 1989, pp. 296–302.

The Intel 80x86 microprocessors

Boling, Douglas. "Bringing It All Together: A Look Inside The 486 Chip." *PC Magazine*, November 13, 1990, pp. 463–483.

Intel Corporation. *Introduction to the 80286*. Santa Clara, CA: Intel Corporation, 1982.

Intel Corporation. *80286 Programmer's Reference Manual*. Santa Clara, CA: Intel Corporation, 1983.

continued

The Intel 80x86 microprocessors, cont'd

Intel Corporation. *80287 Programmer's Reference Manual*. Santa Clara, CA: Intel Corporation, 1984.

Intel Corporation. *Introduction to the 80386*. Santa Clara, CA: Intel Corporation, 1985.

Intel Corporation. *80386 Programmer's Reference Manual*. Santa Clara, CA: Intel Corporation, 1986.

Intel Corporation. *80387 Programmer's Reference Manual*. Santa Clara, CA: Intel Corporation, 1987.

Intel Corporation. *i486 Microprocessor*. Santa Clara, CA: Intel Corporation, 1989.

Intel Corporation. *i486 Microprocessor Programmer's Reference Manual*. Santa Clara, CA: Intel Corporation, 1990.

Morse, Stephen P. *The 8086/8088 Primer*. Rochelle Park, NJ: Hayden Book Company, 1982.

Morse, Stephen P. and Douglas J. Albert. *The 80286 Architecture*. New York: John Wiley and Sons, Inc., 1986.

Morse, Stephen P., Eric J. Isaacson, and Douglas J. Albert. *The 80386/387 Architecture*. New York: John Wiley and Sons, Inc., 1987.

Sartore, Ron. "The 80486: A Hardware Perspective." *BYTE — IBM Special Edition*, Fall 1989, pp. 67–74.

Smith, Bud. "The Intel 80486." *MIPS*, June 1989, pp. 57–59.

Strauss, Edmund. *Inside the 80286*. New York: Brady Books, a division of Simon and Schuster, 1986.

DOS

Angermeyer, John, et al. *The Waite Group's MS-DOS Developer's Guide, 2nd ed.* Indianapolis: Howard W. Sams and Company, 1989.

Brooks, William. "Leaving 640KB Behind." *PC Tech Journal*, April 1989, pp. 34–45.

Dettman, Terry R., and Jim Kyle. *DOS Programmer's Reference, 2nd ed.* Carmel, IN: Que Corporation, 1989.

continued

DOS, cont'd

Duncan, Ray. *Advanced MS–DOS Programming*. Redmond, WA: Microsoft Press, 1986.

Duncan, Ray, ed. *The MS-DOS Encyclopedia*. Redmond, WA: Microsoft Press, 1988

Duncan, Ray, et al. *Extending DOS*. Reading, MA: Addison–Wesley Publishing Co., Inc., 1990.

Duncan, Ray. "An Introduction to The DOS Protected Mode Interface." *PC Magazine*, February 12, 1991, pp. 365–391.

Forney, James. *MS-DOS Beyond 640K*. Blue Ridge Summit, PA: Windcrest Books, 1989.

Fried, Stephen. "Accessing Hardware from 80386 Protected Mode Part I." *Dr. Dobb's Journal*, May 1990, pp. 92–98.

Fried, Stephen. "Accessing Hardware from 80386 Protected Mode Part II." *Dr. Dobb's Journal*, June 1990, pp. 78–84.

Holtzman, Jeff. "Expanding the Limits." *BYTE*, March 1990, pp. 205–214.

Schulman, Andrew, et al. *Undocumented DOS*. Reading, MA: Addison–Wesley Publishing Co., Inc., 1990.

Yancich, David. "Using Expanded Memory." *BYTE — IBM Special Edition*, Fall 1989, pp. 123–128.

Components and peripherals

Armbrust, Steven, and Ted Forgerson. "Memory in the Hot Seat." *PC Tech Journal*, February 1988, pp. 84–95.

Campbell, Joe. *The RS-232 Solution*, Alameda, CA: SYBEX, Inc., 1984.

Dyke, Bruce Van. "SCSI: The I/O Standard Evolves." *BYTE — IBM Special Edition*, Fall 1990, pp. 187–191.

EIA. *RS-232C Interface Between Data Terminal Equipment and Data Communication Equipment Employing Serial Binary Data Interchange*. Washington, DC: Electronic Industries Association, 1969.

continued

Components and peripherals, *cont'd*

Ferraro, Richard F. *Programmer's Guide to the EGA and VGA Cards.* Reading, MA: Addison–Wesley Publishing Co., Inc., 1988.

Grofton, Peter W. *Mastering Serial Communications,* Alameda, CA: SYBEX, Inc., 1986.

McNamara, John E. *Technical Aspects of Data Communication, 2nd ed.* Bedford, MA: Digital Press, 1982.

Rosch, Winn L. "Math Coprocessors: Fact or Fantasy." *PC Magazine,* February 12, 1991, pp. 301–335.

Rosch, Winn L. *The Winn Rosch Hardware Bible.* New York: Brady Books, a division of Simon and Schuster, 1989.

Simon, Barry. "Learning Your Way Around the Keyboard Under DOS, Part 1." *PC Magazine,* December 25, 1990, pp. 383–388.

Simon, Barry. "Learning Your Way Around the Keyboard Under DOS, Part 2." *PC Magazine,* January 15, 1991, pp. 409–414.

Teja, Edward R. *The Designer's Guide to Disk Drives.* Reston, VA: Reston Publishing, 1985.

Wilson, Ron. "Will the search for the ideal memory architecture ever end?" *Computer Design,* July 1, 1990, pp. 78–90.

Index

Controller RAM Diagnostic, 215
device service routines. *See* Device service routines
Diagnostics 1: Read Test Buffer, 211
Diagnostics 2: Write Test Buffer, 212
error handling for, 195—196
Format Bad Track, 203
Format Disk Cylinder, 202
Format Drive, 204
Initialize Drive Parameters, 206
Read Disk Sectors, 199
Read Disk Status, 198
Read Disk Type, 218
Read Drive Parameters, 205
Read Long Sector, 207
Recalibrate Drive, 214
Reset Fixed Disk System, 197
Seek to Cylinder, 209
Test Drive Ready, 213
Verify Sectors, 201
Write Disk Sectors, 200
Write Long Sector, 208

Fixed disks and disk drives, components
controller, 24
cylinder, 190
head, 190
sector, 190
track, 190

Flags, shift, 126, 131, 136

Foreign keyboard support, 112

Format Bad Track, Fixed Disk Service, 203

Format Disk Cylinder, Fixed Disk Service, 202

Format Diskette Track, Diskette Service, 180—181

Format Drive, Fixed Disk Service, 204—205

Formats, character code, 111

Frames, transmission of, 220

Function keys, 111

G

Global Descriptor Table, 240, 243—244, 246—247

GPIB register, 81, 91

Graphic video format, 140

H

Hardware, port addresses for, 70—91

Heads, fixed disk drive, registers for, 79, 81

Hercules display adapter (HGC), 140
configuration switch register for, 83

Horizontal resolution, display screen, 138

Horizontal total, video port for, 92—93

I

I/O ports, addresses, 69—93
for hardware, 70—91
for System Services, 231

IBM BIOS POST and boot messages
AT, 312
XT, 328

Index register
for CRT controller, 82—83, 92—93
for video sequencer, 83
port, for CMOS RAM, 76

Informational messages
AT, 318
XT, 330

Real-time clock, 22, 27

Recalibrate Drive, Fixed Disk Service, 214

Recalibration of diskette drives, 170

Receive One Character function, 226

Receiver buffer register for serial port, 85—86

Reset, system, 111

Reset Diskette System, Diskette Service, 175

Reset Fixed Disk System, Fixed Disk Service, 197

Reset pointing device, System Services subfunction, 254

Return Extended BIOS Data Area Segment Address, System Services, 251

Return Extended Keyboard Status, Keyboard Service, 135

Return Extended Shift Flags Status, Keyboard Service, 136

Return Serial Port Status function, 227

Return Shift Flag Status, Keyboard Service, 131

Return status, System Services subfunction, 257—258

Return System Configuration Parameters Address, System Services, 250

Return Video Status, Video Service, 163

Right shift pressed shift flag, 131, 136

Rolling ones test during POST, 319

Rolling zeros test during POST, 319

ROM BIOS data, 53—68

ROM BIOS multitasking support, 171

RS–232C, 11, 220

RTC, 22, 27

RTS, 220

Run–time messages
  AT, 325—326
  XT, 331

S

Scan codes, 112—123

Scan lines for text mode, maximum, 92—93

Scroll Current Page Down, Video Service, 153

Scroll Current Page Up, Video Service, 152

Scroll Lock key, shift flag for, 131, 136

Sectors, fixed disk
  count for, 79—80
  number for, 79—80

Seek to Cylinder, Fixed Disk Service, 209

Select New Video Page, Video Service, 151

Send Character function, 225

Sequencer registers, 83

Serial Communications Service, 11, 220
  description, 219, 221
  error conditions
    parameter related errors, 222
    time–out errors, 222
  Initialize serial adapter function, 223
  invoking the DSR, 221
  Receive one character function, 226
  Return serial port status function, 227
  Send character function, 225

T

U

V

V

Wait, System Services, 239

Write Character Only to Screen, Video Service, 157

Write Character/Attribute to Screen, Video Service, 155—156

Write configuration storage, System Services subfunction, 272

Write Disk Sectors, Fixed Disk Service, 200

Write Diskette Sectors, Diskette Service, 178

Write Long Sector, Fixed Disk Service, 208

Write Pixel, Video Service, 159

Write String, Video Service, 164

Write Teletype to Active Page, Video Service, 161—162

X